Building a Church Counseling Ministry | without Killing the Pastor

A Collaborative Model for Local Churches, Pastors, and Biblical Counselors

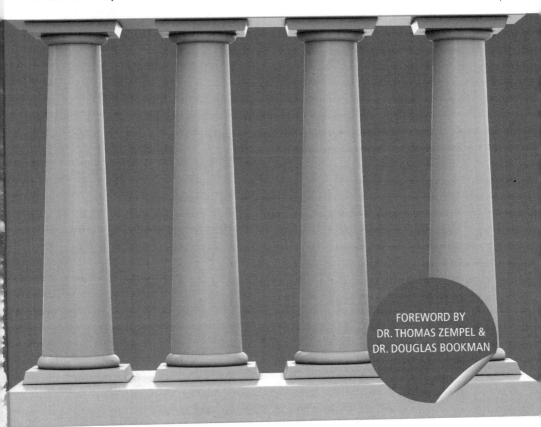

FOREWORD BY
DR. THOMAS ZEMPEL &
DR. DOUGLAS BOOKMAN

Sue Nicewander Biblical Counselor
with Pastor Jonathan Jenks and Pastor Stephen Steinmetz

DayOne

© Sue Nicewander 2012
Published by Day One Publications 2012
First printed 2012
Reprinted 2017
Library of Congress Cataloging-in-Publication Data
Nicewander, Sue, 1954–
Building a Church Counseling Ministry without Killing the Pastor: A Collaborative
Model For Local Churches, Pastors, and Biblical Counselors / Sue Nicewander

ISBN 978-1-84625-353-9

Published by Day One Publications
Ryelands Road, Leominster, HR6 8NZ
☎ 01568 613 740   FAX 01568 611 473
☎ Toll Free 888 329 6630 (North America)
email—sales@dayone.co.uk
web site—www.dayone.co.uk

Cover design by Wayne McMaster

Biblical Counseling Ministries, Inc. is a non-profit ministry located at Calvary Baptist
Church, 469 Airport Avenue, Wisconsin Rapids, WI 54494,
USA. E-mail: info@bcmin.org. Web site: www.bcmin.org

Biblical Counseling Ministries, Inc. has a vibrant ministry in Central Wisconsin. God has used this solid biblical counseling ministry and model as the means for change toward sanctification in the lives of many Christians. Over the years it has been a privilege to observe the God-honoring ministries of Sue Nicewander and the pastors of the BCM churches.

Pastors and qualified biblical counselors: read this book for useful information toward the development of a biblical counseling ministry that will serve your people and also other Christians from like-minded churches.

Wayne Johnston, ACBC Fellow Director of Training Center, Certification Association of Certified Biblical Counselors

This book is much needed. BCM has proven through hard work and careful development that its model works. I trust that this book will soon be on the shelves of many small churches all over the world. It definitely will be a required text for the Foundations Course here at the Shepherds Seminary and at Central Baptist Theological Seminary.

Dr. Thomas Zempel, ACBC Fellow, Pastor of Care Ministries at Colonial Baptist Church, Cary, NC, and Adjunct Professor of Biblical Counseling at Central Baptist Theological Seminary, USA

The whole organization of BCM—involving the cooperation of five churches—is a remarkable accomplishment. I sincerely hope that this book will be used to transplant this model into other areas. It really is a marvelous model.

Dr. Kevin T. Bauder, Research Professor and past President at Central Baptist Theological Seminary, Plymouth, MN, USA

Appreciations

Building a Church Counseling Ministry Without Killing the Pastor presents a wonderful vision for local churches of like mind to scripturally help people. The author defines and describes biblical counseling and then explains how a biblical counseling ministry can be developed in practice. While her emphasis is upon local churches in a region cooperative in such a ministry, there is much in this book which would benefit every kind of biblical counseling ministry—whether in a counseling center or a church-staff-based counseling ministry. The author is very practical and incredibly thorough. She thinks of everything! If you are involved in a biblical counseling ministry or if you are considering starting one, you will greatly benefit from this book.

Dr. Jim Newheiser, ACBC Fellow, and Pastor and Director of the Institute for Biblical Counseling and Discipleship, Escondido, CA, USA

To Jim,
my beloved husband:
Through your faithful love God has blessed our family,
and through your selfless support of BCM and of me, many others know God's
blessings as well.

Also to Jenni and Jodi,
my dearly loved daughters,
and to your families,
for freely and sincerely living for Christ. I have no greater joy.

Contents

Contents

Contents

Contents

Working together for the cause of Christ

Sue Nicewander is the ACBC-certified executive director, biblical counselor, and discipleship-development instructor with Biblical Counseling Ministries, Inc (BCM). Sue has a BA in biblical counseling from Trinity Bible College in Newburg, IN, and an MA in biblical counseling from Central Baptist Theological Seminary in Plymouth (Minneapolis), MN.

A women's ministry leader for over thirty years and biblical counselor for more than eighteen years, Sue counsels, writes, speaks, and teaches, providing a counseling resource for small local churches. Her published works include a monthly e-newsletter, three articles in the *Journal of Biblical Counseling* and the booklet *Help! I Feel Ashamed* in Day One Publications' Living in a Fallen World series. Sue has been married to Jim since 1973 and they have two married daughters and six grandchildren. Sue and Jim serve as members of Berea Baptist Church in Stevens Point, WI.

Stephen Steinmetz has served in pastoral ministry since 1985 in Illinois and Wisconsin. He is a graduate of Pillsbury Baptist Bible College (BS in Bible) and Calvary Baptist Theological Seminary (MDiv). He and Sharon, his wife of nearly thirty years, have six children and two grandchildren.

Steve Steinmetz served in pastoral ministry in First Baptist Church of Rockford, IL, for eight years, and has served in his current position as pastor of Faith Baptist Church of Wisconsin Rapids, WI, since 1993. He serves on the BCM board of directors and teaches the BCM Basic Skills parenting curriculum, which he developed. A gifted teacher, Steve also presents workshops at BCM seminars.

Jonathan Jenks, a native of upstate New York, graduated from Cedarville University in Ohio, where he met his wife, Jeniffer. Jon graduated from Baptist Bible Seminary in 1996 after completing an internship at Calvary Baptist Church in Wisconsin Rapids. He then served at CBC in the area of Church Education from May 1996 to December 2000, when he was called to be senior pastor.

Jon serves on the BCM board of directors and as counseling supervisor at BCM's home church. He also teaches the BCM seminar "Pastor's Toolbox: Developing Leaders in Your Church." A gifted administrator and teacher, Jon leads Calvary Baptist Church to focus on discipleship and growing one another in Christ using his "Spiritual Development Plan." He coordinates the teen ministry at Calvary and serves as Wisconsin state director for Talents for Christ. Jon enjoys wilderness camping and spending time with his family. He and Jeniffer have three children.

Acknowledgments

Thanks are due to the current BCM board of directors for their testimonials and suggestions, and, more importantly, for working together to form a vehicle of ministry that some said would never work: Pastor Corey Brookins, Berea Baptist Church of Stevens Point, WI; Pastor Larry Gross, First Baptist Church of Waupaca, WI; Pastor Jon Jenks, Calvary Baptist Church of Wisconsin Rapids, WI; Mrs. Kathy Parker, R.N., Calvary Baptist Church of Wisconsin Rapids, WI; Mrs. Lucy Runnells, Faith Baptist Church of Wisconsin Rapids, WI; Pastor Steve Steinmetz, Faith Baptist Church of Wisconsin Rapids, WI; Pastor Steve Svendsen, Rice Lake Baptist Church of Rice Lake, WI; and Mr. Robert Veldhoff, Grace Baptist Church of Plover, WI.

The BCM board of directors and I shall be ever grateful to our former directors and liaisons who so patiently and diligently brought this model together: Mrs. Denyne Carey, Dr. Richard Houg, Mr. Robert Oikarinen, Mrs. Juanita Purcell, Mrs. M. Jane Shaurette, Pastor Jeffrey Sheeks, Pastor Earl Swigart, Mr. Charles Whitmarsh.

Special thanks also go to Dr. Thomas Zempel, my teacher, mentor, ACBC supervisor, and friend; and to Dr. Kevin Bauder, for pointing me toward great poetry and sound theology. Thanks, too, to Wayne Johnston, Dr. Jim Newheiser, Dr. Jeff Newman, and Dr. Douglas Bookman, for your godly wisdom and direction with this book. My great affection goes to Pastor and Mrs. Harold Reemstma, under whose pastoral ministry my whole family came to Christ many years ago.

To Calvary Baptist Church of Wisconsin Rapids goes heartfelt gratitude for patiently enduring the start-up and continuance of BCM. Your organizational support and incredible spirit have been indispensable! And to Liz Bravick, Kathy Parker, and Amy Knoll, who have enthusiastically served BCM in countless ways: thank you.

Many thanks to our resource center at Faith Baptist Church of Wisconsin Rapids, with special thanks to Julie Landowski, resource center secretary, for your many cheerfully supplied hours of help with our recommended resources list, textbooks, and counseling materials, booklets, and brochures.

To Grace Baptist Church of Plover, our training center: thank you, with special thanks to Kristen Akright and the numerous past and present volunteers who have made classes more enjoyable and more smoothly run.

To First Baptist Church of Waupaca, our support center, and Berea Baptist Church of Stevens Point, my church of membership, thank you for your ongoing support of biblical counseling and for helping us with mailings, printing, audits, and other necessities.

Much gratitude goes to Brian Landowski and Wade Beavers for Web site building and maintenance; Art Napgezek and Gideon Mayhak for audio/video work and technological consultations; Pastor Steve Barton, Pastor Jack Austin, and Randy White for home office advice and support in lots of areas; Don and Steve Yusten, John and Donna Wilhorn, Jim Orth, and Tony Shilka for crafting and finishing office furnishings; Pastor Earl and Ellie Swigart for building a beautiful display board; Dean and Heidi Hartman for BCM Sunday presentations; Linda Dougherty and Marie and Eileen Trylick for lunches at our seminars; Jolean Gross for coordinating at our support center; and Betsy Carlson for her patient editing and faithful heart of service.

Thank you to the many unnamed disciple-makers at our home and host churches who are living out the principles of the Word as presented in this book. You are all a blessing!

I have long been persuaded that the remarkably God-honoring, many-faceted, and generally delightful but occasionally frustrating undertaking which may be broadly denominated the "Biblical Counseling Movement" will not reach its maturity until its focus moves beyond "parking an ambulance at the bottom of the cliff" to "building a fence at the top of the cliff." That is to say, counseling is currently perceived as intended for those who have, in some way and in some measure, crashed and burned. But would not the biblical principles which have been "systematized" in the entirely noble effort to help those whose lives are thus broken be just as effective in *keeping* folk from wandering (or plunging themselves) into habits of mind and life that result in such a sorry state of affairs? In other words, the movement has from its recent beginnings sought to identify and make functionally applicable those scriptural principles which are necessary to deliver individuals from deep-rutted habits of sinful and destructive behavior, to repair relationships fractured seemingly beyond repair by years of selfish and hurtful priorities and reactions, and to liberate those in bondage to the culture's lying solutions for the emptiness and hopelessness which is the certain lot of the person who will not give God His place. If those principles alone are effective to rescue people from such tragedies, would not those same realities function as the only dependable safeguard against that witches' brew of personal disasters? In short, would it not be wise to apply the palliative as a preventative?

But that step—from surgical-crisis counseling to broad-based preemptive inculcation of the principles of progressive sanctification—is by any measure an intimidating project. It is, indeed, if not a "paradigm shift," at least a paradigm recalibration on several counts. Primarily, it involves refocusing the ministry not only from the professionally licensed practitioner to the pastorally trained minister of soul-care, but also from the larger, resource-rich churches (where most of the attention is) to the smaller, resource-restricted churches (where most of the believers are).

Furthermore, such a recalibration demands that those who—in no pejorative sense whatever—function as the "high priests" of the movement, and who thus tend to move among thinkers and movers and shakers, resist the impulse to fixate on those more visible and impressive elements of the effort and strategize ways to take the dynamic of the movement to the believing community at large.

Enter Sue Nicewander. What began as a gleam in her eye has, by God's grace, Sue's perseverance, and the adventurous spirit of a handful of pastors and lay-leaders, metamorphosed into a remarkably well-conceived, carefully framed, and happily communicable methodology of doing just that—taking the movement to the street! The title she has given the book is only slightly tongue-in-cheek: in most churches any new ministry means most fundamentally more work for the pastor, and a ministry as ambitious as what is involved here might well portend a premature funeral! The solution suggested in this book is well synthesized in the tagline—"Working Together for the Cause of Christ." That tagline could hardly be more descriptive first of all of what God has wrought among a circle of smaller churches in central Wisconsin, and, second, of what needs to be implemented among churches elsewhere if the movement is to be taken to the streets. And this work is a how-to guidebook for causing that to happen, a comprehensive manual describing a strategic method for making widely available the all-important teachings of progressive sanctification as articulated in the context of the biblical counseling movement. There may emerge other ways of doing that, to be sure: the more the merrier (as it were!). But here is a strategy which was worked out first in theory and then in practice, which has been refined and corrected in the real world of local-church ministry, and which has been herein reduced to a well-written and far-sighted handbook for getting it done. Our Lord is to be praised, Sue and her coworkers are to be congratulated, and this book is to be commended as a very important step in the way God is working providentially to equip pastors and churches to live out the reality that He has indeed "given to us all things that pertain to life and godliness, through the knowledge of Him who called us by glory and virtue" (2 Peter 1:3).

Dr. Douglas Bookman
Professor of New Testament
Shepherds Seminary, Cary, NC
Formerly on staff at The Master's College

As a former senior pastor of one church for nearly ten years and a professor of counseling in a seminary for sixteen years, I hold up the Bible as sufficient for life and godliness. It is *the* resource for helping people to grow and change formally and informally. However, it has become evident that the ministry of discipleship is facing a twofold problem. First, most pastors have not been trained to do formal or informal discipleship well. Second, since the average church in the U.S. has a congregation numbering between seventy-five and 150 members, the possibility of placing a staff member with training in this kind of ministry is not realistic financially. I was trained to do formal biblical discipleship, which resulted in my being led into the seminary milieu to establish a counseling program that would also train others for the primary ministry of doing discipleship both formally and informally.

This is where I find Sue Nicewander and Biblical Counseling Ministries exciting. Sue was a student of mine. After graduating with her MBC degree, she began the process of finding opportunities to apply what she learned about biblical counseling and training. It was through that journey that God laid on her heart the possibility of serving several small churches rather than being on the staff of one local church. Through the counsel of her pastor and connecting with area pastors, the BCM ministry that Sue reveals in this book came to fruition.

This book is not about how to set up a counseling center in your church, but about training church members how to be involved in the formal and informal ministry of discipleship. Sue has submitted herself to the guidance of her pastor as well as the guidance of several other pastors in the Wisconsin area who compile the board members of BCM.

Most churches are limited in what they can do in counseling ministry, but Sue has proven through hard work and careful implementation that there is a way! Churches now have a model to help with formulating effective discipleship/counseling even if the congregation is small. Every church needs to be practicing Ephesians 4:11–12, and Sue has helped us discover how to do this strategically and effectively.

Do yourself a real service: read this book and learn from one who has been creative in her efforts and strategic in her plans to help meet an untapped need in most small churches.

Dr. Thomas Zempel
Administrative Pastor of Care, Colonial Baptist Church
and Professor of Counseling, Shepherds Seminary, Cary, NC
Adjunct Professor of Biblical Counseling at Central Baptist Theological Seminary, Plymouth, Minnesota.

Biblical Counseling Ministries (BCM) is a bit of an anomaly. We are neither a counseling center nor a local church. We work closely in, with, and through local churches to provide supplementary biblical counseling resources, including one-on-one biblical counseling, discipleship training, and literature recommendations. We counsel and train as part of those churches, rather than from the outside looking in.

The concept of BCM began with a couple of realizations. First, we have observed that pastors of small-to-average-sized local churches need more help with the growing demands of counseling. Second, well-trained biblical counselors are coming out of our Bible colleges and seminaries to a silent job market. How might the two groups be brought together?

We started BCM with a small group of central Wisconsin Baptist pastors and lay-leaders from ordinary churches whose size ranged from roughly forty to 300 members. The five pastors who started on our advisory board were extremely busy men with multi-faceted ministries that included regular counseling. As a biblical counselor, I brought the idea of BCM to them. They all loved the thought of having such resources available, but they also agreed that they had neither the time nor the energy to take on such a project.

> "… I cannot escape the suspicion that the vast majority of the Lord's work is being accomplished in little churches led by pastors whose names are seldom heard outside their own ministries. These are faithful men, laboring without human commendation, sometimes under heartbreaking circumstances. They are the ones I admire most. If there is any hope for the future, it almost certainly lies with them. Hold such in esteem."
>
> **Dr. Kevin Bauder, Research Professor and past President of Central Baptist Theological Seminary, Plymouth, MN, "In the Nick of Time" e-newsletter**

However, when I offered to do the legwork, they were intrigued, and we began to discuss the possibilities. The concept that would have overwhelmed a single pastor actually energized the group. Now, ten years later, we have together built a uniquely effective model that supplies counseling resources through a trained biblical counselor for each of their churches as well as consultations, training, and/or referrals for nearly sixty others.

During our inception, five core churches hammered out the BCM structure while I chased down information, engaged help, developed materials, and wrote documents. Once the ministry opened its doors, my responsibilities shifted to BCM administration, counseling, curriculum writing, speaking, and mentoring. The ministry now requires regular travel to each core church for on-site counseling, pastoral consultation, and some student mentoring. BCM also teaches discipleship classes and seminars at a central location. Our activities are framed to carefully honor all biblical norms and appropriate leadership in each church as we help them to develop disciple-makers.

As with many other ministries, our counseling philosophy is Christ-centered and biblical (specifically, "nouthetic"[1]). Therefore, you will find the principles and practices of BCM to be useful in a variety of church and geographical settings. Our organizational model, however, is uniquely collaborative. Each BCM core church hosts part of the ministry and provides for specific needs, both financial and otherwise. We know of no other such ministry model, but we are convinced that churches everywhere could benefit from what we have learned (adapted, if necessary, to fit their situation).

As you can imagine, others are becoming curious about the BCM model and want to explore how it might work in their setting. We are excited about the possibilities.

> "Nothing is too small for God ... and no one is too small for Him to use."
> **Earl Swigart, Former Senior Pastor and BCM Secretary, Berea Baptist Church, Stevens Point, WI**

- The benefits of the BCM model to small and average-sized churches in rural and urban settings include refreshing collaborative fellowship, shared resources, counseling consultations and referrals, and discipleship training they could not otherwise afford.

- Our experience is also useful for larger churches. For example, we present practical tools and tips to consider when adding a biblical counselor to your staff. The BCM vision may also help a larger church to effectively share resources, mentoring, training, and community outreach with its smaller counterparts, while respecting each church's autonomy and value.

- Biblical counselors can learn how to work effectively with churches using BCM's practical tips, forms, and outlines for administrative guidance and thorough record-keeping.

This book shares our vision along with the nuts and bolts of setting up and running a healthy counseling ministry. To that end, *Building a Church Counseling Ministry Without Killing the Pastor* speaks to two main audiences: pastors and biblical counselors. Because both groups are intricately involved in the model, we recommend that both groups read the entire book. However, some sections target one audience more than the other.

> The BCM model was built with pastors, so we will use the term "pastors" throughout the book. But the role of "elder" would also easily fit into our collaborative model, as long as one elder is named as liaison and given some decision-making authority by the church.

- Part 1 speaks to pastors, under whose direct authority the local church's ministry lives and breathes. Chapters 1–3 present the need to develop biblical discipleship in the church, where our model is designed to function. BCM would not have happened without area pastors who valued biblical counseling resources and who were willing to work together to bring those resources (including me) into their churches.

- Part 2 is important for both audiences. Chapters 4–7 provide a set of specific organizational pillars, steps, and tools necessary for a well-run ministry. Here we unpack our model, offering suggestions for building dialogue and collaboration among like-minded church leaders. We also offer some modifications if you are not able to collaborate as we have done.

- Part 3 brings the biblical counselor into the conversation. Chapters 8–13 offer experientially tested tips for walking alongside pastors throughout the design and implementation of a local-church counseling ministry. We recommend that a counselor be brought into the organizational plan as early as possible, because a working knowledge of the ministry's vision, needs, and structure can contribute to balance and unity in the Lord's work.
- Finally, the appendices offer a wealth of useful biblical resources. We include concise outlines to help pastors develop church leadership and discipleship, a checklist for building your ministry model, as well as a brief theology of biblical counseling and a general structure for offering biblical counsel. In addition, we include a variety of our most widely used forms to save you hours of time and headaches.

International readers will find some of our materials to be specific to the USA. Nevertheless, we believe that our organizational principles and rich experiences will be helpful as you adapt our ideas and methods to fit your region.

We are excited about sharing what we have learned through developing the BCM model. The Lord has guided our group on this pioneer journey, and this book is our attempt to leave our trail well marked for those who care to follow. May you find many ideas that will enhance the Lord's work in your own local church. Without killing the pastor.

Note

1 "Nouthetic counseling" comes from the Greek words *nouthesia and* noutheteo, meaning to warn, admonish or instruct (see Acts 20:31; Rom. 15:14; Col. 1:28; 3:16; 1 Cor. 4:14).

AN OVERVIEW OF COLLABORATION USING THE BCM MODEL

Biblical Counseling Ministries

BCM provides biblical counseling on site at our core churches by pastoral referral. We also provide consultations, speaking, writing, discipleship training, administration, and resource recommendations. We produce most of our written materials (including curriculum), promotional materials, and administrative tools.

Home Church

Our home church houses our administrative office and provides our primary clerical support, audio/visual services, a room for counseling sessions, an office, and a counseling supervisor. BCM operates under the authority of the deacon board at our home church. The senior pastor serves on our board of directors as a BCM liaison with his church.

Host Churches

Each of our three host churches has a liaison on the BCM board of directors to facilitate communication and coordination of efforts at each location. Each BCM church gives its liaison the authority to speak for the church on matters pertaining to the counseling ministry. The liaison, the church secretary, and designated volunteers at each host church work with BCM to meet specific ministry needs.

- *The training center* provides classroom space, supplies copying for training-related needs, cares for class and seminar materials, and handles class registrations.
- *The resource center* is responsible for books and other literature that we use in seminars, classes, and counseling. It also publishes BCM brochures and booklets. A volunteer at our resource center maintains our Web site.
- *The support center* helps with miscellaneous needs such as mailings, brochure development, and fundraising.

Travailing ... for Souls
by John Newton

What contradictions meet
In ministers' employ;
It is a bitter sweet,
A sorrow full of joy:
No other post affords a place
For equal honor, or disgrace.

Who can describe the pain
Which faithful preachers feel;
Constrained to speak in vain
To hearts as cold as steel?
Or who can tell the pleasures felt
When stubborn hearts begin to melt?

The Savior's dying love,
The soul's amazing worth;
Their utmost efforts move,
And draw their passions[1] forth:
They pray, they strive, their rest departs,
Till CHRIST be formed in sinners' hearts.

If some small hope appear,
They still are not content;
But, with a jealous fear,
They watch for the event:

Too oft they find their hopes deceived,
Then how their inmost souls are grieved!

But when their pains succeed,
And from the tender blade,
The rip'ning ear proceeds,
Their toils are overpaid:
No harvest-joy can equal theirs
To find the fruit of all their cares.

On what has now been sown
Thy blessing, LORD, bestow;
The pow'r is Thine alone,
To make it spring[2] and grow:
Do thou the gracious harvest raise,
And thou, alone, shalt have all the praise.[3]

Notes

1 "Bowels" in original.
2 "Bloom" in original.
3 *Olney Hymns*, Book 2, Hymn 26. Public domain. From Christian Classics Ethereal Library, www.ccel.org/. Accessed May 2012.

Pastor, the last thing you need is another item for your to-do list! Even so, your list seems to grow by leaps and bounds.

Pastors are incredibly busy people with full and complex lives. Balance is precarious. Everybody seems to want a piece of your time, whether to complete tasks, ask for ministry help, seek personal advice, pose questions, lodge complaints, or simply to quell loneliness.

In particular, people come to you when life gets hard. Considering the complexity of today's society, the counseling issues that you confront are more intense now than ever before. Even if you have biblical counseling education and years of experience, you find that the demands of counseling and discipleship are great. It would be helpful to train some mature believers to share the load, particularly to reach out to newer believers or those who are struggling with trials. But you are already so buried that you can scarcely consider—much less implement—another program.

> "Most churches ... tend to buy into the pastor-driven ministry model, where you hire talented staff as the doers of all that is considered 'qualified ministry' in a church ... you can attract large crowds and not see transformed lives as a result. The church health movement taught us that if you work on your weaknesses, you'll be healthy. But neither of those things is enough ...
>
> "Jesus said if you want to gain your life, lose it; for a seed to grow, it must die; if you want to be first, be last; if you want to lead, serve. The role of the pastor in the local church is to act like a fuse that ignites the church to reach its potential. You are the catalyst, not the center of ministry."
>
> **Alan Nelson, *Me to We: A Pastor's Discovery of the Power of Partnership*** (Loveland, CO: Group, 2007) pp. 31, 37.

Yet you know something has to be done. Your carefully prepared sermons don't seem to be enough. People aren't changing. But it is difficult to know why not. People are attending services, the church is teaching scripturally and providing solid programs, and you are making calls and visits, but the spiritual depth remains about the same. In your heart you know something is wrong.

So you, the conscientious pastor, take on more and more until you can barely balance church demands, attend to your family, reach out to the community, and still spend time with the Lord. Keeping up this pace will lead to burnout, you fear. But what else can you do? Everyone wants you to be there for them.

Discipleship is the model exemplified by the Lord Jesus Christ, commanded in Matthew 28:19–20, and expanded on in Titus 2. Mature believers are to reach out from their resources in Christ to those who need help. But, practically speaking, how can a pastor facilitate a discipleship-driven church? How can you teach people to think in such a way that scriptural responses naturally spill over into the way they live?

If you are a pastor/elder or a biblical counselor who wants to help the local church to fulfill Christ's Great Commission, this book is for you. We will define and explore why biblical discipleship is important for a local church, and sketch a plan to develop and maintain strong disciple-makers. We will consider some possible ways you could develop biblical counseling in your church. Finally, we will describe the creative Biblical Counseling Ministries model for sharing counseling resources through a group of like-minded churches. The BCM model makes it possible for smaller churches to have a trained biblical counselor available for counseling and discipleship training. It also provides a way for churches of any size to work together to impact their communities.

The Pastor's Friend

We don't want the BCM model to be another item on your to-do list, but, rather, a tool in your toolbox. Our counseling and discipleship plan directly assists the pastors in our core churches, as you will see from the testimonials throughout this book.

Who are we? BCM is the combined effort of five ordinary Baptist churches that have pooled their resources to share a biblical counselor to assist their pastors. The BCM counselor provides on-site one-on-one counseling by pastoral referral and under pastoral supervision. We also offer discipleship training to build up each church's ability to disciple and counsel its own people. Our reading list recommends reliable counseling and discipleship literature for informal discipleship and church ministry use. All of this is carried out under the authority of the local church.

We at BCM believe that God's kind of counseling is gospel-centered and biblical. We also believe that God has given authority and purpose to the New Testament local church as His vehicle of ministry. Therefore, we are working together upon these foundations.

> "Obviously, a biblical counseling ministry brings impact in the lives of counselees. Biblical counseling is beginning discipleship that readies counselees for more discipleship in their lives, and they naturally then bring it to others in their home and church family because their worldview and proficiencies have changed. Some former counselees are now the best counselors, mentors, and confronters in our church, which has deepened the health of our church, stopped disunity, and removed burden from our pastors. Remember, though, they will want solid training and regular discipleship, so be ready to provide this."
>
> **Jonathan Jenks, Senior Pastor, Calvary Baptist Church, Wisconsin Rapids, WI**

HOW THE BCM MODEL HELPS PASTORS

The BCM model helps pastors:

- We carefully respect the pastor's authority and his accountability to God for the well-being of his fold, so BCM offers one-on-one counseling only by pastoral referral. We also ask counselees to give us permission to communicate with their referring pastors.
- Because the BCM counselor is female, BCM provides an important ministry to pastors' wives and female counselees in the spirit of Titus 2.

- BCM offers high-quality biblical counseling that pastors can trust. Unlike most outside counseling services, we are careful to reinforce the church's biblical teaching.
- The church offers resources necessary for the counselee's spiritual walk, so we require counselees to attend church services while in counseling, as an act of obedience to God. Therefore, we have seen our churches and our counselees grow as a result of the counseling ministry.
- BCM provides discipleship training to develop the people-helping skills of church leaders and spiritually mature members. Pastors sign our class registration forms, so we know that the pastors are aware of the training our students receive. Pastors may ask their trained workers to help with discipleship at their ability level—for example, to have a Bible study with a particular counselee after formal counseling is done. Thus, strong Christian relationships are nurtured in the church with counselees, discipleship ministry is strengthened, and biblical growth is more likely to continue.
- Our free recommended reading list is easily accessible at our Web site. It contains reliable resources that pastors can use to equip their people. The literature is suitable for Sunday Bible classes, midweek Bible studies, counseling, discipleship, and personal spiritual growth.

> "About half of the adults saved at our church in the last few years have come out of the counseling ministry. Many other families that would have left our church, or that left other non-gospel-preaching churches in disarray, have been salvaged and have become productive body members. Jesus reached those who knew they were lost—the desperate. This ministry targets those 'readied' by God."
>
> **Jonathan Jenks, Senior Pastor, Calvary Baptist Church, Wisconsin Rapids, WI**

The Impact

We schedule our BCM counselor to

work at our five core churches on a weekly basis, as needed. We also open our doors to other local churches through pastoral consultations, one-on-one counseling at our five locations, and discipleship classes and seminars.

IN OUR CORE CHURCHES

Our churches have consulted the BCM recommended reading list when choosing teaching materials for Sunday Bible classes and Bible study, as well as for pastoral counseling and discipleship. Through discipleship training and modeling, mature believers are becoming committed to Bible-centered leadership and their skills and participation in one-on-one soul care have increased. Pastors are seeing people offer wise scriptural advice. Evangelism has increased and the lost are receiving Christ. Biblical counseling is part of that impact as it has drawn in people from the community who are hurting and looking for help. With trained disciple-makers and biblical counseling resources available in the church, people are receiving care as never before.

BEYOND OURSELVES

We have also made a difference statewide. In our first five years, we directly helped nearly sixty churches, hundreds of students and counselees, as well as countless others through our e-newsletters and other materials. We have trained Bible camp counselors and have spoken at numerous events around our state. Our training center is certified by the Association of Certified Biblical Counselors (ACBC).[1] We rejoice in the impact God is making through our little group of ordinary churches.

Sharing the Model

To our knowledge, no one else is doing what we are doing—that is, collaborating to provide supplementary counseling resources designed with small or average-sized churches in mind. God's blessings have been rich. Since a significant segment of local churches are small or average-sized,[2] we think many more could benefit from what we have learned.

Larger churches—even mega-churches—may benefit from our model as well. This book provides some practical materials that are helpful for keeping counseling and discipleship ministries well organized and efficient. In addition, the BCM model helps you to collaborate with other like-minded churches to offer biblical counseling for your community. The cooperative spirit of our model lends itself to a respectful partnership with smaller churches that might otherwise feel dominated or patronized by their larger neighbors.

We do not claim that our model is the only way biblical counseling and discipleship can be done.[3] Our purpose is not to tell you how to run your church. We simply want to share what God has taught us as He has built up discipleship in our five churches through the BCM model. We pray that you will benefit from our experience as you develop your own discipleship resources.

If you have questions after reading this book and looking at our Web site and Facebook page, please give us a call. We would be delighted to help.

- BCM Web site: www.bcmin.org
- BCM Facebook page: Biblical Counseling Ministries
- E-mail: info@bcmin.org
- Home office phone: 715–423–7190 (M–F 9–12 & 1–3)

> "Jesus came and spoke to them, saying, 'All authority has been given to Me in heaven and on earth. *Go therefore and make disciples ...'"* (Matt. 28:18–19a, emphasis added)

Notes

1 The Association of Certified Biblical Counselors (ACBC) certifies individual biblical counselors through a rigorous program of education, testing, and counseling practicum. BCM is a certified ACBC training center. Students who successfully complete our seminar and six Basic Skills classes have fulfilled the educational requirement and may elect to progress in the ACBC counselor certification process.

2 Fifty-nine percent of American Christian churches have attendance under 100. See "Church Size Statistics ... Small Churches Rule!" at Good Church Design, Jan. 5, 2011, at http://goodchurchdesign.blogspot.com/.

3 The terms "biblical counseling" and "biblical discipleship" are used somewhat interchangeably throughout this book, since both offer the same scriptural content and form of ministry. However, for clarity's sake, some distinctions may apply. The term "biblical counseling" often refers to intensive one-on-one help offered through a certified biblical counselor by pastoral referral, while "biblical discipleship" usually refers to help that is offered less formally or even casually by members in the local churches.

P astor Paul Samuelson raised his head from his open Bible as the phone rang for the fourth time since he had sat down an hour ago. Leaning back in his chair, he stretched his arms. As he reached for the receiver with a cheerful hello, in the back of his mind he wondered where Laura was today. The volunteer secretary had said she would be in this morning, but it was already 2:30 p.m. and he hadn't heard from her. His call to her house had produced no answers.

"Hi, Pastor! John here," the familiar voice of his head deacon greeted him. "Just wanted you to know I'll be late for tonight's meeting." John gave no reason, but Pastor Paul was used to that. Anytime the pastor had pressed further, John smoothly sidestepped his questions. Pastor Paul concluded that he didn't like to be tied down.

"OK, John. Thanks for letting me know. Say, where's that wife of yours today?" The pastor's question was lighthearted, almost too much so. "I expected her this morning but haven't seen her in the office." He heard the soft ticking of the clock for a few seconds in the pause.

"Laura didn't call you? Oh ..." John's voice trailed. "Um, well, she meant to let you know that she's taken a job to help pay off the kids' tuition. I thought she told you ... she isn't going to be able to help out in the office as much."

"I see. She did mention last week that she was thinking about part-time work, but I thought … well, it doesn't matter. I hope she enjoys the job. Would you please have her call to let me know what her schedule will be? And I have a few questions about office stuff."

John was a hard worker at Glory Baptist Church. He and his wife, Laura, were among the faithful few who were at every service and who consistently stepped up to help. But lately Pastor Paul had been a little mystified to see their enthusiasm fading. He had been trying to draw them in, but the harder he tried the more they seemed to slip away. Were they burning out? Their children were getting older now and much more active in sports. He knew the game schedule could be rigorous on parents, as well as on the kids.

Pastor Paul tossed his pen aside as he hung up the phone, then lowered his head and stared at the well-worn pages of his beloved Bible. A sigh escaped his lips, along with a prayer for strength and wisdom. He knew his wife, Jenny, would take care of the clerical work for him, and for that he was grateful. But lately they had been handed many tasks that he felt could—and should—have been shouldered by others who were very capable of doing so.

Am I equipping the saints? he thought. *It seems they are more interested in letting me do the work.* Not that he minded. After all, he was called to be their senior pastor. Still, he had a nagging feeling that all was not well. His most gifted people were not inclined to work very hard at ministry. Others had potential, but they didn't seem to be growing. The faithful few were being worked to the bone, he among them, while the rest quietly observed or drifted away. He felt a little helpless.

As Pastor Paul turned to his outline for Sunday's sermon, the phone rang yet again, and an ache crawled into his chest. He let the call go to the answering machine as his mind began to swirl with the decisions he had to make, his ever growing task list, the financial pressures, the loss of his study time to people who called or stopped by unannounced, the family time that evaporated every week. But he didn't resent any of it. God had called him here, of that he was sure. Still, he was growing weary, and he even felt a little torn, being pulled in a hundred directions at once. Jenny rarely complained, but lately his family had been asked to sacrifice their time with him too often.

There are just a few of us who are willing to do the work of ministry, he thought. *And we're kind of a ragtag group. But God said He has fully equipped His church. Why has it been so difficult to motivate people to get involved? What is the secret?*

With a start, Pastor Paul overheard the church answering machine recording a message. Wendy's son was near death—would the pastor come right away? In a flash, he grabbed his overcoat and keys.

Part 1

Discipleship Development in the Church

Go and Make Disciples

"Go therefore and make disciples ... baptizing them ... teaching them to observe all things that I have commanded you ..."

Matthew 28:19–20

A disciple is "one who accepts and assists in spreading the doctrines of another."[1] When we hear the word "disciples," most of us probably think of Christ's inner circle of twelve. But Christ's command in Matthew 28:19–20 extends beyond those twelve men. He commissioned his original disciples to make more disciples, who, by definition, would continue to produce disciples until Christ's return. Therefore, today all believers are to be active disciple-makers. That is, all believers are commissioned to share the gospel with unbelievers. They are also called to work with individuals within the body to establish them in the biblical doctrines, as did Jesus Christ. And the pastor-teachers of each local church

---

ISN'T PREACHING ENOUGH?

The need for disciple-makers goes back to Old Testament times, such as when Ezra read the Scriptures to Israel. Nehemiah 8:7–8 records teachers going into the crowd to help the people understand what they were hearing from the pulpit: "Also Jeshua, Bani, Sherebiah, Jamin, Akkub, Shabbethai, Hodijah, Maaseiah, Klita, Azariah, Jozabad, Hanan, Pelaiah, and the Levites, helped the people to understand the Law ... So they read distinctly from the book, in the Law of God; and they gave the sense, and helped them to understand the reading." These men went among the people to help them make sense of the Word Ezra was presenting to them. Their job probably included answering questions and correcting wrong thinking.

In a similar way, through counseling and focused discipleship training, BCM has deliberately set out to help pastors equip believers to disciple people one-on-one so they will understand and live out the Word that has been well taught in the pulpit. Every believer is to be a disciple. That's a huge job. We think our model can help.

---

have been charged to equip the saints to do that work (Eph. 4:11–12).

This book will first address the value of biblical church-driven discipleship before briefly describing how skillful biblical disciple-making may be built into the church. We will also discuss some options for those times when you need some extra help with your counseling load. Finally, we will observe how the BCM model may be implemented or modified to provide biblical counseling resources in local churches of any size and in any place.

> "There are some pastors who have developed the thinking that their counseling takes place solely from the pulpit. While there is a priority in preaching, the fact is that every sermon cannot possibly address every individual's needs. One-on-one counsel is not merely a side ministry for some churches—it is an essential part of shepherding the church."
>
> **Corey Brookins, Senior Pastor, Berea Baptist Church, Stevens Point, WI**

Christ's Example of Discipleship

Preaching/teaching and discipleship may be carried out in several ways, as Christ Himself demonstrated. Jesus preached to thousands on the hillsides, taught smaller groups in the temple, intensively trained His inner circle of twelve men, and worked with a few individuals one-on-one. While He preached broad concepts and spiritual principles to larger groups, it was in the smaller venues that He addressed specific doctrines and needs, provided explanations, and demonstrated applications. The church follows His example by preaching from the pulpit to large groups, teaching small groups in Bible studies and classes, and providing discipleship for those who need individualized exhortation and instruction.

Significantly, Christ did not do all the work himself. He trained His followers, and then sent them out to teach others in a perpetual cycle described in Titus 2. This is the model He has exemplified for His church, as seen throughout His prayer in John 17 (see also Luke 9:23; Eph. 4:11–13; 2 Tim. 2:2; Titus 2:1–10; Gal. 6:1–2).

The Value of Church-Based Biblical Discipleship

Although we will use the terms "discipler," "disciple-maker" or "biblical counselor" here, the terms "soul-care provider" or "mentor" are also appropriate to describe a person who disciples others. A mentor or disciple-maker cares about people, conveys wisdom and skill, corrects error, and provides fellowship and relationship.[2] Every church should deliberately develop mentoring skills in its people. But why exert such effort when (as most church members believe) the pastor has been hired to do that work? Or why not send people to counseling centers outside the church?

THE BIBLE PRESENTS DISCIPLESHIP AS A NORM FOR THE CHURCH

For three years after his conversion, the apostle Paul (formerly Saul the Pharisee) was individually discipled by Ananias, followed by Barnabas, Peter, and others (Acts 9:15–19; Gal. 1:13–24). As a high-ranking Pharisee, Saul had an impressive educational background and knew the Old Testament Scriptures well (Phil. 3:5). But, like many churchgoers today, he did not know how to rightly interpret and apply what he had learned about the Scriptures. Therefore, after Paul received Christ, God immediately sent him to be individually equipped for ministry through the early local

> "… Speak the things which are proper for sound doctrine: that the **older men** be sober, reverent, temperate, sound in faith, in love, in patience; the **older women** likewise, that they be reverent in behavior, not slanderers, not given to much wine, teachers of good things— that they admonish the **young women** to love their husbands, to love their children, to be discreet, chaste, homemakers, good, obedient to their own husbands, that the word of God may not be blasphemed. Likewise, exhort the **young men** to be sober-minded, in all good things showing yourself to be a pattern of good works; in doctrine showing integrity, reverence, incorruptibility, sound speech that cannot be condemned, that one who is an opponent may be ashamed, having nothing evil to say of you."
> (Titus 2:1–8, emphasis added)

church. The fruit of his discipleship was plentiful: Paul brought scores of people to Christ and taught them to follow Him.

The same principles hold true today. Untaught people come into the local church with broken lives built upon false ideas about God, themselves, and others, and about the purpose of suffering. They need to learn the truth and how it applies to their lives. The local church is best equipped to do that work through the ministry of the Word of God.

INVOLVEMENT IN DISCIPLESHIP IS NOT OPTIONAL

All mature believers—not just the pastor—are required to disciple others. Notice that Titus 2 (see box on previous page) exhorts *every* believer to reach out—old and young, male and female, from all walks of life—to share the gospel and to teach individuals who are spiritually younger than themselves. In other words, the Bible calls for the whole church to be involved. Each person is

> "Let nothing be done through selfish ambition or conceit, but in lowliness of mind let each esteem others better than himself. Let each of you look out not only for his own interests, but also for the interests of others. Let this mind be in you which was also in Christ Jesus ..."
> (Phil. 2:3–5)

to receive scriptural teaching and share what he or she has received. Thus belief, accountability, and obedience are perpetuated across all generations.

BIBLICAL DISCIPLESHIP LEADS PEOPLE TO CONSIDER THE WELL-BEING OF OTHERS RATHER THAN TO LIVE FOR SELF

In specific ways, God commands believers to care for one another.[3] Christ is emulated through the practice of sacrificial love, and unity is encouraged in the body. Will we obey?

BIBLICAL DISCIPLESHIP RESTORES BROKEN LIVES THROUGH CHRIST, AND HELPS PEOPLE SHARE OTHERS' BURDENS

The pastor is not the only person called to this work; every mature believer is to evangelize, to forgive, to ask forgiveness, and to gently restore souls. The message of the gospel rings true in that context. The reality of Christ's ever present grace and power are demonstrated in the process of sanctification.

> "Brethren, if a man is overtaken in any trespass, you who are spiritual restore such a one in a spirit of gentleness, considering yourself lest you also be tempted. Bear one another's burdens, and so fulfill the law of Christ." (Gal. 6:1–2)

BIBLICAL DISCIPLESHIP AVERTS FALSE DOCTRINE BY TEACHING PEOPLE HOW TO UNDERSTAND AND APPLY THE TRUTH OF SCRIPTURE

Truth takes root when an individual's beliefs are addressed in the context of his or her way of life. A person must learn to accept and apply (not just hear) what the Bible says. In the process, he or she will develop a biblical perspective on the basic questions of life:

> Who is God? Who am I? What are my responsibilities toward other people? For example, how is the character of God reflected in parental love and discipline when my child has disobeyed? Or in my marriage to an unfaithful spouse? How does Scripture apply in complex relationships at work? What does it mean to follow Christ when dealing with abuse? How does the Bible speak concerning eating disorders, poor health, addictions, rebellious teens, depression, troubled marriages, and domestic violence? What does any of this have to do with the grace and forgiveness of Jesus Christ?

BIBLICAL DISCIPLESHIP TEACHES PEOPLE HOW TO FOLLOW CHRIST, NOT JUST IN CONCEPT BUT IN CLOSE RELATIONSHIP

Dr. Steve Viars says, "God meets us where we are, but He doesn't want us to stay there."4 God's purpose is to grow believers in His image. People often embrace life-changing scriptural principles through direct instruction that demonstrates the impact of the gospel to real life. Thus they learn to seek Christ, to apply the biblical teaching and preaching they receive in large- and small-group settings at church, and thereby to grow in His likeness.

> How does Christ's message relate to the everyday situations faced by Christians today—e.g., when they are tempted to become angry at being caught in traffic, making financial decisions at clearance sales, facing marital conflict over where to go for their vacation, experiencing church conflicts over music choices, or deciding how to help someone diagnosed with bipolar disorder? Biblical discipleship employs practical applications of Scripture with individuals to address real-life issues like these.

Below we will look at the necessity for careful biblical equipping so that "help" does not do more harm than good. Then we will discuss a few ways you can train your leaders. But first we need to address a question that may be dancing in your mind right now.

Counseling Outside the Church

Why work this hard? Why not just send people outside the church for counseling and discipleship? After all, it is fine to consult a physician about physical ailments, and it is appropriate to learn vocational skills from a technical college. Counseling, however, should occur within the local church, for several reasons.

First, the heart, soul, mind, spirit, and emotions are part of the inner man; thus, all fall within the realm of spiritual or soul care.5 The inner man is the part which counseling of any kind seeks to instruct and correct. Scripture says that that realm belongs to the Holy Spirit (John 14:16–17). Further, the local church, the organism that is called the temple of the Holy Spirit (made up of Spirit-indwelled individual temples), is to address these areas biblically (1 Cor. 6:19–20; Eph. 2:21–22; Gal. 6:1–2).[6] In Chapter 2 we will look at how biblical counseling accomplishes that goal.

Second, there are hundreds of varieties of counseling outside the church, and the outside counselor is rarely if ever held accountable for his or her doctrine. Certainly, a secular counselor will not even pretend to advocate or teach a biblical perspective. But even counsel that is given by Christians may be founded on secular psychology more than (or instead of) Scripture. How can you be sure what will be taught to the people for whom you are responsible (1 Peter 5:2–4; Heb. 13:17)?

Finally, counseling that is done outside the local church usually dampens or even denies the authority and accountability of the local church in the life of a given individual. For example, if a husband is found to be in an adulterous relationship, the local church is commanded to seek to restore him (Gal. 6:1–2). However, confiding in an outside counselor may prevent the church from learning about the problem and fulfilling its biblical mandate. In addition, the church is called to come alongside to provide godly fellowship, friendship, accountability, mentoring, examples, prayer, and direct Bible teaching. The active involvement of the local church is not commonly on the agenda of an out-of-church counselor.

In the next chapter we will discuss some further considerations related to outsourced counseling.

> "And He Himself gave some to be apostles, some prophets, some evangelists, and some pastors and teachers, for the equipping of the saints for the work of ministry, for the edifying of the body of Christ."
> (Eph. 4:11–12)

The Importance of Biblical Equipping

A PASTOR'S STRUGGLE

Most pastors are well trained by seminaries to accurately exegete passages, teach effective lessons, and preach biblical sermons. Like you, they have a godly heart for people. But often pastors have not been specifically trained to disciple at a personal level or to counsel individuals as Christ did. Perhaps no one has ever personally discipled them, so they have not seen the model in action. Therefore, they may find it difficult to equip others for the work of discipleship.

A young pastor recently expressed his need for help: "I have been well trained to counsel from my pulpit," he said, "but I'm finding that one-on-one in my office requires a different set of skills." From Ephesians 4:11–12, this pastor realizes with alarm that he is to equip the saints with the very discipleship skills he lacks. Although he knows that God has put into His church people with the potential to carry out Christ's Great Commission, he wonders how to best prepare them for service (1 Cor. 12:4–31, esp. vv. 11, 18, 24, 27–28). Maybe you identify with him.

> "In His marvelous wisdom, God has given us the blessing of the local church as a multifaceted means of helping believers carry out the Great Commission. BCM recognizes that biblical counseling is not an end in itself, but one important factor in the overall function of the church as we seek to 'make disciples.' I have appreciated the value of biblical counseling as a complement and supplement to the preaching, teaching, and other ministries at our church. Those who struggle in particular areas can have their specific needs addressed, while at the same time getting a wider biblical foundation and receiving support through the body as it 'edifies itself in love.' I'm grateful for the commitment that BCM has shown to the biblical pattern for the local church and its leadership. Our church is much stronger for it."
> **Stephen Steinmetz, Senior Pastor, Faith Baptist Church, Wisconsin Rapids, WI**

CHURCH RESOURCES

A thorough examination of biblical teaching responsibilities goes beyond the scope of this book, but they are important, and biblical churches practice them. As a conscientious pastor, you are already in the process of equipping people in a variety of important ways. No doubt you direct purposeful biblical teaching through preaching, adult Bible fellowships, care groups, Bible studies, age-specific Bible classes and ministries, devotions at special events, Scripture memory, music, church discipline, evangelism, the practices of baptism and the Lord's Table, and, sometimes, through individual discipleship.

Individual discipleship is listed last, because that is where it normally lands on the priority list in many churches. Laborers are few—especially in smaller churches—so that each willing worker wears many hats. It seems expedient to maximize each one's efforts by teaching groups. Therefore, one-on-one discipleship is practiced solely during times of crisis, and exclusively in the form of pastoral counseling.

In other words, people receive individual help only during times of crisis. At a practical everyday level, if one-on-one discipleship is considered at all, it is left to family and friends in an undirected manner, almost always outside of the church setting. Why should the church take the lead instead of leaving discipleship to friends and family?

PROBLEMS WITH UNDIRECTED DISCIPLESHIP

Friends and family do, in fact, regularly offer counsel, and their help is normally given in a loving and well intentioned way. Certainly, biblical Christian help should be encouraged in every setting. But Christ commanded disciple-making to be the central role of the church (Matt. 28:19–20; Eph. 4:15–16). Without biblical equipping by the church, three problems may occur:

> "A majority of churches don't do any serious teaching or training in the area of spiritual gifts and service. They're fine to let the pastor run the show and add some token time here and there whenever a plea for more help shows up in the bulletin ... something like 50 to 60 percent of people in churches say they never use their gifts and skills in ministry roles ... No wonder most churches hurt for workers ..."
> **Alan Nelson, *Me to We: A Pastor's Discovery of the Power of Partnership*** (Loveland, CO: Group, 2007) pp. 144-145, 166.

First, undirected discipleship may not be grounded in Scripture. Many friends, even churchgoers (especially new believers), have little or no Bible background and usually have been significantly influenced by an eclectic mix of secular and "religious" thinking. Most do not spend daily time in the Word, and even those who do so may not interpret life from a biblical worldview. Therefore, like Saul (see above under heading "The Bible Presents discipleship as a Norm for the Church"), they do not correctly understand or apply the Word. When trouble comes, well-meaning family members or friends offer personal opinions that may directly contradict God's Word. Without the ability to biblically discern truth from error, untaught believers may become very confused and frustrated, and their faith may be weakened. Skepticism and factions may result from this kind of discipleship. Divisions are a real possibility when personal advice is challenged by the teachings of Scripture.

Second, secular psychology has crept into the church at an alarming rate, often with a Christian veneer that looks attractive and even spiritual. Many unsuspecting believers are drawn into a secular worldview through cultural influences, including "Christian" books, cable channels, magazines, and radio stations. They bring that perspective into their

> "It cannot be stated too strongly that the primary vehicle for God's work during this age is not Christian radio, not evangelistic crusades, not Bible colleges, but the local church."
> **Corey Brookins, Senior Pastor, Berea Baptist Church, Stevens Point, WI**

churches, typically using God's Word, prayer, music, good works, and church attendance to meet felt needs. Their goal is to fix earthly problems more than to trust and honor Christ in the trials of life.

Psychologized Christian counseling, or integrationism, minimizes, changes, or omits the true gospel.[7] If Christ is mentioned at all, He is viewed as a divine therapist whose primary purpose is for every believer to be happy, rather than to learn to manifest the fruit of the Holy Spirit (Gal.

5:22–25). The underlying integrationist philosophy maximizes the lie that Christ died to alleviate earthly suffering. At the same time, it tends to minimize (or ignore) the truth that Christ died to atone for our sin, necessitating admission of our depravity and need for forgiveness. People are presumed to be innocent and deserving of much better, rather than sinners who are accountable to a faithful God. Therefore, with psychological approaches, blame-shifting is common and relief is sought by means of manipulating people, physical factors, or circumstances. For this reason, psychologized advice often leads to depression, confusion, crushing disappointment, or loss of faith and hope when circumstances do not improve. We will briefly look again at integrationism in the next chapter.

Third, even Christian friends and family members who know and follow Scripture may not take into account the whole counsel of God. The general approach among well-meaning Christians is to hear the problem, offer advice about achieving a desirable result, and find some verses dealing with the subject at hand. This approach falls tragically short of a biblical worldview, because the gospel of Jesus Christ is almost never the primary theme of discussion. This kind of discipleship usually relies on one of two extremes: some level of works righteousness (working hard to merit God's approval or favors, usually with the primary desire for Him to fix the problem) or mysticism ("letting go" of spiritual disciplines and expecting God to meet self-defined personal needs). The goal is to fulfill the desires of the sufferer, as long as those desires are biblically defensible. Thus, the person is taught to use Scripture to fix problems, rather than to see his or her circumstances through a biblical lens—as opportunities to follow Christ and to build relationships with Him and our neighbors for His glory.

Our intention here is not to discourage discipleship in everyday settings, but to offer caution. Believers need to be biblically based and Christ-centered as they give advice, in any environment. And Scripture clearly discloses that God has commissioned the church to train them

(Matt. 28:19–20; Eph. 4:11–12). Therefore, the church needs to be at the center of such ministry.

THE CHURCH'S UNIQUE ABILITY

A church is only as sound as the individuals that comprise it, because the church is its people. Churches grow in Christ only when individuals are walking closely with the Lord, are well founded on scriptural principles, and are using their spiritual gifts to reach out to the unsaved and to minister to the body of Christ. The biblical pattern of Titus 2 indicates individual mentoring. All mature believers are exhorted to help those who are younger in the Lord, and not just while they are in a crisis. Because a church-wide development of individualized discipleship is so important, Chapter 3 is devoted to that subject.

> "The BCM training and counseling of our church members causes them to be more sensitive to sin, the truth of the Word, and care for one another. This brings accountability between friends and ministry partners in a more consistent way because they believe change is possible and commanded, and because hope has become part of their way of life. This does mean that as a pastor you need to be ready for some hard questions that may get personal. But the return from this sharpening is beautiful. The steps of church discipline happen naturally and many are restored before public destruction—and who knows how many are protected from evil altogether?"
>
> **Jonathan Jenks, Senior Pastor, Calvary Baptist Church, Wisconsin Rapids, WI**

Vibrant relationship with Jesus Christ, founded upon the true gospel, is the bedrock of biblical discipleship in all settings. Unfortunately, weak biblical foundations are the norm in American society, even among those who call themselves Christians. Few people have ever looked at life through God's Word. Their worldview is so gummed up that they have difficulty correctly understanding and applying even the simplest principles from Scripture.

But God empowers transformation by faith in Christ, and He has commissioned the local church to be the New Testament center of ministry. The church represents Him through the preaching and teaching of Scripture. Upon that basis and for that purpose, He uses the church to evangelize and to extend Christ-centered fellowship, godly friendships, spiritual mentoring, Scripture-based accountability, structured restoration, love-driven discipline, and meaningful opportunities to serve. Nowhere else are these essential elements so powerfully brought together in one place. There, people can receive individual guidance to replace wrong thinking with truth and to change self-serving habits to gospel-centered ones. As individual disciples grow, the church is naturally strengthened and broadened.

A stronger church

As we have seen, biblical discipleship contributes to a spiritually healthy church by encouraging every believer to consistently walk with Christ. Biblical living produces unity and faithfulness, discourages error and isolation, and demonstrates the practicality and importance of receiving scriptural instruction. Not only that, but biblical discipleship has been used of God to bring numerous people to Jesus Christ for salvation.

Through biblical discipleship, people usually develop healthier relationships, both personally and collectively. Thus, some forms of crisis are prevented altogether. Furthermore, when people see firsthand how biblical theology relates to real life, they give better advice and reject poor advice when they hear it. During times of crisis, rather than requiring crisis counseling, maturing disciples typically begin to offer biblical crisis intervention within their churches.

As their walk with Christ deepens and their discipleship skills increase, believers become better leaders, teachers, and co-laborers. Additional workers naturally emerge. Thus, biblical discipleship feeds a maturing staff pool for youth groups, Sunday school classes, and Bible studies, as well as for future pastors and missionaries.

Does This Sound Too Good To Be True?

We are practicing what we preach. Our group of ordinary churches has been learning to enhance and reinforce discipleship through the pulpit, biblical counseling, discipleship training classes and seminars, and biblical literature. With plans that fit their particular churches, our pastors are deliberately presenting not only the careful exposition of scriptural text, but its relevance to the everyday lives of the people in the pews. In concert with that, our pastors are personally discipling key leaders, and are providing biblical discipleship training for other mature church workers. We are seeing our churches growing stronger as the discipleship base grows broader. People with biblical skills are spontaneously reaching out to those around them, encouraging others to follow their example as they follow Christ. As a result, the pastor's load has been changing.

It hasn't been easy. But biblical discipleship is happening, and it is exciting to watch!

> **HERE'S MORE FOR YOU:**
>
> **Appendix C: Questions to Help Church Leaders Assess Church Health and Direction**
> Use this list of questions to evaluate the general strengths and weaknesses of your church and to plan for growth.

Notes

1 *Merriam-Webster's Collegiate Dictionary* (10th edn.; Springfield, MA: Merriam-Webster, Inc., 1999), 330.
2 Adapted from "Discipleship—Or Mentoring?" in *The Word in Life Study Bible* (Nashville: Thomas Nelson, 1993), 444.
3 See Appendix D endnotes for a list of "one anothers."
4 **Steve Viars,** "How Can A Church Help Those With Psychiatric Disorders?," notes from a live

workshop at the Biblical Counseling Training Conference, Faith Church, Lafayette, IN, February 15, 2012.

5 Gen. 6:6; Exod. 35:26; Deut. 15:9; Ps. 45:1; Matt. 5:8; 6:21; 22:37; Acts 2:37; Mark 12:30; Jer. 31:33; Heb. 8:10; 10:16; 1 Peter 1:13; Luke 24:45; 10:27; Rom. 8:6–7, 27; 2 Cor. 4:4; 13:14; Phil. 4:7.

6 For a more thorough discussion of the role of the Holy Spirit in counseling, see **Jay Adams,** "The Role of the Holy Spirit in Counseling," Chap. 2 in *Competent to Counsel: Introduction to Nouthetic Counseling* (Grand Rapids, MI: Zondervan, 1970), 20–25.

7 The true gospel is effectual not just in securing salvation, but also in spiritual growth. Therefore, the gospel must be central in biblical discipleship to lead people to put off their sinful natures and to recognize their ongoing need for forgiveness and grace, Christ's unfailing provision and strength, and the importance of obedience as a consistently diligent expression of gratitude to God.

Wendy's grief was palpable as Pastor Paul walked into the hospital room. Her son, Jordan, was her only child. Mother and son had grown very close since Wendy's husband left her, two years earlier. As the pastor prayed with Wendy, he could sense how deeply her heart was breaking as the boy's life waned before her eyes.

Pastor Paul had thought she was recovering well from her husband Larry's departure. She had continued to teach her Sunday school class, although her attendance at worship services had dropped a little. He had asked how she was, and he and Jenny had gone to visit her. Jenny called Wendy frequently for a while until the pressing needs of home and church clamored for her attention. Wendy kept plodding along, with a brave gentle smile for him every Sunday morning. Women at church brought meals and invited her to their Bible studies and activities. She came to church services and activities, but she always looked a little out of place, as though she didn't know how to relate to them anymore. Pastor Paul had faithfully prayed for her.

But today, with Jordan's life ebbing, Wendy's composure was gone. She came unglued, crying and screaming hysterically, "Oh, Pastor, what will I do without Jordan? What is there to live for? How could God do this to me?" She ran to her pastor and buried her head in his chest.

Pastor Paul felt uncomfortable. "Where is your sister, Wendy? Is she on her way?" he asked quietly as he gently drew away from her. Wendy's sister, Sandra, an atheist, could offer only limited help, but she was family. His mind raced. He could be here for her for a while, but he needed help. Who could he call? He didn't want to leave Wendy alone with Sandra while she was in this state. He wondered what kind of advice she had received from her sister in the past. Had her husband's unfaithfulness provoked doubt about God? Sandra would certainly have pounced on that. Her mother would have encouraged her faith, but with her eclectic background and love of pop psychologists, she probably viewed Wendy primarily as a victim. And what would that have done to Wendy's view of a sovereign God?

With a pang of sorrow, Pastor Paul wished he had found a godly woman to walk with Wendy through her divorce. But everyone had felt intimidated by the situation and inadequate to get involved.

And what now, after Jordan's cancer claimed his life?

What Is Biblical Counseling? A Closer Look

Why consider biblical counseling as the foundation for building church discipleship? Before answering that question we will define more clearly what we mean when we use the terms "biblical discipleship" and "biblical counseling." Generally, "biblical discipleship" refers to general scriptural help given by any mature believer to teach another person how to follow Christ more closely. On the other hand, "biblical counseling" involves more training and is more formally conducted to scripturally target specific concerns. Biblical Counseling Ministries sometimes makes a distinction by referring to biblical counseling as focused discipleship.

> "I have told others that while we recognize our position in Christ, while we may know/spend time in God's Word, while we may know what we need to do, working with [my biblical counselor] has helped me apply [Scripture] and grow in ways I never have before."
> **BCM counselee**

The biblical counseling described in this chapter is also known as "nouthetic counseling," from the Greek words *nouthesia* and *noutheteo*, meaning to warn, admonish, or instruct.[1] When used to describe biblical counseling, "nouthetic" signifies a method of biblical change brought about through confrontation out of concern. In other words, the nouthetic counselor helps a person to change his or her thinking and behavior to follow the Christ of Scripture more fully, warning and admonishing where sin is involved, with compassionate concern for the well-being of that person and a primary desire for the glory of God.

Principles of Biblical Counseling

Now we are ready to look more closely at what makes biblical counseling biblical and thus not only perfectly suited but also very important for the spiritual well-being of the local church. The following points apply to any nouthetic skill level, whether in casual discipleship or formal counseling. These qualities contrast with popular psychological and psychosocial approaches to counseling.

First, biblical counseling is Christ-centered rather than problem-centered. The overarching goal of biblical discipleship or biblical counseling is to bring glory to God in the process of addressing concerns, whether at a general level or with a specific difficulty. The primary objective is not to facilitate human comfort or pleasure, but to please God. For example, although someone receives biblical help to change his or her thoughts and behaviors, and although those changes result in joy, joy is not the primary goal of the counsel. Tara Barthel observes, "We don't worship God because He makes us happy, but when we worship God, we are happy."[2] The central figure in biblical counseling is the God of the Bible. People are taught to see their situations and their responsibilities from God's perspective and to respond accordingly.

Second, Christ is the model. Biblical counseling focuses on Jesus Christ, who simultaneously incarnates God's glory and exemplifies humanity at its best. Therefore, the purpose of biblical

> "Biblical counseling expects failure and change, and the capacity for both to function together. This is the grace of the gospel. Your church will have public sinners changed and wanting to serve. This forces the entire body to have a grace mindset so they do not judge others or look down on them. Without strong grace teaching, those being changed will have a hard time productively mainstreaming into your church. But when this path of grace happens, they then add to the wave of impact."
>
> **Jonathan Jenks, Senior Pastor, Calvary Baptist Church, Wisconsin Rapids, WI**

counseling is to help someone receive and follow Jesus Christ from the heart. Such change transforms people, being manifested in Christlike thinking and behavior.

Third, Scripture is the authority and source of counsel. Because God is our Creator, He knows us best. He has declared that His Word is sufficient for all of life and godliness (2 Peter 1:3). Biblical doctrine, reproof, correction, and instruction in righteousness bring human beings to maturity and thoroughly equip them for every good work (2 Tim. 3:16–17). Biblical discipleship rests its full weight upon scriptural wisdom, commands, and principles that guide a person to relationship with God and a Christ-centered way of life.

On the other hand, counsel from psychological research is neither authoritative nor reliable because of the depravity of human wisdom and the limitations of human knowledge.[3] God's Word provides everything needed for abundant life and godliness, but the benefits of science extend only to the physical realm, and then only when interpreted from a biblical perspective.[4]

Fourth, the gospel mediates life change. In biblical counseling, change is sought and evaluated through the lens of the gospel. Biblical counselors share the gospel right from the first session, and we continually point out its relevance to all the issues of life. Therefore, through the counseling ministry many people have bowed before Christ by faith to receive His gift of eternal life (John 1:12; 14:6).

As sinners, we are completely dependent upon God's grace for forgiveness and growth. Yet we are also responsible to participate in God's work: first, to receive Christ, and then to faithfully follow His example. Authors Jerry Bridges and Bob Bevington use the term "dependent responsibility" to describe this relationship. They write, "When we become united to Christ by faith, God places a set of bookends on the bookshelf of our lives. One bookend is *the righteousness of Christ*; the other is *the power of the Holy Spirit*" (his emphasis).[5] Bridges and

Bevington explain that the believer is completely dependent upon God for justification, adoption, and glorification. The imputed righteousness of Christ is the basis of a believer's confidence. Therefore, a believer who recognizes that he or she is eternally secure in Christ will trust God for his or her well-being. Such a person understands that he or she is completely dependent on God. On the other hand, the power of the Holy Spirit gives every believer the ability to follow Christ's example, and thus he or she is also responsible to God to live faithfully. That responsibility leads people to diligently apply Scripture in every situation they face, as Christ did—even when doing so requires painful self-sacrifice.

A gospel focus directs a nouthetic counselor to correct unbiblical beliefs about God, self, purpose in life, and relationships with others. People learn about their dependent responsibility before God, and how His grace is freely given to those who put their faith in Him. No longer must they rely upon their own efforts to justify themselves, but on Christ's righteousness. They learn how their wrong beliefs show up in their thoughts, speech, and behaviors. They are also taught how to replace sinful responses with right living in the context of their troubling circumstances, so that they follow Christ more faithfully. As they grow, they find the Holy Spirit empowering their scriptural efforts.

Fifth, worship is targeted. Recently, while scolding our dog, my husband remarked, "You rascal!" Then he paused and reflected, "We're all rascals at heart." Biblical counseling recognizes that there is a rascal in us all that flows from selfish desires of the heart.

The heart of worship is the central issue in a human life—who or what does the person live for, and how is that worship showing up in the context of the current struggle? God's greatest command is to love Him wholeheartedly, but our reaction to trials or blessings points to the true object of our faith. Biblical counselors are alert to ways in which people may be craving something—good or bad—to the point that when they lose or cannot obtain what they want, they are willing to sin. Any time sin is present, a person has set his or her heart on something other than Christ.

Of course, not every difficult situation is the result of the sin or idolatry of the sufferer. Consider Christ, who suffered without sinning (Heb. 4:15). However, every problem has a spiritual dimension that should be addressed in a biblical, Christ-centered way. Heart desires are active all the time and can be easily provoked. Even when the original problem is not due to personal sin, people may react with vengeance, despair, or fear, rather than faith and love. The biblical counselor will lead a sufferer to honor Christ in response to life's conundrums.

Christ-centeredness marks all biblical discipleship. People often focus on their desires without considering Christ at all, except to ask Him to change their circumstances to satisfy themselves. Biblical counseling leads people to depend upon Christ and accept appropriate personal responsibility.

To see how these principles work, consider the following scenario.

A Comparative Illustration

Mary, a Christian, wants to change her son Billy's embarrassing behaviors at restaurants. Appropriate behavior is a reasonable and good objective, so she prays for Christ's help and seeks assistance from XYZ Christian Counseling (integrationists).[6] The counselor works with Mary to change the child's behaviors using manipulative techniques. She cites Scripture to punctuate her counseling techniques and to warn Billy about God's watchful eye. On one hand, Mary is happy if Billy responds well. Behavior management helps in public places and also makes home more enjoyable. However, if Billy won't change, Mary's hopes are dashed. She becomes frustrated, embarrassed, and anxious.

Now Mary decides to seek biblical counseling. Her biblical counselor leads Mary to examine herself as she works with her son. Together, they find that Mary's primary objective is to prevent humiliation, because she wants others to think well of her. As a result, when Billy misbehaves in a restaurant, Mary reacts angrily because she feels personally disgraced. "What will people think?" she wonders, as the color rises in her face. Mary's motive is to avoid further embarrassment, not to honor Christ. She sees Billy's behavior as the cause of the problem, so her solution is to change her child.

The biblical counselor uses Scripture's definition of love to teach Mary to seek the well-being of her child above her own feelings (see 1 Cor. 13:1–8). They go to Scripture to define what is best for Billy, and then how to pursue Christlikeness for everyone in the family. If she is to be Christ-centered as a parent, Mary must realize that her little boy is fundamentally sinful and therefore needs a Savior. She knows that sin fuels Billy's disobedience, but she learns that sin fuels her responses to him as well.[7]

With this in mind, Mary is taught to see the restaurant scene as a teaching moment. Behavior modification is employed, but the motivation and methods are now biblically based. As she learns to discipline Billy in an age-appropriate way, the young mother also points out the child's sin and his need of the Savior. She relies upon Christ as she urges Billy to receive the gospel and follow God's good wisdom for his lifetime.

When Mary's goals are centered in Christ, there is hope. Later, even if the child ultimately chooses to reject Christ and act foolishly, Mary knows she has fulfilled her biblical role in Billy's life.[8] She also knows that a wise and sovereign Savior cares for Billy, so she prays with an enduring hope.

The major thrust of biblical counseling points to the sufficiency of Christ in the context of a current trial. Biblical counselors urge people to turn away from inflated personal desires in order to follow the true Savior. For Mary, that means consistently expressing love for God and her son as Scripture defines love, not as a reaction to what other people may think.

A growing relationship with Jesus Christ is the key. Mary will be most effective as a parent when she sees Billy from God's perspective: as a sinner in need of the Savior. Therefore, biblical counselors consult Scripture to correct any misunderstandings of God's character and sufficiency, to present the gospel, and to define the person's view of purpose and self in that light.

The biblical counselor also helps people to apply biblical knowledge. Mary has to learn specifically how to respond as Christ would in the situation at hand. So her counselor teaches her how to treat Billy with grace, yet to address his sinful behaviors appropriately and lead him to obey. Love and truth should drive the process.

During each meeting, Mary and her counselor go over the challenges that Mary has faced. They discuss Mary's motives and personal responses. She learns not only how to trust and follow the Lord, but how to lead Billy gracefully toward Christ as well. She fulfills her responsibilities in light of God's sovereignty over her son. When Mary understands, embraces, and applies dependent responsibility, her parenting becomes biblical, and lasting changes occur.

A Word about Christian Counseling, or Integrationism

In our fictional example, XYZ Christian Counseling represents integrationism, a philosophy that attempts to bring Scripture into psychological constructs. You should be aware of the differences between biblical counseling and Christian counseling, or integrationism.

Integrationism has its roots in secular psychology, but it carries a Christianized tone. Problems are usually identified according to terms and definitions from the latest version of the Diagnostic and Statistical Manual (DSM)[9]. Once a problem is identified, counseling focuses on solving that problem by defining and meeting the needs of the client in psychological terms. An integrationist may consult the Bible for solutions and encouragement, and may pray to God for help to meet those psychological needs.

David Powlison broaches the subject of integrationism by acknowledging that man does have legitimate needs for forgiveness and care. He explains the difference between needs-based counseling (integrationism) and Christ-centered counseling (biblical counseling) by referring to C. S. Lewis's *The Four Loves*:

> Lewis captures something that has numerous implications. For example, he says that man's love for God is a "Need-love," but the way he unpacks it is exactly the opposite of the need theology and need psychology [now commonly called integrationism] that is popular in our contemporary culture. When Lewis speaks of a need love, it is not a need for self-esteem, a need to feel loved, a need to feel significant, or a need for excitement in our lives. He's referring to our need for forgiveness of our sins and a need for support in our tribulations. Lewis turns on its head the entire way that our modern world thinks about the nature of how God's love and human need meet.[10]

Integrationists elevate human worth and define human desires as "needs." Those needs seem reasonable and good, even biblical, so it seems right to expect God to fulfill them. However, the approach is upside down: man is presumed to be innocent, human needs are considered to be primary and are defined psychologically, and God is implored to serve those self-defined needs.

In our example above, Mary's self-defined need was for Billy to behave. While obedience is good and should be pursued, her fundamental premise was flawed. Through biblical counseling, Mary learned that neither she nor Billy was innocent. Both operated out of selfish desires. Their true needs were for God's forgiveness and grace, as well as His wisdom. As Mary confessed her sin and pursued God's agenda, she fulfilled His purposes as a parent and was freed from the notion that her well-being was tied to her son's behavior (Isa. 43:7; Col. 2:9–10).

In contrast to integrationism, a biblical counselor elevates Christ. People are led to evaluate self biblically, first, according to a true and ongoing need for God's forgiveness and grace, and, second, in light of God's declared purpose for His children to glorify Him (Phil. 2:1–11; 2 Cor. 5:9, 15). Believers glorify God by faith as they trust in His character and cooperate with His agenda in the context of their lives (Eph. 1:13–14; Phil. 1:6). Thus, God causes them to grow in Christlikeness by manifesting the fruit of the Spirit: love, joy, peace, patience, gentleness, goodness, faithfulness, kindness, and self-control (Rom. 3:10, 23; 8:28–29; 1 Cor. 10:13; Gal. 5:22–23). These results exceed all earthly goals and do not depend upon situational change (though they do affect our circumstances), as Mary discovered.[11]

More about Biblical Counseling

Much more about biblical counseling could be said, but a complete explanation is not possible here. Further resources are listed in Appendix H. You may also go to the BCM Web site (www.bcmin.org) and click on the "Resources" tab for our free "Recommended Reading List." Look for the subject "Counseling" to find books on biblical counseling. Paul David Tripp's *Instruments in the Redeemer's Hands* and John MacArthur's *Counseling: How to Counsel Biblically* are two of our

---

HERE'S MORE FOR YOU:

Appendix A: A Brief Theology of Biblical Counseling
Learn more about the foundational beliefs behind biblical counseling with this concise outline. Compare them with the counseling and discipleship that your church offers.

Appendix B: A General Outline for Offering Biblical Counsel
Learn what biblical counseling generally looks like in a session, so you can assess your skills and your need for additional training. This appendix will also help you to interview potential counselees and ask good questions of counselors when making a referral.

---

favorite texts. In addition, BCM offers a one-day training seminar called "Basic Skills for Giving Wise Counsel" that covers the basics of biblical discipleship and is particularly aimed

> "Get the help. It's important to have someone show you how Scripture applies."
> **BCM counselee**

at church leaders. Click on the "Training" tab at the BCM Web site for current seminar information and registration.

Notes

1 For example, see Acts 20:31; Rom. 15:14; Col. 1:28; 3:16; 1 Cor. 4:14.

2 **Tara Barthel,** *The Peacemaking Church Women's Study: Living the Gospel in Relationships* (Billings, MT: Peacemaker Ministries, 2007), 28.

3 God alone knows the heart (Jer. 17:9–10). Therefore, His Word is the only reliable source of help for the spiritual needs of the inner man.

4 For a more complete discussion of this subject, consult **Douglas Bookman,** "The Scriptures and Biblical Counseling," in **John MacArthur and Wayne Mack, (eds.),** *Introduction to Biblical Counseling* (Dallas: Word, 1994).

5 **Jerry Bridges and Bob Bevington,** *The Bookends of the Christian Life* (Wheaton, IL: Crossway, 2009), 15.

6 This agency name is fictional.

7 This statement is made in reference to this illustration and does not necessarily apply to all cases.

8 This example is sketchy. For more information on the subject of Christ-centered parenting and heart motives, see **Tedd Tripp,** *Shepherding A Child's Heart* (Wapwallopen, PA: Shepherds Press, 2009).

9 The Diagnostic and Statistical Manual of Mental Disorders (current version: DSM IV-TR) is used as a standard by the psychiatric community to evaluate and diagnose mental disorders.

10 **David Powlison,** "CCEF Presents," in *CCEF Now* (magazine of Christian Counseling & Educational Foundation), 2012, 3; quoted from a CCEF video at www.goo.gl/dTNGN.

11 For more comparisons between biblical counseling and integrationism, consult **Richard Ganz,** *PsychoBabble: The Failure of Modern Psychology—and the Biblical Alternative* (Wheaton, IL: Crossway, 1993).

Jordan's funeral was the saddest that Pastor Paul had ever experienced. Wendy was overwhelmed with grief, to the extent that she had to be hospitalized for several days. When she returned, the church, shocked and grieved, sent women to deliver meals, care for Wendy's house, and stay with her day and night. Pastor Paul put Wendy on his counseling calendar for weekly sessions, and he and Jenny dropped in to see her every few days.

Although he appreciated the attentive care that was given to Wendy, Pastor Paul wondered about the content of the solace being offered during those evening hours at Wendy's home. Were the women sympathizing in a way that built up Wendy's faith in God, or did they pity her? Essentially, he knew that too much pity would reinforce the idea that God had not been faithful or loving toward her. Would they give her hope or platitudes? Would they help her to express her grief through the eyes of faith? Would they point to Christ, or center themselves in emotionalism? He shuddered at his next thought. Through their well-meaning tears and pity, would they unintentionally reinforce what Sandra had undoubtedly told Wendy: that God couldn't be trusted (if He existed at all)?

As Pastor Paul turned the situation over in his mind, he could see the necessity of discipleship training. Wendy needed hope in Christ, and the message must be reinforced as often as possible. He knew his counseling would be more effective if the women attending her were skilled to support what she was receiving from him.

Compassion flooded him. Many of Wendy's comforters were struggling too, in conflicts, difficult situations, and poor health. How might he equip them to meet those trials biblically? He knew that with some encouragement they could be reaching out to each other more effectively. Meals and emotional support should not be ends in themselves, but rather doors for sharing hope in Christ and guidance from Scripture.

The office chair squeaked in protest as Pastor Paul suddenly straightened up—he realized that the men needed help to develop meaningful ministry in their relationships, too.

The phone rang, shaking Pastor Paul from his reverie. A shot of panic hit him as he realized how chaotic his schedule had become now. But something had to be done. Reaching across the paper-laden desk for his cell phone, he breathed out a prayer: *Lord, show me where to begin.*

Church Discipleship Development

Christ-centered discipleship development trains people how to think and act biblically, reinforces your pastoral preaching and teaching, and holds church ministry objectives in view. All believers are to be diligently taught to prioritize their personal relationship with Christ so that their desires, activities, and human relationships are defined by Scripture.

In this chapter we will unpack some ways you can purposefully organize discipleship development to fulfill your biblical mandate. We will explore how you can be a catalyst for leadership development that will perpetuate itself. In other words, we will give you a few ideas for making disciples who will, in turn, make more disciples as Christ intended, so that your whole church becomes involved in discipleship at some level.

> "That's our job as pastors and teachers, not to do works of service for people, but rather to prepare, to train, to empower God's people for works of service. But for what outcome? Here it is [in Eph. 4:12–14]: 'so that the body of Christ may be built up until we all reach unity in the faith and in the knowledge of the Son of God and become mature, attaining to the whole measure of the fullness of Christ. Then we will no longer be infants, tossed back and forth by the waves, and blown here and there by every wind of teaching and by the cunning and craftiness of men in their deceitful scheming' [NIV 1984]."
> **Alan Nelson, *Me to We: A Pastor's Discovery of the Power of Partnership*** (Loveland, CO: Group, 2007) p. 48.

Pastor's Toolbox: Getting Started Developing Qualified Leaders

Godly leaders are not usually just found; they must be developed, in Titus

2 and 2 Timothy 2:2 style. We urge you to take the initiative to identify believers with leadership and discipleship potential. If possible, arrange for your church to cover all or part of the costs to get them some biblical counseling training.

Biblical Counseling Ministries' "Pastor's Toolbox" seminar is designed for pastors and deacons/elders to set up a plan for leadership development in their churches. This chapter will briefly touch the high points. However, we encourage you, if possible, to come for the seminar, which is taught by pastors, for a more thorough and tailored treatment of this important subject. Also, see Appendices C, D, and E of this book for additional help with discipleship evaluation and implementation.

> **HANDS-ON HELP FOR PASTORS WHO WANT TO DEVELOP CHURCH LEADERS**
> BCM's "Pastor's Toolbox" seminar helps pastors and deacons to write a leadership plan that will work for them. Every church is different, so every plan will differ also. Our "Pastor's Toolbox" seminar track is built around that premise. Check the BCM Web site (www.bcmin.org) for seminar information.

Identifying and Developing Leaders

Your first step is to identify leadership potential among your current members and then systematically to encourage the development of their latent spiritual gifts and abilities.

Discover leaders by observing people during regular activities. As a pastor, you can redeem the time simply by being alert to what is going on around you. Prayer breakfasts, home visits, retreats, fellowship activities, and deacons' meetings can all be good opportunities to discover who is teachable, maturing, and willing to

> "And the things that you have heard from me among many witnesses, commit these to faithful men who will be able to teach others also."
> 2 Timothy 2:2

work. Look for a growing walk with Christ, interest in the Word, evidence of repentance for sin, humility, compassion, perseverance, and willingness to work at biblical change. You will probably see these qualities only in seed form; hence the need for discipleship. Test for leadership qualities like wisdom, a teachable spirit, and biblical knowledge by discussing one or two difficult hypothetical scenarios and biblical solutions.[1] Ask some of the strategic questions from the appendices at the back of this book. These questions will heighten interest in biblical thinking and spur discussion among those who are interested in maturing spiritually.

Once identified, you can train and exhort teachable men through one-on-one discipleship with you. To develop women's leadership, a godly woman such as your wife could be trained to offer discipleship.

Develop potential leaders through deliberate personal efforts. Be creative and purposeful with personal discipleship. One pastor structures his budget so that he can take teachable men out to breakfast to talk about spiritual things. Another pastor arranges for morning prayers with a few men at his office, while his wife invites a woman to their home to pray before work. Yet another pastor invites men for hunting and fishing trips to discuss their relationship with God. His wife schedules fun activities with their wives, during which they pray and discuss spiritual issues. By utilizing some creative ideas like these, you can personally assist capable men

"Whenever the body gets serious with God's Word, it will require and desire strong biblical leadership that helps it obey the commands of outreach, discipleship, and holiness. The people will want order because God is orderly. They will love a gracious, gentle leadership unmovable in the truth. They will hold you accountable to this. They will listen to your preaching in a better way and be expecting sound biblical application for life."

Jonathan Jenks, Senior Pastor, Calvary Baptist Church, Wisconsin Rapids, WI

and women to become biblical leaders in their homes and workplaces, while simultaneously building leaders in your church.

For specific help with leadership development beyond what is covered in this chapter, see Appendices C and D. These resources will help you to assess your strengths and weaknesses as a church, spur spiritual depth in your leaders, and strengthen relationships in your church (especially among the church leadership).

Develop leaders through team building. You can train one or two potential leaders by including them in your current work. For example, together you can minister the Word during home or hospital visits, Bible research for a message, evangelism with the waitress who serves you breakfast, or team counseling sessions. As your potential leader develops people-helping skills, God will bring disciples to him. Now he can walk alongside others to purposefully nurture and train them, just as you have walked with him.

Develop leaders through discipleship training courses and biblical counseling seminars. You should encourage your disciples to get the training necessary to minister to their fullest potential. If possible, the church should cover the cost of their training.

Several viable training options could be used. Some pastors write their own curriculum for Sunday Bible classes or evening services. You may choose to

> "BCM impacts this area [equipping the saints] directly by training people to think biblically about problems and to build healthy life patterns. You can use the seminars to introduce people to the big picture of how to address problems through biblical discipleship, as well as to introduce them to great books. We encourage all our leaders to take some of the seminars as a refresher and as a way to whet their appetite for more training. The greatest thing people tend to take away from the seminars is something for them to personally resolve with God. Don't forget—leaders at peace produce."
>
> **Jonathan Jenks, Senior Pastor, Calvary Baptist Church, Wisconsin Rapids, WI**

host weekend leadership conferences and invite other churches to join you. Small groups or evening Bible studies can teach biblical perspectives on marriage, parenting, or emotions. Other training could involve BCM classes, courses at reputable seminaries, or conferences such as the ACBC annual conference or the Biblical Counseling Training Conference in Lafayette, Indiana.[2] Additional options include reading reliable literature[3] or taking online or DVD training in biblical counseling.[4] These resources are all worthy of exploration.[5]

BCM Discipleship Training

One way for pastors to offer discipleship training is through BCM. We have designed valuable supplementary resources to train people to disciple others biblically. We offer help through recommending books, telephone consultation, and, if the pastor prefers, classes and seminars in discipleship development. Many of our classes are streamed live.[6]

BCM originally started with a one-day seminar that is now called "Basic Skills for Giving Wise Counsel." This seminar covers elemental teaching about biblical counseling, including its definition, discovering heart issues, dealing with wrong thinking, and going through the basic steps of biblical change. This seminar is now offered on the road.

Responses to our first seminar revealed that people were hungry to learn more. So we wrote a curriculum that is now offered on a two-year cycle. If you live too far away to travel to central Wisconsin every week, you can gather together a small group of church leaders around a table for our live-streamed classes.

BCM training is certified by the Association of Certified Biblical Counselors (ACBC). We chose to associate with ACBC because of that organization's high level of commitment to the Word of God as the foundation for discipleship. We also like ACBC's high educational standards, their rigorous certification process, their excellent training conferences, the integrity of their organizational structure, their vision for worldwide impact, and the legal recognition that comes with ongoing accountability to an internationally recognized certifying organization. We also appreciate how the everyday believer can become better equipped to disciple others through the ACBC certification process.

Of course, we realize that not everyone wants to become a full-time biblical counselor. Therefore, BCM offers training that is appropriate for a variety of skills and ministry objectives:

- Some people simply want to increase their everyday discipleship skills to offer biblical advice in informal settings. Our seminars and everyday discipleship classes are designed for them. Training helps them to think biblically, to avoid foolish decisions, and to informally advise others to live in God-honoring ways.

- Some students take our "Basic Skills" classes to help them minister well in their Sunday Bible classes or midweek Bible studies, youth groups, deacon/deaconess roles, or other church work. Trained disciplers in our area are helping their churches with conflict resolution, marriage and family problems, meaningful person-to-person Bible studies, and ongoing discipleship for counselees who have completed sessions with a certified biblical counselor.

- "Basic Skills" classes may be

BCM seminars are normally held in late fall, followed by "Focused Discipleship" classes during winter and spring. We also offer our seminar on the road to those who are unable to travel to us. At the time of writing, our classes are held on weekends and Tuesday evenings in central Wisconsin. Through live streaming, our classroom options extend beyond our region. Check our Web site for developments, upcoming class schedules, and other training information. For direct e-mail notification of upcoming training events and other ministry opportunities, ask for our free e-newsletter. E-mail your name, address, and e-mail address to info@bcmin.org with the subject line E-NEWSLETTER.

taken for Bible college credit or to prepare for ACBC certification. We are excited to see our certified students taking active roles in their local church soul care and outreach ministries. With their pastors' direction and supervision, they are able to serve in leadership roles, community outreach, and biblical counseling sessions in their churches.

BCM instructors teach students to ask good questions, define problems biblically, search Scripture for solutions, demonstrate the relevance of the gospel, and skillfully communicate how to apply biblical principles to help individuals grow in grace.

Our students are challenged to apply Scripture in their personal lives, as well as to help others. That should come as good news to pastors like you. Whatever the level of study, our goal is to better equip each student to follow Christ and reach out with Bible-based advice, thereby strengthening the local churches they serve.

Persevere by Faith and Allow Time for Your Discipleship Efforts to Bear Fruit

Developing leaders and nurturing discipleship in your church is not neat and tidy work. Expect some disappointments and setbacks. Finding leaders may seem next to impossible, but remind yourself that all things are possible with God (Matt. 9:37–38; 19:26).

Remember Christ's example and consider the job that lay ahead of Him when He chose His twelve disciples. He, the Son of God, personally selected a group of unimpressive men and took three years to train them. Follow Christ's discipleship development

> "Being equipped to do the work of the ministry seems to be everyone's ideal goal for church leaders.
> "Everyone but Christ. His pastoral ministry description demands the ability to equip others to do the work of the ministry."
> **Robert Kellemen,** *Equipping Counselors for Your Church*

model. Pray, pray, pray (Luke 18:1; John 17). Teach again and again with patience and mercy (2 Tim. 2:1–10). Keep God's purposes clearly in view (Heb. 10:35–38). And don't give up (Gal. 6:9).

Spiritual growth is not instant, but when you follow God's plan you can expect that perseverance for Christ will produce fruit in His time (John

> "I invited our congregation to join me on a journey of catching God's vision for every-member disciple-making. Because of that focus, this family received both formal biblical counseling and informal one-another ministry."
> **Robert Kellemen, *Equipping Counselors for Your Church***

15:4–8). Christ patiently taught lessons over and over, using many teaching styles. He persevered in love, even when they didn't understand what He was trying to do, and even though one of them rejected and betrayed Him, one denied knowing Him, and all of them ran away at one point. Follow Christ's pattern, remembering that every Christian church worldwide has grown out of that group of twelve unlikely men.

Discipleship As a Whole Church Environment

After consistent prayer, pastoral involvement, perseverance, and discipleship training over the course of a few years, the pastors at BCM's core churches have seen God raising up solid leaders from among their men and women—some from unexpected places. Those believers are now trained leaders who spontaneously reach out in line with the Titus 2 and 2 Timothy 2:2 example, just as their pastors reached out to them. As a result, we are seeing a broader base of leadership and growth in church unity.

As leadership becomes stronger and as members become more involved in discipling one another, we have found that the pastor's burden is lighter and fewer people are slipping through the cracks.

Depending upon the size of your church, as more people get involved in discipleship you may want to provide a flowchart to guide your people to find the help they need. For example, let's say that Jaclyn, a Sunday Bible class teacher, notices that one of her students, Kerri, appears troubled. She goes to Kerri, inquires about her concerns, and offers to pray with her. Jaclyn has been trained to ask good questions, to share the gospel, and to open Scripture with Kerri to address her concerns. They spend some time together, and Jaclyn encourages Kerri to grow in her relationship with Christ as she deals with the challenges in her life.

It isn't long before Jaclyn realizes that Kerri needs additional help. The flowchart provided by her pastor tells Jaclyn where to take Kerri next for assistance. So she introduces Kerri to Alicia, a deaconess in her care group. Alicia, too, knows whom to consult, if necessary ... and so on, up to the pastor.[7] Each church member Kerri meets reinforces the same biblical worldview, which helps her to gain hope in Christ even as she struggles with her problems.

The BCM model also offers counseling assistance to the pastor who is asked to see Kerri. The pastor can consult with the BCM counselor, or he may directly refer Kerri for one-on-one sessions. As her referring pastor, he may participate in sessions if Kerri agrees. When sessions are complete, the biblical counselor asks the pastor to find someone at church to continue to walk closely alongside Kerri for a while. His choice is usually fairly obvious. In this case, since Kerri is in Jaclyn's Sunday Bible class, and since Jaclyn is a mature believer who has had some discipleship training, the pastor logically chooses her. Kerri's biblical counselor helps Jaclyn find pertinent Bible study materials to use. The counselor may also meet with Jaclyn and Kerri a few times, if necessary, to help establish a comfortable relationship and to clarify goals.

Thinking Through Your Resource Options

It will take time and patient endurance to equip your people well. As your discipleship plan takes shape, you will probably need someone to help with consultations and counseling for people like Kerri. Before moving on, we should look at some of the options that pastors choose to fill that gap.

LEAVE PEOPLE TO PURSUE UNDIRECTED DISCIPLESHIP

We have already pointed out some concerns regarding undirected discipleship, especially if it lacks a biblical foundation (see Chapter 1). This option—though commonly practiced—falls far short of the standard of care commanded in Scripture for the church (see Luke 10:25–37). Most pastors recognize the dangers and do not actively make this choice. Still, people "fall through the cracks" when their struggles are not adequately addressed through local church avenues. A church's lack of energy, skills, compassion, and/or resources may leave people to consult sources that are not spiritually prepared to help them. Fortunately, other alternatives are available.

HIRE A BIBLICAL COUNSELOR TO JOIN THE CHURCH STAFF

A staff counselor can help you with consultations, counseling cases, discipleship development and training, as well as recommending reliable literature. Other biblical counselors will emerge as the men and women in your church respond to the training, personal attention, and exemplary roles modeled by you and your staff counselor.

Finances usually prevent the average church from bringing in more paid staff. Indeed, a great many churches cannot afford to pay a part-time church secretary, let alone a biblical counselor.[8] However, if God allows for your church to call additional staff, this book will help you to think through how to organize your counseling ministry and prepare well for your new counselor.

REFER PEOPLE TO COUNSELORS OUTSIDE YOUR CHURCH

We have already pointed out some of the problems with making referrals outside your church. First, it is difficult to ascertain whether the quality or content of sessions will hold to biblical standards. Second, counseling occurs apart from the authority of the local church and may preclude appropriate church involvement or biblical accountability for both counselor and counselee (see Chapter 2).

If you do choose to refer, we urge you to become familiar with the basics of biblical counseling so that you will know what to look for in a counselor. You may find access to reliable biblical counselors outside your church in the following ways:

- Contact a nearby church of like faith and practice that has a biblical counselor on staff to see if he or she is able to take your referrals. (If your church is blessed with a staff biblical counselor, please consider helping smaller churches in your area with biblical discipleship training and one-on-one counseling by pastoral referral. The BCM model may help you to organize your efforts.)
- Refer people to a biblically sound organization such as the Biblical Counseling Center (BCC) in Arlington Heights, Illinois.[9] Be aware that nouthetic counseling centers are few and far between, whereas integrationism is common. So before referring (even to a reputable church or organization), we recommend that you read its doctrinal statement. In addition, inquire where your counselor was educated and discuss his or her philosophy of counseling (see Chapter 2).
- Organize a counseling center to which you may refer people from your church. Although biblical counseling is growing, it may be difficult to find qualified biblical counselors in your area. In that case, you may consider starting a counseling center at your church and hiring a biblical counselor to whom you and your community can refer. Often a center is operated independently, but it can be started and maintained by a church or a group of churches. If you choose to start a center, you should seriously consider locating it in a local church, in line with the New Testament pattern. Having your counseling center located in your church building sends the

message that the local church (as God's representative) has answers for the problems that people face. It also encourages church involvement, Scripture-centered fellowship, and church membership. We do recognize, though, that there are legitimate reasons for locating a counseling center outside the church building (e.g., on a college campus, where student transportation to a church is not possible).

Although BCM is not a counseling center, the BCM model may be adapted to form a church-based center for biblical counseling. The following chapters offer some suggestions for doing so.

BRING IN BIBLICAL COUNSELORS

BCM's biblical counselor travels to five churches for sessions. We know of only one other ministry model that sends biblical counselors to local churches: Truth in Love Ministries.[10] Their model trains teams that travel from church to church. They differ organizationally from BCM, particularly in their relationship with the churches they serve.

UTILIZE THE BCM MODEL

BCM functions in, with, and through local churches. We work directly with pastors, under church authority. Pastors decide whom to refer and whom to send for training. Therefore, the ministry is church-driven.

BCM's model can be an invaluable help to local churches because:
- BCM is fully accountable to the core churches we serve.
- BCM counsel carefully upholds the biblical doctrines of its governing churches.
- Pastors/elders decide whom to refer for counseling, and the referring pastor is usually part of the counseling process.
- BCM counselors serve pastors by providing resources for literature, teaching materials, and consultation when needed.
- Mentoring is available for pastors and advanced students.[11]

- Our female counselors provide a helpful option for counseling women.
- Female BCM counselors model godly submission to authority within a role of responsibility in the church.
- We are a biblical option for the counselee who has difficulty opening up with someone from his or her church about sensitive subjects.
- BCM training assists pastors to equip their members for biblical discipleship. We also encourage ACBC certification for qualified people, with a goal of building a pool of skilled biblical counselors in our churches.
- BCM initiates discipleship relationships to encourage continuing counselee support in the local church.
- Because our counselor is female, co-counsel is required for men and married couples. Usually the referring pastor provides co-counsel, but other trained godly church leaders may also take that role. The role of co-counselor is a helpful vehicle for building experience and personal growth in discipleship skills.
- We make a biblical impact in our community by accepting some counseling referrals from pastors outside our core churches. These pastors learn about biblical counseling via consultations and co-counseling.

The BCM model offers resources to fill the gap when pastors, church leaders, and teachers are stretched thin. We suggest reliable literature, provide training, and supplement pastoral counseling when needed. Because our model works under the authority of the local church, the pastor can be confident that the care

> "God will one day fulfill every good intention prompted by faith (2 Thes. 1:11)."
> **David Powlison, *Seeing With New Eyes***

we offer will be compliant with Scripture. These qualities make our model unique and very effective.

Moving Forward

We have shown that discipleship is essential to fulfill the God-given purposes of every local church. As pastor, you are responsible for equipping your people. You may effectively begin by pursuing personal discipleship with actual and potential church leaders, teaching them to reach out to others in the same way. The goal is for the whole church to catch on: to become actively involved with helping one another to grow in God's grace and wisdom.

It is important to start now. Every obedient step you take toward fulfilling God's command is worth the effort (Matt. 28:19–20; Eph. 4:11–12), no matter how small that step may seem.

The appendices in this book provide some outlines and checklists to help you proceed in an organized way. For additional assistance, the

---

HERE'S MORE FOR YOU:

Appendix C: *Questions to Help Church Leaders Assess Church Health and Direction*
Use this list of questions to evaluate the strengths and weaknesses of your church and to plan for growth.

Appendix D: Key Components for Pastors Developing Disciple-Makers
An outline/checklist for pastors to work on discipleship skills with potential church leaders. This is what discipleship development looks like in action.

Appendix E: The Disciple-Maker's Task: Building Christ-Centered Relationships
Essential elements of godly relationships and how to nurture them in the church family. In today's isolationist society, use this appendix to help your people build stronger relationships.

Appendix F: A Checklist for Setting Up Your Ministry Model
An outline of the steps in this book for use as a checklist to help you to be thorough when organizing your ministry.

Chapter 3

BCM "Pastor's Toolbox Developing Leaders in Your Church" seminar can help you to write a leadership and discipleship plan specifically to fit your church. Contact BCM for more information about that seminar.

The BCM model shows you how a biblical counselor can help you to carry out your plan. You may choose to follow our model, utilizing collaboration among several churches to share a resource counselor. Alternatively, you might choose to hire a staff biblical counselor or to start a counseling center at your church. As we share how the BCM model was developed, we will indicate some ways that our model may be adapted for either of the last two resource options. We will also speak directly to biblical counselors, offering practical tips to work as a team in any of these environments.

Notes

1 This is also an effective way to teach biblical problem-solving.

2 Biblical Counseling Training Conference (BCTC) is held at Faith Baptist Church in Lafayette, Indiana, for a week in February. The BCTC Track 1 training is also held at various other locations in the U.S.

3 See our "Recommended Reading List" under the "Resources" tab at www.bcmin.org.

4 For example, IBCD offers ACBC classes online (audio with pdf notes) at www.ibcd.org. Twelve Stones Ministries and Harvest Bible Chapel produce the DVD set *Biblical Soul Care*: visit www.biblicalsoulcare.com.

5 For international students, BCM offers live streamed classes that may be taken from anywhere in the world (with the exception of our Basic Skills 102 "Skill-Building" class, which features role playing that requires on-site participation). Students who do not speak English must find their own translators in order to participate in live streaming. Other training options include contacting the Association of Certified Biblical Counselors (https://biblicalcounseling.com), which is in the process of building a global network of biblical counseling teachers and materials in various languages. We expect that the resources offered by ACBC will continue to grow in number and content. Finally, international students may purchase a lesson series on DVD from such sources as the Institute of Nouthetic Studies (Jay Adams), or they may download classes from the Institute for Biblical Counseling & Discipleship (www.ibcd.org). Currently, these resources are in English and will require

translation. See also footnote 3 on page 148.

6 For more information on our live-streamed option, see the "Online Class Fact Sheet" in the "Training" section at www.bcmin.org.

7 Care must be taken not to start a gossip chain. We have not found that to be a problem among godly leaders. However, to avoid gossip, some pastors prefer that all their people come directly to them.

8 This has been a discouragement to qualified biblical counselors coming out of our seminaries right now.

9 www.biblicalcounselingcenter.org. Founded by Dr. Ron Allchin, a ACBC Fellow.

10 www.truthinloveministries.org. Founded by Dr. Mark Shaw. Dr. Shaw explains his model in *Strength in Numbers: The Team Approach to Biblical Counseling* (Bemidji, MN: Focus, 2010).

11 By application, with BCM board approval.

O ver the next several months, Pastor Paul gave himself to prayer. The "Pastor's Toolbox" seminar had helped him to assess his goals and begin to form a plan. He had gone alone to the BCM seminar this year, grateful that BCM seminars are free to pastors. While there, he realized that he should bring his church board next time. God's plan from Ephesians 4 meant his style of leadership had to change. He was not meant to lead alone. He had to equip his church to work as a team.

As he left the seminar, Pastor Paul turned his key in the ignition and felt his old Chevrolet Impala sputter to life. He drove away challenged and a little overwhelmed, but with a sense of direction that had been lacking throughout his pastorate. He drew courage because he could see which step to take next and he had an idea where the church should head. A long-neglected passion flickered inside and new hope awakened.

When Pastor Paul returned to his office the next day, he thoughtfully prepared for the afternoon deacons' meeting. Of course, time was allotted to discuss church business. But he added a few minutes at the beginning to ask the men what they thought were the strengths and weaknesses of the church as a whole. He was careful not to let them resort to gossip and he determined ahead of time that he would not internalize their criticisms. As a result, he gained a lot of helpful information that he turned over in his mind during the following weeks. His prayers became more specific, and direction began to form. In preparation for the next meetings, he spent half an hour a few times a week to record his thoughts and observations about his church. Often he asked Jenny for input as he wrote. She had drawn out the perspectives of some of the women and came up with some valuable insights of her own.

As time went on, deacons' meetings became a training ground. Before the men closed in prayer, Pastor Paul spent ten minutes presenting an imaginary scenario. For example, at one meeting he said, "A teen girl approaches you in the church parking lot after morning service. She says she has a problem, and she asks you not to tell her parents. When you promise, she tells you she thinks she may be pregnant. What should you do?" The pastor had some Scriptures and a biblical perspective ready. But he did not spoon-feed the men. He let them figure it out. By asking questions, he led them away from personal opinion toward wisdom from the Word.

Pastor Paul shifted in his chair as he thought about their first few scenario attempts. He had been surprised at how difficult scriptural application was for the men. But as they had learned to expect a new scenario at each meeting, he noticed their attitudes changing. Some of them had spent more time in the Word, reading for the purpose of knowing how to handle situations and using the materials he had sent home with them.

Pastor Paul was beginning to understand where each one of the deacons was spiritually. John seemed to benefit most from the scenario exercises. Pastor Paul could see a teachable spirit arising in him, along with a degree of interest that the pastor knew he should nurture. Pastor Paul remembered John's surprise when he suggested they get together for prayer before work on Tuesdays. The younger man's eyes had flashed with mild skepticism, but he scheduled the appointment. They had been meeting for almost a month now. Pastor

Paul sensed that John's reluctance had lifted and a measure of enjoyment was taking its place.

Pastor Paul also started a twenty-minute prayer time early on Sunday mornings. He invited the church family to come, and was encouraged when a half dozen people showed up. Of those six, four continued to come each week. Those four were put on an e-mail update list, where Pastor Paul recorded answers to prayer and made further prayer requests throughout the week (again, carefully avoiding gossip or confidential information). He encouraged each of them to uphold one another in prayer, hoping to see some buds of discipleship begin to develop among the group.

His wife, Jenny, asked Laura and a newer believer named Carole to help her host an occasional craft night. Carole had been living on the fringes ever since her conversion and baptism a few months earlier, but Jenny perceived that she wanted to be more involved. As the women worked on their crafts, Jenny brought up a marriage role scenario. The feedback was very revealing. She could see a lack of connection between their Scripture study and the application of biblical knowledge to their marriages. Jenny also observed that the ladies viewed their church ministries temporally rather than eternally. They gave devotions, served meals, and cared for children, but meaningful discipleship was not on their radar. In addition, when trials came, the women usually had trouble asking for prayer or reaching out to help others. Considering Wendy's situation, Jenny knew most of them wouldn't know what to do to help anyway. They needed training.

Pastor Paul realized that Wendy's struggle continued to be very intense. He could see that she needed more counsel than he was able to provide, even with the collective help of his church. Perhaps he could get some ideas from a counselor at BCM. He picked up the phone.

Part 2. Working Together

Pastor Paul received some helpful advice from BCM, but his church was too far away to send Wendy for individual sessions. He thought about what he could do. At the last church association conference, he had spoken with one of the pastors from a BCM core church. Pastor Paul had liked what he heard and wondered about the possibility of developing such a group in his area. He was turning over an idea in his mind for hosting a BCM seminar, and wondered how his people would respond.

Pastor Paul shook his head and chuckled to himself. Where would he find the time to work at developing a counseling resource ministry? Yet he knew such resources could be invaluable for churches like his—churches that housed a world of need but had very limited resources. Working together with others of like faith and practice could help everyone. He and his deacon board decided to host the seminar and see what developed.

Pastor Paul thought of Bill Gray, a pastor across town. And Ken Peterson, pastor of a little church about an hour away. There were several others who crossed his mind. God had done a good work with the small churches that made up the growing ministry of BCM. Why not here?

Pastor Paul picked up a BCM brochure and slowly leafed through it. His next church association meeting was coming up next month. He would see about having lunch with Bill and Ken at the conference to discuss the possibilities. Perhaps their churches could come to the BCM seminar at Glory Baptist, to get a taste for biblical counseling.

The story of Pastor Paul is fictional, as you may have guessed. Pastor Paul represents counseling ministry inception through a pastor, who goes on to follow the path taken by BCM. Our ministry construction has played into every facet of this fictional scenario, except for the fact that the start-up person for BCM was a counselor rather than a pastor.

After finishing my degrees in biblical counseling, I assembled a group of five Baptist pastors and two godly women in central Wisconsin. We began to discuss the extent of need for biblical counseling resources in our region. Each of them was eager to explore the possibilities.

Either type of initiator, whether a pastor or a biblical counselor, may realistically start the process. Chapter 4 presents these two possibilities in more detail.

Building a Team

Now that you have begun to establish a foundation of biblical discipleship among your church leaders, we will dive into the "nuts and bolts" of putting together your resource counseling ministry, based on the experience we gained as we built Biblical Counseling Ministries. Most of what we have learned is directly applicable to any biblical counseling ministry. However, we include some adaptations to consider if you are hiring a staff biblical counselor (see notes labeled STAFF) or starting a biblical counseling center in your church (see notes labeled CENTER). Here is a sample box to illustrate.

> STAFF: If you are able to hire a biblical counselor to serve on staff at your church, you are indeed blessed. But to be most effective, you should carefully consider which policies and organizational plan you will follow. We will help you to think through how you can prepare for your new staff member so you can function most effectively as a team in the Lord's work. CENTER: Our experience is specific to the BCM model. Therefore, in addition to reading our suggestions for starting your center, we strongly recommend that you contact a functioning biblical counseling center for more help. (Visit the ACBC website at https://biblicalcounseling.com for names of some biblical counseling centers.) Their advice can save you time and help you avoid trouble.

In all cases, please keep in mind that we are writing on the basis of our experience and for the purpose of education, not as legal or financial consultants. Laws vary from state to state and country to country, so consult an experienced attorney for legal counsel. You should also ask an accountant for financial guidance.

Enjoying the Biblical Counseling Ministries Model

One of the benefits of the BCM model is the cooperation that has been established among small to average-sized Baptist churches in central Wisconsin. Working together for the cause of Christ is a worthy endeavor, and our model demonstrates both the means and the rewards that accompany that pursuit. As a group, we have enjoyed our unity in the gospel. On our shared doctrinal foundation, our five churches have pooled their resources to provide evening and weekend discipleship classes, a biblical counselor/consultant, and a growing list of recommended literature for use in Bible studies, discipleship, and other church teaching. We present a detailed look at our division of labor in Chapter 5.

Our directors have found BCM to be a vehicle of encouragement and support for one another in ministry. God has used BCM to develop some healthy pastoral friendships, so we do more than run BCM. We also pray together, share burdens, gain ideas from one another, and offer assistance where needed. We sharpen one another and keep one another accountable, too. In America's culture of individualism and isolationism, our bond is refreshing. And we don't think it should be unique.

> "I have been greatly blessed by the counsel I have received from the other pastors I serve with on the BCM board. As a young pastor shepherding my first church, it has been very helpful to develop relationships with these men that may not have happened otherwise. When facing a situation that I haven't faced before, I don't hesitate to contact one of these men for godly counsel. Without already having those relationships, I certainly would not have obtained their counsel. Although our meetings always deal with the business of BCM, they also help in developing mentoring relationships among the pastors on the board."
>
> **Corey Brookins, Senior Pastor, Berea Baptist Church, Stevens Point, WI**

> "... The New Testament teaches a pattern of churches cooperating with each other ... For example, the book of Acts narrates an ongoing exchange between Jerusalem and Antioch, in which the so-called Jerusalem Council (really a local church's business meeting, Acts 15) is only one episode. The churches of Macedonia and Achaia clearly cooperated in a voluntary endeavor to raise funds for the poor saints at Jerusalem (2 Cor. 9:1–15) ... Individual church members [also] appear to have cooperated for the advancement of New Testament Christianity ... Paul's circle displayed its own kind of organization and accountability. While it reported to churches, it operated independently of their direct oversight. In a sense, this circle could be called the first parachurch organization. Voluntary cooperation between churches of like faith and order has good precedent in the New Testament. So does cooperation between members of those churches, even to the point of creating organization outside the churches proper ...
> "The apostle Paul declares the local church to be the 'pillar and ground of the truth' (1 Tim. 3:15). God has not ordained any other institution for the completion of His plan during the present dispensation. Sooner or later, the responsibility for the advancement of the Lord's work must be shouldered by local churches. They must take leadership, and their prerogatives must be respected in any form of interchurch cooperation ..."
> **Dr. Kevin Bauder, "Herding Baptist Cats," in The Baptist Bulletin**

Getting Started

For a busy pastor like you, the thought of adding responsibility probably seems daunting. No pastor needs more to do, least of all something major like trying to get a group of churches to work together on a counseling ministry. We understand this because that's where we started, too. Our pastors have said that they probably would not have considered starting BCM were it not for two factors:

- First, the need is great. All the pastors wanted the counseling support. They all had people who required more care than they knew how to provide. The pastors also recognized that biblical counseling builds up the church body, and that outreach through counseling is a valuable evangelistic tool.

- Second, our counselor (myself) did the legwork. None of our pastors is singularly able to bear the load of starting such a ministry and probably would not have been interested in the idea of BCM had I not served as administrator and go-to person.

Who Should Get the Ball Rolling?

BCM pastors emphasize that the senior pastor or a senior elder should be contacted first, and that he is much more likely to receive the idea from another pastor than from anyone else. Ideally, a pastor should make the first contact.

We hasten to point out that BCM was initiated through a biblical counselor, not a pastor. But we agree that a counselor alone will probably have difficulty garnering pastoral interest unless strong relationships are in place and the counselor is already well known and trusted by the local churches that he or she approaches.

> Bear in mind the distance of churches that you invite. This is important if you want your counselor to provide on-site counseling. Those who live in an urban area will probably have numerous choices within a reasonable distance. Rural churches tend to be much farther apart. We chose a maximum radius of half an hour's drive from our central point to the farthest church. We hold training sessions at that central point, making travel easier for students from our core churches, too.

At the inception of BCM, I had lived in the area for about thirty years and was already acquainted with the pastors in all but one of the churches I contacted. To strengthen those relationships, I kept in touch and shared resources with those pastors while I was in seminary. Thus they were aware not only of my personal reputation, but also of my educational qualifications and my willingness to serve. When I eventually invited them to join an advisory board, the pastors were eager to hear about the biblical counseling resources I could provide.

If you are an initiating counselor, prayerfully strengthen your personal relationships with potential churches. Friendly phone calls, letters, résumés, and office visits[1] with pastors will not only build acquaintances, but will also let you know the extent of their knowledge and interest in biblical counseling. Patiently seek their perspectives without being pushy about your ideas or combative when you disagree. Respect their opinions and their position, and express gratitude for their time and attention. Gentle, thoughtful efforts like these helped me to gain access so I could discern who might work best together. I invited those churches that were compatible with the one in which I am a member.

Pastor, you could do the same. A pastor (or a team of pastor and biblical counselor or pastor and other church leader) with a working knowledge of nouthetic counseling may be in the best position to organize an advisory board. We recommend that you personally phone area colleagues that you think may be able to work together with you. You may also want to

STAFF: You need unity on your staff. First, discuss the hire of a counselor with your pastoral staff and other church leaders. Be sure they know what biblical counseling is. Then brainstorm with them about ministry vision for your church. Finally, share how you might collaborate with smaller churches of like faith to help them and to broaden your collective impact for Christ in your community.

CENTER: If your church members will fill the ministry board, you will not have to contact other pastors right away. However, if your church is not able to sustain a counseling center on its own, we suggest that you contact like-minded pastors rather than involving an eclectic mix of denominations. Doctrinal unity is an important foundation for a biblical counseling ministry, creating a spirit of harmony among your board members and defining your counselor's approach. (We will return to this later.)

arrange for some clerical help and simple follow-up work from someone with administrative abilities (preferably, but not necessarily, from your church).

If consensus is difficult, remember that this is God's work. Bathe your efforts in prayer, seek God's will and direction, and faithfully follow scriptural principles. Take the time to identify pastors and other church leaders who agree with your objectives and who are biblical in their worldview (or who are willing to learn). Consider distance realistically, knowing that your counselor will be asked to travel regularly to your core churches. Give thanks throughout the process, and leave the timing and the results with Him.

Choosing an Advisory Board

The advisory board usually becomes the ministry's board of directors. Therefore, choosing members is important. Every member should be a wise, mature believer from a like-minded church located within your anticipated radius. Beyond that we also recommend that you consider a mix of business professionals, health professionals, lawyers, pastors, and other church leaders of like faith, and at least one certified biblical counselor. A wealthy advisor may be able to help out in lean times. Bear in mind the personalities of the people that you invite, too. Some advisors are deliberately cautious, and some are energetic go-getters. One tends to

> Be creative when time and distance are a problem. Would telephone conferencing or online video connections such as Skype help? If necessary, could you borrow a laptop for that purpose?

> "The BCM process of incorporation has been carefully and thoughtfully laid out. The advisory board saw the need of being not only biblically sound, but also legally sound. We anticipate being a model for other similar ministries to look to for help in their incorporation."
> **Larry Gross, Senior Pastor, First Baptist Church, Waupaca, WI**

moderate the other. While there have been some challenges as we have learned to work together, we have come to appreciate having a variety of personality types on the board.

Initially, we asked the senior pastors from all five of our core churches (rather than another church representative) to serve on the advisory board. This decision has facilitated a bond among the churches that has endured beyond the scope of BCM itself. That decision has also had a direct bearing on the relatively large number of directors on the board of our small ministry.[2] We began with five pastors, plus a registered nurse, a biblical counselor, and the wife of a state association representative.

Early meetings focused on learning together about biblical counseling, and exploring each person's perceived need for counseling resources in each of the churches.[3] I took responsibility for recording and distributing meeting minutes until a board of directors was formed and a ministry secretary was elected.

Once formed, your advisory group should continue to broaden their understanding of nouthetic ministry[4]

STAFF: Even if you serve your church exclusively and choose not to incorporate, it is wise to have an overseeing board within your church for the counseling ministry. In addition, if you intend to invite other like-minded, doctrinally sound churches to refer, consider giving them a voice in your plans by including them on your advisory board. Your board may be an effective way to build trust, solidify bonds, communicate respect, and share ideas. You can choose to write a ministry plan together, or you can write your plans and ask for their input as you polish those plans. If you follow the BCM model, your staff biblical counselor could initially serve as the shared resource until more certified counselors are developed. Your church would naturally be named as the home church.

CENTER: Our experience has shown that pastoral input is very important when putting together an advisory board. If you want churches to refer their members to your center, pastors have to know they can trust you. Engaging like-minded pastors as advisors is one way you can demonstrate your commitment to the local church. Your center will then be well placed to involve local churches in the counseling process.

and narrow down their ideas for organizing. To facilitate discussion, I wrote a formal proposal based upon findings from preliminary contacts with area pastors. It contained the ministry vision, along with ideas for organization, division of labor, and a financial structure. Also included were a definition of biblical counseling, a resource list, a sample brochure, and a business card. Though many of our initial concepts changed along the way, the prospectus gave us momentum and saved us a lot of time during meetings.

If possible, the counselor/church ministry bonds should be established early on so that you can learn to work as a team. Therefore, your advisory board would be wise to discuss a realistic time line for hiring a counselor, and to arrange for an initial source of income. Support could include monthly church giving (e.g., through missions budgets), individual gifts, and, if needed, assistance with a job search for additional income for your counselor. The counselor should be asked to help with the preliminary setup of the ministry because the group will probably work best together if they have walked through the process from the outset. During BCM's setup, I drafted the documents for the ministry, conferred with pastors, completed clerical work, and led board meetings.

> STAFF: Project what you hope to accomplish in the first year, after five years, and so on. Strategically plan how you will meet your goals. What preparations should you make before bringing in your new staff member? Take time to learn more about biblical counseling so you know what to look for in a counselor and so that you will function as a team. CENTER: Depending upon the background of your ministry board, you should spend some time learning about biblical counseling to be sure you are all in agreement about the nature of the counseling you will provide. A proposal such as the one BCM used will serve to keep you focused and forward-thinking. Talk through your purposes and list ideas. Discuss and decide who you are and what you want to accomplish.

We invited our core churches to refer people for evening sessions during ministry formation, to a maximum of three cases per week to avoid overload. To facilitate this arrangement, I was named as a staff counselor at my church, and counseling was provided free, as stipulated in my church's insurance policy. Although my church was unable to provide a salary, remuneration is preferable, perhaps via donations from the churches represented on the ministry board.

During our ministry's inception process, I held a full-time day job until our doors opened and BCM could provide regular paychecks. My husband's income has been essential, especially during our start-up and in lean times when BCM paychecks have been thin.

Persevere by Faith on God's Time Line

It took us about two years, meeting three or four times per year, to make all the necessary preparations to get BCM off the ground. We do not claim that every ministry will take a similar amount of time, but we do advise lots of prayer and careful planning.

Remember that biblical counseling is God's work and that He will direct you when you trust Him and follow His Word (Prov. 3:5–6). BCM was founded upon the firm conviction that biblical discipleship is what God wants in His churches. We moved toward that goal one step at a time, careful to stay biblical, with only a rough idea where God would take us organizationally. All along our journey, we have found Him to be consistently faithful to light the way.

Pastor, stand upon truth, knowing that God has chosen you to be His tool and has commanded you to equip your church. Start now to move steadily forward. Take that next step of faith and trust God to lead you where He wants you to go. Begin to work with your church leaders (or potential leaders) so your church will develop a working knowledge of biblical counseling and grow in discipleship. Plan ahead. Talk to area pastors. Arrange for biblical counseling sessions to occur while you organize. Since BCM has done some pioneer work, we hope that our experiences will make your ministry formation more expedient.

Therefore let us pursue the things which make for peace and the things by which one may edify another. (Rom. 14:19)

Building a Team in Various Settings

(*Note:* Advantages, disadvantages, and suggestions in this chart generally apply to building collaborative ministry but may not be true in all cases.)

Large Churches

Advantages: Relatively large number of human and material resources. Potentially broad range of influence.

Disadvantages: Unity and accountability may be elusive. Pastors may not know their people well. Churchgoers may "hide" or "fall through the cracks." Smaller churches may feel overshadowed, inadequate, and defensive in comparison with their larger neighbors, making collaboration more difficult.

Suggestions: Develop discipleship skills from the top down, starting with training for your leaders. BCM's "Pastor's Toolbox" may help with church organization and unity. Use personal contacts to build collaboration with your smaller sister churches. Resist the urge to dominate: verbally acknowledge their value, respect their resources, and invite their input. Lead gently, but stand on truth. Depending upon what each church can offer, your church's staff biblical counselor will likely be the go-to person as you build your collaborative ministry. Your large church may be in the best position to house the ministry, and other like-minded area churches of any size may participate as host churches. As an alternative, consider whether your large church should completely house the ministry, and invite other like-minded churches to join your ministry board. Follow the four pillars of organization set out in Chapter 5.

Urban Areas

Advantages: Churches are close together; distance is not usually a problem. New ideas are welcomed.

Disadvantages: New ideas (and people) come and go quickly. Competitive, hurried, impersonal spirit.

Suggestions: We recommend that you invite discussion with pastors whom you believe to be like-minded, rather than sending out a general appeal. Begin with some friendly one-on-one conversations to explore their views about the importance of biblical foundations for counseling. Then choose a small group from among those who agree on the authority and sufficiency of Scripture. Meet once or twice monthly to discuss scenarios to discover counseling philosophy, or take some biblical counseling training together and review together what you learn. See Appendix H for books (such as this one) to discuss. As you meet, brainstorm with your group about the need for a biblical counseling ministry in your area. At this point, make no promises and avoid building expectations until you have narrowed down your choices for an advisory board. Remember, as pastors you won't agree on everything, but you should agree on matters of biblical dogma, such as the nature of God and each Person of the Trinity, the definition of the gospel, the sufficiency of Scripture in counseling, and your hermeneutic. Use the four pillars of Chapter 5 to help you come together further.

Small to Average-Sized Churches

Advantages: People usually know one another well. The pastor is familiar with all (or nearly all) of his people.

Disadvantages: Limited material and human resources. Workers bear many responsibilities.

Suggestions: This book is written largely from your perspective, because BCM was created by small and average-sized local churches. Review Chapters 1–3 for many suggestions for how to build leadership and discipleship in your church. At every level, preach and teach a biblical approach to the challenges your church faces. As you equip your own people, contact other pastors to assess the need for establishing a collaborative ministry.

Rural Settings

Advantages: Tendency to be hardworking, loyal to decisions made, and patient with the process of change.

Disadvantages: Distance between churches. Hesitant to accept unfamiliar ideas or people. Cliques.

Suggestions: The key to building understanding is trust. To allow for people to accept you and the idea of collaborative ministry, stress the timelessness of the biblical model (biblical counseling is not a new fad). Set aside one or two mornings per month to meet for breakfast at a central location with an area pastor or two (or invite them to your home). If possible, take a deacon or two along. (Budget creatively for gas and meals, e.g., from your expense allowance, an individual donor, or a temporary job.) Get to know the pastors, their beliefs, and their counseling needs. Pray with them. Encourage pastors to read this book and others on biblical counseling (see Appendix H). Share with them what you are learning about biblical counseling, and invite them to share their questions and concerns with you. At church conferences, informally talk to pastors and their wives about biblical counseling. Present a workshop. Get to know their churches, if possible, remembering the importance of the family unit in rural communities. Host a training event on a Saturday or a Sunday evening, and invite other churches. Demonstrate collaborative spirit by offering to help with a neighboring church's needs, such as painting or roofing their building or housing a missionary for them. Start now and don't give up. Press on gently, patiently, yet relentlessly, seeking God's timing and enjoying the fellowship He builds. In so doing, people will eventually recognize the validity of your message and may choose to listen. Follow the four pillars of Chapter 5 to move forward purposefully.

Chapter 4

Notes

1 Electronic communication is less effective, but may be useful for follow-up.

2 Expect the face of the board to change in time. Because we live in a transient culture, our board has undergone many changes as directors have moved out of our area. Care should be taken to avoid depending upon any particular board member too much.

3 For example, members of the group could read and discuss **Paul David Tripp's** *Instruments in the Redeemer's Hands: People in Need of Change Helping People in Need of Change* (Phillipsburg, NJ: P&R, 2002) to familiarize themselves with biblical counseling philosophy. In addition, they could invite a ACBC representative to speak and answer their questions.

4 Our experience has shown that a true understanding of nouthetic biblical counseling is rare. We recommend taking time to define and establish a biblical approach to discipleship (rather than an integrationist approach), so that everyone is on the same page.

azy drops of rain smudged together as the Chevrolet's windshield wipers dragged across the glass. Pastor Paul absently rolled up his window as he turned out of the church driveway. This year's state association conference had concluded, and his mind was full. The three pastors had enjoyed exchanging ideas at lunch. Their churches had a pool of resources that looked promising, and they had even thought of three or four other nearby pastors who might be interested in exploring the BCM model. They arranged to call their colleagues. They also planned to meet with the BCM trainer after the seminar about how to begin finding a resource counselor for their area.

Pastor Paul knew that Jenny would be happy to hear the news, but he wasn't sure what his deacons would think. Most of them were already aware of the demands on his time and would be concerned about distraction or ministry overload. However, one of them thought the pastor had little to do besides preaching his Sunday morning sermon; that leader was not inclined to have the pastor seek out help with counseling, even with his most difficult cases.

Pastor Paul reached for his coffee cup and sipped the hot liquid as he considered the value of a resource counselor. He would have appreciated a woman's help with Wendy, but her grief intimidated the ladies who had reached out to her so far. Even Jenny found her difficult to understand. Although Wendy had responded well to her pastor, he was concerned about protecting them both from temptation, or even the appearance of impropriety. He shifted in his seat. A pastor's reputation is easily damaged.

Rain began to pelt the car in a steady rhythm, then to drum harshly. Visibility became difficult. As he eased his foot off the gas, his mind moved back to his deacons. He knew that they were finding their scenarios and discussions somewhat unsettling. Most of the deacons realized they needed to think more biblically. They were sharing his scenarios with their wives, who had become interested as well. The pastor hoped that the BCM seminar would demonstrate the heart of biblical thinking and awaken a pulse of discipleship they had not yet experienced. If they responded well to the training, he considered taking a group to Faith Baptist Church in Lafayette, Indiana, for the Biblical Counseling Training Conference in February.

Pastor Paul prayed enthusiastically for wisdom for Jenny and himself, for Wendy, for Glory Baptist Church, and for Bill and Ken as they considered the ideas they had discussed at lunch. And for the counselor that God was maybe—just maybe—preparing for them.

But when Pastor Paul walked into the house, reality hit him sharply. Jenny and the kids had the flu, Wendy had called in a panic, and the church basement was full of water from the rainstorm. The pastor breathed another prayer and went for the buckets.

After two days at home caring for his family, Pastor Paul was back at his office, trying to put together a message for Sunday before rushing off to visit Wendy in the hospital. He had spent a couple of hours Tuesday night mopping up water in the church basement before he realized that he should have called one of the trustees. (*Teamwork is not my strength,* he mused. He still had a lot to learn.) He was grateful that before the conference he had asked John to prepare something for Wednesday's prayer meeting. That decision allowed him some time to work on his messages and the Sunday afternoon deacons' meeting.

He noticed that the familiar squeak of his chair was less irritating now that he was making deliberate changes and watching his time more closely. The thought of teamwork and discipleship development seemed to energize him, even though his schedule continued to be challenging. A warm wave flushed through his body. Was his stomach feeling a little queasy?

Out of the chaos of the week stepped a quiet answer to prayer. Carole had phoned to express interest in helping at the office. Laura was willing to come in to train her this week. Pastor Paul was so relieved, he almost shouted a whoop into the receiver. The seminar was coming up. Carole had some office experience, and she had arrived just in time. It was so like God!

Four Pillars: Pillars 1–3

Any good contractor knows that solid structures don't build themselves. To endure, they must be carefully planned and faithfully constructed to withstand storms and everyday wear and tear.

> "Coordinated effort without organization is impossible."
> **Dr. Kevin Bauder, "Herding Baptist Cats," in *The Baptist Bulletin***

Solid ministry organization doesn't build itself, either. Like a well-constructed building, a ministry's foundations must be sound, and its organizational structure must be sturdy. The principles in this chapter can help you to be thorough, realistic, and careful as you structure your counseling ministry.

We built Biblical Counseling Ministries upon four foundational pillars that help us to achieve our ministry objectives. Each is important to the structural integrity and stability of the ministry. These pillars are doctrinal agreement, unity in purpose and philosophy, commitment to function according to our plan, and shared responsibility to meet ministry needs. A ministry's success is much more likely when these four factors are present.

FOUR PILLARS
- Doctrinal Unity
- Unity in Purpose and Philosophy
- Commitment to Method
- Sharing Ministry Needs

Pillar 1: Doctrinal Unity

Your board of directors must be in agreement doctrinally so that the ministry will travel in a biblical direction. Disunity in doctrine dishonors God, breeds conflict, and contaminates counseling quality and content. To succeed, the governing board of any ministry model must be in harmony on this pillar.

After our advisory board brainstormed some general ideas for Biblical Counseling Ministries, one of the first steps we took was to write a doctrinal statement.[1] Following earnest prayer, we settled on a baptistic doctrinal base. Now that we have incorporated, each director is required to sign our covenant annually to affirm compliance with those doctrines. You are welcome to use our statement as a basis for your group ministry, if you choose. However, we urge you to go over every point together to be sure that you agree, especially on the dogmatic doctrines of the Scriptures and the hermeneutic that you will use.

> Sound doctrine is the foundation of biblical counseling. Therefore, multichurch ministry must emphasize doctrinal unity in all matters pertaining to counseling, which excludes very little. Ecumenical ties set you up for significant doctrinal compromise and conflict. Do not join with those who teach a false or "different" gospel (see 2 Cor. 6:14–18). Be sure your governing group of churches is compatible with all four pillars, but especially Pillar 1.

One way to test doctrinal unity is to have your advisors write down beliefs that they think are necessary for anyone who is to be part of the organization. Discuss the statements, biblically evaluating each one. Note which doctrines, if any, are missing and the significance of their omission. This will not only establish your doctrinal base, but will also tell you a lot about the way that you will function together in ministry.

Pillar 2: Unity of Purpose and Philosophy

UNITY OF PHILOSOPHY

We have discovered that most people think they know what biblical counseling is, but few actually grasp its concepts sufficiently to make effective application. Before settling on a course of action, your advisory board must understand biblical counseling and its value to the local church. That is why a large portion of Part 1 of this book defined biblical counseling and explained how it can be developed in a local-church setting.

This pillar should be carefully and prayerfully built, whether you are seeking new staff, setting up a counseling center, or following the BCM model. Our advisors were not at the same place in their knowledge and practices when we started. Book recommendations and a biblical counseling training seminar helped them and their churches to form an accurate picture of nouthetic counseling. This knowledge brought us to greater unity as we learned to trust one another upon the foundation of God's Word.

> "BCM has been greatly blessed to have a board of directors with a vision for meeting the needs of people through nouthetic counseling. As a charter member of the board, I see a great sense of unity among the board and the BCM director Sue Nicewander. Five Baptist churches currently have representatives on the BCM board. We stand united in doctrine and strive as one to help make disciples. We all recognize the sufficiency of Scripture to meet man's desperate needs."
> **Larry Gross, Senior Pastor, First Baptist Church, Waupaca, WI**

STAFF: Do not assume that every member of your church staff understands the principles and practice of biblical counseling. Take time to learn together. *Note:* If you have an integrationist on staff already, we advise that you pray and carefully assess how to proceed. To employ both biblical counseling and integrationism will foster division among your staff and confusion in your church.
CENTER: This may be your most difficult pillar. Take the time to train together as a board so that you will move together toward biblical goals. It is better to hash out your differences and come to consensus now. It won't become easier later. Philosophical unity will help you and your biblical counselor to function in a God-pleasing way, with more confidence and less conflict.

Appendix H lists books from which our advisors read and made purchases for their churches. The pastors made this literature the subject of their leadership training and Bible study groups. Then they placed the books in church libraries, where they continue to be available to counselees and counselors in the church body. This list is a starting point for understanding the basic principles of biblical counseling, although it is not exhaustive by any means.

They also ordered booklets on various topics such as ADD, anger, depression, forgiveness, marriage, parenting, sexual sin, pain, and suffering. Most of our churches kept topical booklets on display for their people to read and give to others, until the cost rose too high. Now our pastors keep a supply on hand to use in their counseling. We recommend that you set aside some funds to purchase books and booklets that may be given to your counselees. See Chapter 11 for more ideas about resources.

UNITY OF PURPOSE

Besides learning a biblical philosophy of counseling, you will also need to

"The development of our vision was a process involving prayer, careful consideration, and hours of discussion. The process was perhaps more valuable than the final product, as the founding board members were able to crystallize and clarify their thinking about what God was raising up, what we believed God was calling us to do, and how that could be done. As time went on, we became more and more convinced that God was doing something special in our midst and thus our enthusiasm for the ministry continued to build. God used the painstaking process of vision development to form in our hearts the convictions, excitement, and focus that would be necessary for effective implementation of the ministry in the churches. The mission statement and supporting ministry structure which flowed out of this process became more than a formality. Getting it on paper is valuable, but backing it up with understanding and commitment is vital."

Stephen Steinmetz, Senior Pastor, Faith Baptist Church, Wisconsin Rapids, WI

work on unity of purpose. What do you hope to accomplish overall through this ministry, and how do you envision the pathway to those goals?

Most of our board members came with a perception of what the ministry should entail, but even with a formal proposal in front of them, they each had different approaches. We had to discuss our ideas and come to agreement. The vision statement of Pillar 3 is the end product of this unified purpose. Questions to consider might include:

- What do you want this ministry to do? To what extent?

We wanted to provide biblical counseling, discipleship training, and resource recommendations for our core churches, and to invite other churches to refer counselees and/or to take classes.

Our advisors also decided to carefully protect church autonomy. We therefore chose to build BCM as an arm of the local church, rather than as a counseling center. For this reason, we made sure that the church always drives its own counseling ministry. Eventually, we worked out this principle by requiring that pastors decide who will be referred for counseling and who will be trained in discipleship. Each church also decides who will be asked to counsel its referrals. We work quietly alongside to help them meet their biblical goals.

> STAFF and CENTER: Think bigger than yourself. Pray, pray, pray about your role in your area, especially as a church. Consider how you might impact your community for Christ through biblical counseling. As you train people, how might your ministry broaden? Consider creative ways to raise awareness, such as seminars, conferences, special speakers, topic and discussion nights, video ministry, and marriage and parenting classes to offer to your community. In so doing, you will open the door for further ministry of the Word in your church and in your community.

- How will you offer training? What kind? Will you train only the people in your core churches, or will you offer seminars and classes to others? How will you decide which others you will include?

We wanted to make discipleship training available to Christians who serve in differing roles, both formal and informal. Therefore, we chose to pursue training at two levels: everyday discipleship (for any Christian who wants to learn more about helping others biblically), and focused discipleship (for Christian leaders and teachers who are interested in biblical counseling). To facilitate this objective, we later decided to hold classes at a central location on Saturdays or Tuesday evenings for the convenience of those who have weekday jobs. Because of our commitment to local-church autonomy, we offer our classes to students whose pastors sign the registration form. See Chapter 10 for more on our training program.

Our training program is producing students who are discipling others both formally in their churches and informally in their homes, communities, and workplaces. Many of them serve as advocates for counselees. They may participate in counseling sessions with experienced biblical counselors (including their pastors) and pick up discipleship with counselees who are nearing completion of sessions. In this manner, local churches are being strengthened in the Word.

- Will you give away resources, or will you produce and sell resources such as books, DVDs, or curricula? How will you purchase and/or produce these materials?

We wanted to make reliable resources available, while recognizing and working within our financial constraints. We also wanted to provide a list of biblically sound materials. As a result, we have purchased some books and other literature for use in counseling. We have also written some materials, and we offer a free resource list on our Web site. See Chapter 11 for information on our resources.

- Will community outreach be part of your biblical counseling plan? How?

The BCM board decided to think bigger than their own church buildings. We extend our ministry to the community in two ways. First, people are being brought into sound local churches in a purposeful way. Because we accept counselees only by pastoral referral, unchurched inquirers are directed to a BCM pastor before they can start sessions.[2] Many people have been drawn to Christ through counseling, and most of them have made permanent homes in their referring churches. Second, ACBC-certified BCM students from our core churches are reaching deeply into our community through various church ministries. We are seeing our students taking biblical teaching to places that might not otherwise receive it.

Notice the two factors involved in each question above. First, we decided what we wanted to do (Pillar 2). Then we considered how to build upon those decisions to accomplish our goals (Pillar 3). Pillars 1 and 2 could be thought of as the foundation of the building, while Pillars 3 and 4 form the structure.

Pillar 3: Commitment to Method (Structure and Implementation)

In Pillar 3 we assessed what methods we should use to organize, build, and implement our model. We came up with a vision to build biblical counseling/discipleship in, with, and through the local church. Our objectives flowed from that vision and include one-on-one biblical counseling by pastoral referral, discipleship training for church workers, and the development of a list of recommended resources.

VISION

Once the advisory board was in place, our vision for ministry began to form as we learned the basics of nouthetic counseling and wrote our doctrinal statement. We worked hard at a vision statement (sometimes called a mission statement) that concisely summarizes what our group wants to accomplish. Our name and logo were chosen to reflect that vision. You may use the BCM mission statement as an example,[3] but we highly recommend that you adopt your own. Hammering out your vision helps to focus, unify, and prioritize your group's purpose and heart for the ministry.

STAFF and CENTER: During times of plenty, your vision statement will help you to stay focused. During lean years, your vision will teach you to discern between the essential and the expendable. Share your vision statement freely among all participating churches as you proceed, to bring others along with you in spiritual, financial, and prayer support. Your vision statement lets everyone know who you are, informs your decisions, and leads you to expend your energies as effectively and efficiently as possible.

HOME AND HOST CHURCH DIVISION OF LABOR: STRUCTURE OF THE BCM MINISTRY MODEL

We then had to settle upon division of labor as we considered how each of our core churches could facilitate the ministry at a reasonable and sustainable level. One of the beauties of shared ministry is that no single church bears the load.

- *Counseling: Each of our five churches houses counseling sessions on certain days of the week.*
- Seminars: *All five churches support our seminars by supplying advertising, promotion, child care, video/audio support, music, clerical help, greeters, book tables, instruction, music, housing, and refreshments.*
- Operational needs: *Four of our five churches take responsibility for a specific category of BCM need: home office, resources, training, and support center. The fifth church helps to fill any gaps.*

The burden is light when so many are working together. Our broad base of church involvement strengthens our ministry so that we are not crippled by transitions, such as when a board member or pastor leaves one of our core churches.

> STAFF: Consider each of the areas of need for your counseling ministry and write a well-defined plan for the division of labor for your church staff. Read this chapter carefully to see what will apply to you. For example, you will need a counseling supervisor. Who is willing and able to serve in that capacity? Will you have liaisons from area churches to help with ministry needs? How will they function in your ministry plan? If you choose to set up the BCM model with other participating local churches, you will have a broader base of resources to share. The other churches will take more ownership, too, when they hold a respectable position in the ministry. CENTER: Using the suggestions in this section, consider what is needed by the ministry and what each participating church or individual is able to provide. Write your plan accordingly.

OUR HOME CHURCH

Because we are committed to local-church autonomy, BCM operates under the authority of the deacon board at our home church. The senior pastor of the home church, who is on the BCM board, acts as a liaison. He keeps the home church deacons apprised of BCM decisions and needs. Periodically, the home church deacons will ask me to answer additional questions or concerns, either verbally or in written form. Such communication serves to clarify and unify. I am happy to comply.

To provide accountability for excellence in counseling, the senior pastor of the home church (or a BCM designate) serves as counseling supervisor of our executive director (me). He periodically reviews cases to be sure that my counseling is consistently nouthetic. Other BCM staff, including other counselors and volunteers, report to me.

Our home church provides our primary administrative support, including clerical help, audio/visual services, a location for counseling sessions, and an administrative office.

OUR HOST CHURCHES

Each host church has a liaison on the BCM board of directors to facilitate communication and coordination of efforts. (Most of our liaisons are pastors, but an elder or a deacon would also be an appropriate choice as long as the liaison is given authority to speak for the church on matters pertaining to the counseling ministry.) The liaison, the church secretary, and designated volunteers at each host church work with BCM to meet specific ministry needs.

- The training center provides classroom space, cares for class and seminar materials, and handles class registrations.
- The resource center is responsible for books and other literature that we use in seminars, classes, and counseling. It also publishes BCM brochures and booklets. A volunteer at our resource center maintains our Web site.
- The support center helps with miscellaneous needs such as mailings, brochure development, and fundraising.

The nearby "Table of Organization" illustrates and concisely explains our ministry structure.4 As you can see, our executive director answers directly to the

> "The founding board members all began with a strong theological commitment to the local church, but figuring out how to weave the concept of a counseling ministry into the fabric of each local church was challenging. From our discussions emerged the need for operating under the authority of a home church, but with ministry responsibilities shared with the other churches (host churches). This way the work load would be divided and each of the churches would have a sense of ownership and involvement. It was determined that we would need a training center, a resource center, and a support center, each with a clearly defined purpose and each with representation on the board. The system has worked well and it is a blessing to see the churches cooperating in this way."
>
> **Stephen Steinmetz, Senior Pastor, Faith Baptist Church, Wisconsin Rapids, WI**

board of directors in all areas except counseling supervision. As we move into the counselor section of this book, each of these functions will be explained in more detail.

BCM's organizational arrangement works well for our group, largely because we try to help one another succeed and because we keep communication lines open to detect problems as soon as they arise.

Table of Organization

Home Church
The home church houses the ministry and provides finances, materials, and human resources for clerical and seminar needs. The ministry's board of directors is ultimately answerable to the home church. From time to time the BCM board may present particular needs of the ministry to the deacons of the home church for help.

Counseling Supervisor
The senior pastor of the home church or a BCM board-appointed designate appropriately supervises the counseling done by the executive director.

BCM Board of Directors
The board of directors is responsible for conducting the business and setting the policies of the corporation. Specified liaison directors facilitate and coordinate the areas of responsibility in home and host churches and serve as liaisons between the executive director and home and host churches.

Host Churches
Host churches provide finances, materials, and human resources for the ministry in the areas of fundraising support, resource center, and training center, as agreed. Liaison directors from the BCM board of directors coordinate the ministry's efforts with the host churches.

Executive Director
The executive director oversees the day-to-day operations of the ministry, counsels in home and host churches, works with the board of directors to set direction for the corporation, and communicates with liaison directors concerning the needs of the corporation in particular areas of responsibility with respect to host churches. The executive director reports directly to the board of directors in all areas except in the area of counseling, where he or she is supervised by the senior pastoral counselor of the home church or a board-appointed designate.

Counselors and Staff
Staff, if any, reports directly to the executive director. The staff is responsible for designated duties in line with job descriptions.

Communication is a vital part of success in any group, and ours is no exception. We will address that subject more fully in Chapter 8.

INCORPORATION

Now it was time to formally prepare our paperwork. We sought out several other counseling ministries for help and they allowed us to read their organizational papers. Their wise advice, built upon years of experience, helped us to be thorough as we adapted their policies and other documents to fit our model.

We decided to organize ourselves as a nonprofit corporation (commonly referred to as 501(c)(3)). All legal paperwork had to be carefully constructed and then formally filed. As we compiled the required information and wrote our organizational papers, we consulted an attorney to review our work and complete the maze of documents that had to be filed at state and federal levels. If you choose to incorporate, be sure to consult an attorney who is familiar with incorporation law, so that you comply with all state and federal regulations. We are grateful to the Christian Law Association (CLA) for their assistance with legal documents as we set up our nonprofit

CHOOSING OFFICERS

Your choice of officers is important. The board secretary must be able and willing to keep thorough and clear records and distribute them in a timely manner. I usually type an agenda for the whole board, but I put several extra details on the secretary's copy to make note-taking easier. Our secretary usually has me review the minutes before sending them to the rest of the board.

Your treasurer will be called upon to keep payroll and donation records, pay expenses and payroll-related taxes, and fill out nonprofit reports. We recommend that you find someone who is trained to do these tasks. However, if your treasurer is not familiar with nonprofit requirements, we suggest getting a knowledgeable certified accountant to do some training and consulting with your treasurer.

ministry. For more information, consult their Web site at www.christianlaw.org.

See Appendix G for an outline of the section titles in our incorporation papers: the fruit of our labors.[5]

STAFF: Unless you build a BCM model or decide to start a counseling center in your church, incorporation will probably not be a consideration for you. CENTER: Choose an attorney with knowledge of federal and state corporate law. Ask your attorney whether 501(c)(3) nonprofit incorporation or limited liability corporation (LLC) is the best choice for you.

BOARD OF DIRECTORS

Nonprofit incorporation papers require naming board members, so at this point we had to decide who would become the ministry's directors. Our advisors had worked together to establish the vision and set up the structure, and we all wanted that shared passion and unity to continue. Furthermore, every advisor was in agreement and was willing to continue with the process. Therefore, the entire BCM advisory board constituted the new board of directors. Of course, other organizations may choose to do differently. Bathe this decision in prayer because it will impact your ministry for years to come. Don't put off the hard decisions.

Our board members serve for three-year terms and are responsible for the operation of the ministry as its articles of incorporation, bylaws, and policies dictate. Officers include a secretary and a treasurer. Our executive director also functions as chairman of the board. This arrangement is not ideal, but it is the preference of our directors and is legally permissible.

TROUBLESHOOTING

As we put together our organizational documents, we did some careful troubleshooting to anticipate and answer possible procedural questions. We targeted as many potential trouble spots as we could

> "The development of BCM from an idea to a functioning ministry which is making an impact on our churches was a process completely dependent upon the hand of God. Initially, we faced some difficult issues. How could it be organized? We had no model. How could small churches support it financially? We had limited resources. Is it possible for churches like ours to cooperate on such a scale? We are 'independent' Baptist churches. Could these pastors work together? Each of us was a leader in his own realm, often with strong opinions, and we were active in different fellowships. Could this ministry be a threat to us rather than a blessing? We were well aware of the perils. Would it work? There were those who told us it wouldn't. In spite of all that, we walked through the door of opportunity that God had put before us and we watched Him work in steps. It was, for us, a demonstration of what He had told Moses in Exodus 6:1: 'Now you shall see what I will do …'"
>
> **Stephen Steinmetz, Senior Pastor, Faith Baptist Church, Wisconsin Rapids, WI, and BCM Board of Directors**

think of and wrote reasonable policies to cover each scenario. For example, we considered:

- How to choose home and host churches
- What to do if a home or host church becomes unable or unwilling to house the ministry
- Procedure when a board member leaves
- Addressing lack of consensus or agreement
- Procedure when finances are insufficient
- Handling conflict

Answering questions like these has saved us many headaches as difficult situations have arisen.

> STAFF and CENTER: The more troubleshooting you can do now, the better. Try to anticipate difficulties you may encounter. Be sure to write down what you decide.

Chapter 5

HERE'S MORE FOR YOU:

Appendix F: A Checklist for Setting Up Your Ministry Model
An outline of the steps in this book, for use as a checklist when organizing your ministry.

Appendix G: An Outline of Information to Include in Your Incorporation Papers
A checklist of topics to cover in your various organizational documents.

Appendix H: Further Resources
A list of books on various topics, with notes, to help you learn about biblical counseling and teach your people.

Notes

1   Our doctrinal statement may be read on the BCM Web site (www.bcmin.org).

2   We have a letter prepared for pastors of churches who do not preach the true gospel. The subject of pastoral referrals from churches outside our core group is addressed in Chapter 8.

3   Once your advisory board has been formed, you may contact us for a copy of our mission statement and other helpful documents to use as a model. The BCM board must approve any release of such information, so please allow time for the board to review your request. Some restrictions may apply. We are not legal advisors, but provide this information simply to share our experience with incorporation. Please consult your attorney to be sure you comply with state and federal law before opening your doors.

4   Whatever your organizational structure, your location, or your material or financial resources, flowcharts clarify lines of responsibility and accountability so your ministry can run more smoothly. We recommend that you prepare a chart for each of your church staff and officers. If you are building on the BCM model, write a table for that ministry as well.

5   Our organizational documents may be available for use as a model, with BCM board approval. Certain restrictions may apply.

Pillar 4: Sharing Ministry Needs

So far, we have looked at three of the four pillars of ministry. Pillars 3 and 4 must be built simultaneously, because ministry needs (Pillar 4) have to be met in order for your method (Pillar 3) to work.

> **FOUR PILLARS**
> - Doctrinal Unity
> - Unity in Purpose and Philosophy
> - Commitment to Method
> - Sharing Ministry Needs

Financial Planning

Finances are important in ministry, yet this subject causes significant discomfort and disagreement. Most ministry leaders would tell you that ministry is not about money. Some even believe that it is wrong to accept money for counseling.[1] Others fear that finances will become the focus of their efforts, so they avoid considering the subject as much as possible. No one wants fundraising efforts to sap all the energy from their counseling ministry (1 Tim. 6:10).

SETTING UP YOUR BUDGET

Whatever your perspective on finances, if you want your ministry to succeed you should make arrangements for working capital before you open your doors. To estimate what you will need, carefully set up your anticipated budget expenditures and income. We include the following in our budget:

- *Expenses:* Salary, payroll taxes, office supplies, advertising, postage and shipping, telephone, professional consultation, technology, library (books and videos for use in counseling), professional development training/education, mileage, travel expenses, insurance fees, professional fees, attorney fees, government fees, Internet fees, training videos for classes, classroom supplies, child care for seminars, guest instructor honorariums and guest speaker travel expenses.

> STAFF: Avoid thinking that the expenses of your counseling ministry will be easily absorbed by your church simply because you have a biblical counselor on staff. Instead, write up a reasonable budget for your church to adopt, stay within that budget, and update it annually.
> CENTER: If you locate your center in a church building, work out financial arrangements with the hosting church. Take nothing for granted. Will you pay rent? Hire your own secretary? Pay to make copies? What supplies are you expected to provide?
> If you locate outside a church building, you will have to additionally budget for building expenses, including rent or mortgage, telephone, Internet, building supplies, and utilities. Make provision for custodial and clerical staff, too.

- *Income projection:* Counseling donations, core church support, general donations, seminar and class registrations, books, honorariums, fundraising, endowments.

The difference between your expenses and your income projection should be carefully assessed. (See Appendix I for a budget form to help with that comparison.) Once you open, you will probably find it difficult to raise funds on top of your other administrative and counseling responsibilities unless you can find additional personnel to help with fundraising. Again, we strongly recommend that you have your finances lined up before you officially begin the ministry.

FINANCE-RELATED QUESTIONS TO CONSIDER

1. *Will you suggest a donation amount or charge a fee for counseling? If so, how much?* We ask for a small hourly donation[2] for counseling. (If

you choose to do this, be sure to follow federal and state nonprofit requirements. Check with your attorney.) If a counselee is unable to pay the full amount, referring churches work with our counselees and often supplement the cost. Patient insurance does not cover us because we are not state-licensed.[3] (Consult the laws of your state and your attorney to find out if you qualify to receive insurance payments.) We do not turn people away for lack of ability to pay, but we may limit the number of sessions we can offer.

> CENTER: Depending upon the laws of your state, as an independent center you may be required to function under a state-licensed psychologist. Some biblical counseling centers make such arrangements so that they can accept insurance payments. However, state requirements differ from biblical counseling standards, so it may be more difficult to stay biblical under those conditions.

2. *How much will each core church donate, and when?* Our board determined a minimum support amount for our home and host churches, with our home church providing the most support. We also gratefully accept donations from churches and individuals outside our core group, primarily as we travel to speak and teach.

3. *Will you suggest a donation amount for training or classes? Will you sell books, seek endowments, write grants, or pursue individual donors?* Our board discussed each of these areas and made decisions about what to pursue immediately and what to do later.

4. *What will you do about insurance?* Professional liability insurance from a reputable company is a must. Our five churches all had their insurance from Church Mutual Insurance, so we contacted that company.[4] Church

> STAFF: As long as your staff counselor is on a salary rather than a per-session rate, and he or she has responsibilities beyond counseling, you will probably not have to take out additional professional liability. Check your policy and talk to your insurance agent.

Mutual has tailor-made a policy for our model. Other companies, too, insure counseling centers as well as churches, so we recommend that you do some research to find the one that will work best for you.

RAISING FINANCIAL SUPPORT

Home Missions Support

Home missions support comprises a significant portion of our funding. When presenting the request to their churches, our pastors explained to their people that the need for monthly support for BCM is similar to giving to Bible camps or Christian schools. Churches send regular donations to camps or schools, but individuals must also pay to attend. So, too, our churches support us regularly, but per-session donations are also requested of counselees. Often our churches pay for sessions when they make referrals. We would not be able to survive financially without both sources of income.

We cannot sufficiently stress the importance of each church and each board member taking responsibility to support the ministry financially. Because other sources of income are variable, BCM relies heavily on the steady donations provided by our core churches. Our board sets a minimum support level for home and host churches, but each church votes on the level of support it will provide. Most of our churches generously exceed the minimum set by the board of directors. As people experience the benefits of BCM in their local churches, they enthusiastically support the ministry.

Counseling

BCM counseling is available for a small requested donation amount that is determined by the board of directors. Often the referring church helps the counselee with all or part of that amount. We will send an invoice to the paying church if requested to do so. Otherwise, payment is brought to each session.

Training Events

BCM sponsors training events (such as classes and seminars) at low cost, writes curriculum, teaches workshops at various conferences, and provides speakers for Bible camps and women's events. Each of these efforts introduces the ministry, encourages involvement, and yields some financial support.

Resource Sales

BCM receives a small income from resource sales. We have worked with an area Christian bookstore to stock our seminar book tables. We man the tables and keep track of inventory and sales. The bookstore, in turn, donates a percentage of its seminar sales to the ministry.

Grants and Endowments

Grants are plentiful, but finding ones that fit your ministry may be difficult and time consuming—or strings may be attached. BCM has discussed the pursuit of grants, but so far we have not written any grant applications. If you have computer-savvy volunteers who are willing to do the research, you may be able to find some funding there. Endowments may also be sought if you have individuals able to devote time and effort toward pursuing people with financial means, and if interest rates are high enough to yield sufficient income.

Other Donations

BCM gratefully receives other donations. Several individuals have provided significant one-time gifts at strategic points. Others give monthly, helping to sustain day-to-day operating needs. We have sent mailings to ask for support, but we find that these do not produce enough results to sufficiently offset the cost. Keep in mind that those who have benefited from the ministry are more likely to support it financially. Our BCM Sundays and personal contacts have been more effective than mailings.

> STAFF: After writing your budget, discuss policies for any fundraising that may be needed.
> CENTER: Fundraising will probably be necessary if you have building and staff costs to cover. You will probably have to seek out individuals who can provide start-up capital, and then seek grants or start fundraising events to continue your cash flow. Have your finances in place before you open your doors. A budget sheet is provided in Appendix I, but you will need to add a section for building costs.

THINKING AHEAD

Even with careful financial planning, your ministry must be ready to face lean times. The board should plan how it will cover expenses when funds are low. For example, will you cut back on certain expenses, contact the home church for help, ask individuals for donations, dip into savings, have a fundraiser, borrow money, ask your staff to work without pay, or petition your core churches?

Introducing the Ministry

While we prepared our incorporation documents, we worked to introduce the ministry to our churches and our communities, and to raise support.

> STAFF: Prepare your church for their new staff member. Give them time to consider your reasons for adding a biblical counselor, and take them with you on the journey by projecting your vision for your church and your community. Point out where changes are already taking place through the ministry of the Word, and invite your people to grow along with you.
> CENTER: Opening your doors is not enough; you need a voice in the churches you seek to serve. How will you spread the word about who you are and what you have to offer? If you have pastors on your board, you have a ready field. The following sections offer some ideas.

PREPARING HOME AND HOST CHURCHES TO EMBRACE THE MINISTRY

As we hammered out BCM's organizational structure and put our paperwork in process, all five of the pastors on our board worked to prepare their congregations for the decision that they would soon be making.[5]

Our pastors talked about BCM's plans during deacon board meetings and worship services. The church was informed of my counseling and leadership credentials and was kept aware of the general progress of our ministry formation. Pastors communicated enthusiasm about the need for the ministry and BCM's commitment to the local church. They explained that the church would soon have the opportunity to hear from me about BCM and to pledge prayer and financial support individually and through their church missionary budgets. Each of these steps created interest and ownership in what God was doing in the formation of BCM.

> "My initial process was wrong—I expected people to make dramatic changes without preparing my heart and their hearts for change ... Before you seek to change church structure, seek to shepherd changed hearts ... Before you enlist individuals to be equipped to counsel, invite a congregation to become stewards of a transformational vision."
> **Robert Kellemen, *Equipping Counselors for Your Church***

TALKING WITH DEACONS (OR ELDERS)

First, pastors talked with their deacons about the need for biblical counseling and discipleship. They defined biblical counseling and explained its importance, emphasizing the value of

> "I have appreciated the opportunity to get in on the ground work of BCM. The vision of BCM is to counsel those with needs and to train others to give sound biblical counsel. When first approached by Pastor Steve Steinmetz and Sue Nicewander, I was both honored and excited to be part of this ministry."
> **Larry Gross, Senior Pastor, First Baptist Church, Waupaca, WI**

its resources. Church boards who had received training in biblical counseling (e.g., through the BCM seminar, other biblical counseling conferences, and/or working through scenarios as a deacon board) were more ready to receive the ministry. Leaders who had experienced personal discipleship were also more receptive to BCM.

The process wasn't always smooth. Some of the deacons were ready to move forward, but others were not familiar with biblical counseling and needed more information. A few were skeptical. To help bring the deacons to unity, we developed a PowerPoint presentation, a ministry brochure, and a packet of information. Then I went with another of our directors to present our vision and answer questions. Afterward, we sent follow-up letters to thank the deacons for their attention and to encourage them to continue to learn more about biblical counseling. Their pastors continued to talk with them about the need for biblical counseling resources for their church and their community.

BRINGING THE WHOLE CHURCH ON BOARD
Next, each pastor prepared his church as a whole. First, BCM set up a one-day seminar to introduce biblical counseling.[6] During church announcements, pastors explained the vision for BCM and encouraged their people to attend the training.

In addition, we prepared a church presentation similar to that which a missionary on deputation would bring. Once the presentation had been approved by the BCM advisory board, I visited each church for Sunday morning services. I did not teach at that time, but I did present my personal testimony, our ministry vision, a definition of biblical counseling, and a descriptive account of the need for such counseling and discipleship training. I also explained BCM's organizational structure and described the various counseling resources that BCM would provide. Then I handed out ministry brochures and answered questions.

One item that we found to be especially helpful is our pastor packet—a

BENEFITS OF THE BCM MODEL

To Our Churches

BCM counselees benefit from one-on-one Scripture-based counseling by pastoral referral. Many of our counselees have become members of their referring churches, who have continued to disciple them after formal counseling ended. Pastors appreciate having counseling consultation available. Our churches benefit together when we teach discipleship classes, and every church sends students. In addition, several of our former counselees are interested in training for discipleship now. So our outreach is broadening, and we are seeing discipleship multiplying.

To Our Communities

We are doing some community outreach through seminars with a general audience appeal, such as Tedd Tripp with "Shepherding a Child's Heart," Laura Hendrickson with "Emotions: Getting Off the Roller-Coaster," and Pastor Dan Pugh (Peacemakers Conciliator) with "Getting Along At Work." At such events, people with little or no Bible background receive a powerful taste of Scripture's relevance and also the hope of the gospel, drawing them into the church and sometimes into biblical counseling.

folder of ministry information, flyers for upcoming training, and our recommended reading list. We continue to make these available to pastors at seminars, conferences, and church presentations, as a means of introducing BCM.

There were many opportunities to offer counseling, seminars, and presentations during the time of our ministry's organization. My face became familiar, and I was able to establish more and more relationships. Our churches were already supplying volunteers and some financial resources. Those who had become familiar with biblical counseling were ready to welcome BCM. When our incorporation papers were finished, each of the churches voted to support us through their missions budgets.

MAKING OURSELVES KNOWN IN OUR COMMUNITY

BCM board members made phone calls to area colleagues to introduce the ministry and to encourage their involvement. We also mailed information to area churches and Christian-based businesses, and we traveled with a table display to statewide conferences, camps, and retreats. In addition, we offered workshops and seminars to let others know about the development of BCM. Although we chose not to host dinners or other fundraisers, some ministries have found them to be financially helpful.

Our BCM seminar "Basic Skills for Giving Wise Counsel" was introduced to educate and awaken interest in our community and among our churches. We advertised via newspaper, radio, and television community calendars, as well as through mailings, e-mailing, phone calls, conference displays, and placement of brochures and posters at area businesses and churches. (Radio interviews and conferences with well-known speakers have also been effective.) Imagine our delight when a large group turned up at our first seminar to learn about biblical counseling! Simultaneously, we were surprised at how many had never been introduced to the concept of nouthetic biblical counseling, even among those who had attended Bible-centered churches for years.

HERE'S MORE FOR YOU:
Appendix F: A Checklist for Setting Up Your Ministry Model
A concise outline of the steps in this book, for use as a checklist when organizing your ministry.
Appendix I: Helpful Forms for Ministry Use
A wealth of administrative, counseling, financial, and student forms.

Notes

1 We disagree, based upon 1 Timothy 5:18 and 1 Corinthians 9:7–18.
2 In some states or regions, a nonprofit organization may not charge fees for services but must

rely upon donations for its income. However, for tax purposes, suggested or requested donation amounts may be specified for goods or services rendered. This distinction is important because only donations given above and beyond the quid pro quo (the value of services or goods) may be claimed by the donor as tax exemptions. You should become familiar with laws regarding donations in your area.

3 Note: The terms "professional" or "family counselor" are legally reserved for state-licensed psychologists. You should not use those descriptions unless you legally qualify. Check your state's laws for other restrictions.

4 Church Mutual Insurance Company—phone number: 1–800–554–2642; Web site: www.churchmutual.com.

5 We are also grateful for the two women who served on the BCM board. One, a nurse, advised and taught regarding counseling-related medical issues. The other was the wife of a state association representative, and she brought years of ministry experience. Though these women did not directly prepare churches to receive BCM, their contributions were indispensable.

6 We continue to offer our "Basic Skills for Giving Wise Counsel" seminar at our home church and on the road.

The advisory board meetings were getting more exciting. Pastor Paul had worked with the other two pastors and together they had made a few phone calls to churches in nearby towns. Their colleagues were intrigued by the prospect of counseling and discipleship resources. Each of the previous two meetings had been productive, and now, since attending the seminar and profiting from a helpful time with the BCM instructor, they were on a roll. Two additional pastors had joined their efforts.

The BCM board of directors had told the pastors that they could have copies of BCM documents once they had formed their advisory board and had written their doctrinal statement. The BCM papers saved them a lot of time; the group went to work reading and discussing the documents to be sure that they were all in agreement. They would have to carefully decide if they wanted to incorporate or to work through one church center. The group was leaning toward incorporation, and Pastor Paul hoped Glory Baptist Church would be able to house the ministry. That decision would be up to the board, though, after they determined which facility and staff were best able.

Volunteers were showing up. One of the churches had an attorney in the congregation, another had a registered nurse, and a third was able to provide some technical support. An experienced volunteer offered to build a Web site, and a college student offered to maintain it for them. Each church added counseling ministry information to its church Web site. Carole had been able to devote several hours to design a nice logo and some brochures.

It was time to think about a counselor. Yes, it was still early in the process. They had to seriously discuss raising finances, but the board would let candidates know that the ministry was in its inception. The new counselor would need supplementary work until sufficient support was raised. The advisors would help as much as possible by asking their churches to provide home missions funds right away. They would also assist with the search for a temporary job for the counselor. A couple of the pastors on the board had businessmen in their congregations who were currently hiring.

They were all eager to have the counseling help. By now, under Pastor Paul's guidance, his deacon board was very interested in learning more about biblical counseling. They could now see the value of a resource counselor for their area. The BCM seminar had opened the eyes of the church to the world of biblical discipleship. Coupled with the good preparation that Pastor Paul and Jenny had been doing, the people at Glory Baptist Church seemed ready to welcome the idea of a counseling ministry.

Pastor Paul's office was slowly becoming more ordered because of Carole's competent organizational and clerical skills. Not only that, but Carole had begun to disciple sixteen-year-old Gina. Alongside their Bible studies and casual outings, she was training Gina to serve. The teen was a willing volunteer in assembling worship folders, typing letters and sermon notes, and helping out with mailings. As Carole and Gina worked together, the pastor was happy to hear them discussing spiritual things. He recognized that some of Carole's advice to Gina had been passed on from Jenny, as she and Carole had shared similar conversations during craft nights at their dining-room table.

Pastor Paul was encouraged to see that John's interest in sharing the gospel was growing, too. John had been asking for prayer for people at work and had been more faithful in attending church services. The previous week, after morning worship, the pastor saw John praying with a man whose wife was ill. He also knew that John had made plans to bring the family some fresh vegetables from his garden and to encourage them in the Lord. *That is the way discipleship is supposed to work,* the pastor thought.

These changes brought challenges. With growing interest in biblical counseling among church members, more and more families were seeking help for themselves and for their loved ones. Pastor Paul's counseling schedule was increasing to the point that he had to limit the number of sessions per week in order to have enough study time to prepare for his sermons. But, he thought with satisfaction, this is what I'm here for. The leadership team was helping with discipleship. He was seeing people grow spiritually and become interested in sharing God's help with others. With the prospect of additional resource help and a growing skill level within the church, he could see that biblical counseling could be a wonderful evangelistic outreach in the community.

Preparing to Work with a Resource Biblical Counselor

STAFF and CENTER: Applications from now on will probably be clear to you without additional notes. The following chapters will help you to think through choosing counselors, setting up discipleship training, keeping your resources in order, working with others effectively, organizing your office, keeping accurate records, communicating well, and dealing with conflicts. These should be part of every ministry plan. The appendices will give you some practical tools, checklists, and forms to help you to be thorough and to save you lots of time. After you get started, your plans will undoubtedly have to be tweaked, so be flexible. Evaluate your ministry periodically to see where changes are indicated. You are welcome to contact BCM if you have further questions after reading these resourcs.

The value and advantages of biblical counseling are huge for the local church. Pastors like you can have confidence that nouthetic principles are Bible-centered, practical, and Christ-exalting. With the right resource counselor in place, you do not have to risk sending your treasured people to outside counseling that may undermine the principles of Scripture that you have so carefully taught. The structure of Biblical Counseling Ministries allows you to retain biblical authority and nurture the people for whom you are accountable to God.

However, even the best ministry model will only work if you have a biblical counselor who embraces the ministry vision and possesses the heart, qualifications, and ability to build together with you upon the four pillars of ministry:

- Doctrinal unity
- Unity of purpose and philosophy
- Commitment to method
- Sharing ministry needs

DECIDING WHEN TO START LOOKING FOR A COUNSELOR

1. Pray, pray, pray.
2. Plan to hire early enough for your new resource counselor to be able to participate with your board to build the ministry.
3. Consider how much help you will need with development of ministry vision, writing documents, counseling, raising support, and drawing in other churches.
4. Think realistically about your resources. How much financial support are you able to offer? What other financial or material factors will you need to address?
5. Assess the general interest level and awareness of the people at your potential home and host churches. Are they willing to receive a resource counselor? Will you have volunteers to help with tasks and finances? Is one of your core churches initially ready to add the new counselor to staff?

Your ministry board should carefully time the decision to hire a counselor. Immediate needs and overall goals will vary for each ministry group. See the nearby box for some suggestions.

Working Out a Job Description

You will need to decide responsibilities and salary before you begin your search. Appropriate salary will vary greatly from one church to the next, but generally you should try to pay the counselor roughly the amount that an associate pastor from your area receives.

Your counselor's job description should include the position title, qualifications, expectations for counseling hours at each site, line of responsibility (to whom your counselor will be directly responsible), and duties. Duties should include the following:

- *Counseling: we recommend a 60 percent counseling ceiling per forty-hour week*
- Teaching: *20 percent for developing curriculum and teaching classes*
- Administration: *10 percent for budget setting, board meetings, oversight of personnel, supervision of other counselors, and promotion of ministry*
- Writing and research: *10 percent for reports, articles, newsletters, research, and required forms*

These percentages should be flexible, because demands will vary from month to month. You should also clearly state paid holidays, vacation, skill development allowances, and personal days.

Choosing a Counselor

Not every board will have a highly qualified biblical counselor standing by ready and able to serve a group of churches. You will probably find it necessary to seek one out. Since our biblical counselor initialized the BCM ministry, we did not have to go through the search process. This chapter is therefore not built upon our hiring experience. Rather, we draw upon our years of experience working together to offer some realistic suggestions for finding someone who will fit your ministry needs.

> Consider whether a biblical counseling graduate-level intern might be a good choice for you. Interns are typically temporary employees of a church for a stated time period. They are paid a lower salary because their position is part of their education. You could arrange for your intern to help you set up your ministry, with the intent that the permanent position would be theirs when the ministry's doors open. Work with a few seminaries to find the best candidates for you.

The complexity of serving five churches requires more than a solid seminary education and excellent biblical counseling abilities. Your executive director will also need highly developed organizational and administrative skills, maturity, wisdom, adaptability, humility, flexibility, endurance, versatility, relational skills, integrity, and ability to handle financial responsibilities and manage conflicts.

Resist letting convenience or fear guide you. Avoid choosing someone simply because he or she is a respected member of one of your churches and gives godly advice. The well-educated biblical counselor who already sits in your pews may turn out to be the best choice. Still, the process of thoroughly seeking God's will is worth your effort.

EDUCATIONAL QUALIFICATIONS

1. *Look for someone with a degree in nouthetic biblical counseling from a reputable seminary.*[1] All counseling rests upon the personal application of theology; therefore, a theologically sound education is indispensable if the counselor is to be truly biblical.[2] Thorough biblical knowledge and effective practical application of the Word should be the bedrocks of a local-church counseling ministry. Your counselor should reflect that commitment with unshakable conviction and thorough preparation.

2. *Seek a well-educated person who is passionate about the work, and who, beyond his or her earned degrees, actively pursues an ongoing sharpening of biblical counseling skills through regular attendance at reputable seminars, seminary classes, and conferences.* Look for:

- Attendance at the Biblical Counseling Training Conference (BCTC) at Faith Baptist Church in Lafayette, Indiana
- Attendance at biblical counseling conferences, such as those run by the Association of Certified Biblical Counselors (ACBC)
- Attendance at supplementary Bible college or seminary classes at schools with a high reputation for biblical counseling. Be sure the

school does not teach integrationism, but, rather, a solidly biblical approach to counseling.[3]

3. *Is your candidate certified?* Not all certifying organizations are the same. We require all BCM staff counselors to be certified by ACBC. ACBC is internationally recognized and has rigorous requirements, including references, thirty-two or more hours of ACBC-certified education, two entrance exams, fifty hours of supervised counseling, and approval by the ACBC certifying board. Other certifying organizations, while legitimate and reputable, are far less demanding. For example, the International Association of Biblical Counselors (IABC) and the Association of Biblical Counselors (ABC) accept qualified members by application with references. There are many counseling associations, so be sure that you agree with the counseling philosophy of any certifying organization with which your candidate may be a part.

4. *Is the person a competent counselor?* If possible, observe your candidate in counseling sessions, provide on-the-spot scenarios, and talk to his or her ACBC supervisor.

PERSONAL QUALIFICATIONS

BCM looks for the following qualifications in counselors:

- Is able to give a credible profession of faith in Jesus Christ as his or her Savior and Lord
- Possesses a reputation for a godly Christian walk in his or her daily life
- Participates in continuing fellowship in good standing with a baptistic church
- Is in agreement with the doctrinal statement of the ministry
- Is in agreement with the ministry's statement of mission and its biblical approach to counseling
- Has a sense of God's direction toward this type of ministry
- Is in a growing relationship with our Savior, Jesus Christ
- Has a growing ability to understand and apply the Bible

- Has an active desire to increase his or her counseling skills
- Has an unwavering resolve regarding the sufficiency of Scripture
- Is willing to give of his or her time in order to help people change and grow
- Is aware of his or her potential to sin
- Is willing to be accountable
- Has good administrative abilities
- Is able to work closely with others while exhibiting the fruit of the Spirit at all times (Gal. 5:22–23)
- Is not in bondage to any sin, past or present, and is living blamelessly in the present
- Is able to teach and able to develop curriculum
- Is exemplary in his or her overall life relationships with spouse, children, parents, grandparents, and authority figures

In addition, you should evaluate your applicant's interpersonal skills, maturity, organizational skills, punctuality, work ethic, creativity, teaching ability, and familiarity with church ministry. Practical skills should include an understanding of computers, church office demands, filing, developing forms and advertising materials, and other clerical abilities.

As you conduct your interviews, listen out for the following:

- Does this candidate appear to speak the Word in everyday conversations and consistently apply Scripture in everyday life?
- Can he or she articulate biblically what God is doing in his or her life, including clear and humble identification of personal strengths and weaknesses?
- Are there past sins or failures that might impact this candidate's ability to function in this position?
- How does this person understand and address heart issues, both personally and in counseling sessions?
- Is the candidate's family on board with ministry demands?

REASONS TO CONSIDER HIRING A FEMALE COUNSELOR

Biblical counseling may be provided with excellence by men or women. However, the advantages of a qualified female are worth considering:

- The church already has a male pastor to minister the Word to men.
- A woman's perspective and female skill set can be very helpful in reaching out to other women.
- A female counselor may be a natural help with and to pastors' wives, a ministry that is often neglected in the church.
- She protects the pastor's reputation by counseling women who may otherwise become inappropriately bonded to a male counselor or tempted to falsely accuse their counseling pastors.
- Marriage counseling is enhanced when a male/female team (pastor and resource counselor) works with a married couple so that both husband and wife may feel represented and understood.
- A woman exemplifies and affirms the place of appropriate female leadership in the church. Other women are encouraged and taught when they observe her capable yet submissive leadership. Consider Priscilla's ministry (Acts 18:1–3, 26; Rom. 16:3;1 Cor. 16:19; 2 Tim. 4:19).
- If the counselor's husband is willing and able to fully provide for their living expenses, pressure on the ministry is eased during tight financial times.

There may be some disadvantages:

- One difficulty is in the realm of teaching. Before I speak to a mixed group, we usually have one of the pastors on our board explain that we are not violating 1 Timothy 2:11–12, primarily because BCM is not a church. In addition, I am not usurping authority, because I have been asked to teach under the authority of the BCM board, my pastor, the pastor of our home church, and the pastor of the church hosting the event. Even so, some have difficulty accepting a female instructor. Therefore, we also include some male guest instructors and area pastors to teach some of our seminars and classes. You will need to clearly decide where you stand on this matter and make provision for instructors accordingly.
- Care should be taken that the reputations of the counselor and the pastor are not endangered when they work side by side in the church building.

- Does the person have financial means that can carry him or her during lean times, if necessary?

- Is he or she able to carry pressures and demands with grace?
- In summary, is your candidate thoroughly biblically qualified?

The Decision-Making Process

We recommend that your board appoints a committee to seek candidates, review résumés, and do initial interviews to narrow down viable choices (similar to the process of hiring a pastor). Then the full board may interview the final two or three candidates and hire the new counselor.

Temporary Arrangements

> "Given that I am the only person at our church facility throughout the week, and that my wife has her hands full with our young children, one-on-one counseling with women is nearly an impossible proposition. BCM has been an incredible blessing concerning this problem. When a woman comes with a need for counseling, I can confidently recommend her to BCM, knowing that she will receive the same biblical counsel that I would give, and that I can continue to shepherd her while staying above reproach."
> **Corey Brookins, Senior Pastor, Berea Baptist Church, Stevens Point, WI**

Until your ministry is completely set up, you may decide (as we did) to hire your new counselor as a temporary staff member at one of your core churches. In that case, you should specify the time line of the job, such as you would when hiring an intern, with the end date being the day the ministry expects to open its doors. This arrangement moves the ministry process forward, but also allows for a probationary period for your new counselor. The church should review its procedures and policies and write supplements where needed. Your counselor will need to join the core church and serve under that church's authority as a member, at least for this time period. (Membership at one of the core churches should be required at all times during the counselor's employment.)

The temporary position should be offered with the understanding that a permanent position will be extended first to the new counselor if he or she has met ministry requirements during the probationary period. Donations from each core church should be pledged and regularly sent to the hiring church during this period to cover payroll and expenses for your new counselor.

Pray for God's direction to find a credentialed biblical counselor who is willing to do the work of ministry for a small salary while holding a part-time job. Although finding such a person may be a challenge, keep in mind that many seminary graduates understand a tough work ethic and have a self-sacrificial passion for ministry.

During the formation of BCM, I worked full-time as a school secretary while I served temporarily in an unpaid position at the small church where I was a member (now a BCM helper church). My forty-member church graciously gave me space and office supplies. As a member of the staff, I could counsel under the church's insurance protection as long as I did not charge for sessions. The ministry board could have arranged for me to receive a salary during that time (but not based on a per-session rate). However, my day job paid sufficiently, so I did not ask for any salary from our churches. Any donations during that time period were received by my church and disbursed via the church treasurer to pay our expenses (which were minimal). Once BCM opened its doors, we moved the ministry to our home church, which had larger facilities and could house a growing ministry more comfortably. At that point I quit my day job and began to receive a salary through the ministry.

Working With Your Counselor

BUILDING NEEDS

Administrator's Office Space

Once we opened our doors, we had a formal office set up for BCM in our

> **FINDING OFFICE SPACE**
>
> In many small churches, pastors hardly have the luxury of an adequate office for themselves, let alone the ability to provide a professional office for a counselor. As your board is discussing which of your churches would best serve as the ministry's home church, consider office needs and administrative support staff near the top of the list.
>
> When office space is hard to find (and it usually is), be creative about the possibilities. Rooms may serve double (or triple) duty as long as scheduled uses do not conflict, there is sufficient space for counseling and administrative work, and desks and file cabinets can be locked when the counselor is not there. The BCM office also serves as a Sunday Bible class room, small-group meeting room, and boardroom, among other things. Because our normal office hours are on weekdays, BCM's use of the room does not conflict with the church's use of the room, so the arrangement works well.

home church. There I do administrative work, counsel, and receive visitors. The other four churches provide some secretarial support and a place to counsel, but no office space. BCM counseling sessions are held exclusively in our five core churches (for insurance, financial, and time-management reasons). However, we do offer to speak and teach at other locations.

Your counselor's office should be clean, neat, and well stocked with appropriate furnishings and office supplies, including a desk, bookcases, file cabinets, and a comfortable office chair. Workspace for the counselor should be well lit, professional-looking and large enough to spread out materials comfortably, with computer/printer and files easily accessible.

We recommend that counseling be done in another room, if possible. However, if space limitations require using the counselor's office for sessions, ideally a table and chairs should be set up away from the counselor's desk. If possible, have someone available to answer the phone in another room during session times, to avoid distractions caused by a ringing phone.

Other Space Needs

Filing and storage space are essential. Our home office, training center, and resource center store the files that relate to their area of the ministry. I store some papers at home, and I keep a locked compartment in my car to transport confidential materials to counseling sessions each week.

Our ministry storage space includes two large file cabinets for office supplies, session files, student files, counseling information, and administrative forms. I also have space in various locations for display items, class/seminar books and handouts, BCM Sunday materials, equipment (such as PowerPoint projector and audio/visual items), computer supplies, brochures, and paper. The home church provides most of our filing and storage except for some books and class materials.

> "Space for counseling can sometimes be a challenge. In a small church, the counseling room will quite possibly also serve as a Sunday School room, office, library, etc. When this is the case, it is imperative that the counselor ensures that the facility is appropriate before the counselee arrives. Your church may not have a dedicated space for counseling, but that doesn't necessarily mean there is no space for counseling. If the room can meet the accompanying guidelines, it can be used for counseling."
> **Corey Brookins, Senior Pastor, Berea Baptist Church, Stevens Point, WI**

The home church office also supplies bookshelves for the BCM library, some counselee literature, and a few frequently used reference books and papers.[4]

Counseling Rooms at Each Location

I travel to five churches, usually within certain hours on a specific day of the week so that each church knows when to expect me. While the schedule is flexible and must be modified at times, I try to stay as consistent as possible.

Each church has designated counseling space, according to our written policies. Generally, your counseling rooms should be clean and uncluttered and contain an appropriately sized table and chairs (not a children's table and chairs) and access to a phone (a cell phone is acceptable). For safety and accountability, counseling rooms should have a window in the door or on an inside wall so that your counselor is viewable from outside the room. Seating should be arranged so that the counselee is not visible (or not easily visible) from outside the room. Counseling rooms should be reasonably soundproof, and the door should remain closed for the duration of the session. Temperature and lighting should be set at levels that do not detract from the session. Availability of a copy machine is helpful. BCM asks the church to have someone else in the building while counseling is going on. If these conditions are not present, your counselor may respectfully voice concerns to the appointed board liaison for the church. This has always taken care of any problems for us. However, your board of directors should be notified if your concerns are not addressed by the liaison.

Teaching Space and Equipment for Classes

Our training center provides classroom space for all BCM discipleship training classes and our home office hosts our seminars. Each of these churches graciously allows BCM to use its projectors, whiteboards and markers, coffeemakers, and audio/visual equipment. However, we have to carefully coordinate to be sure the equipment is available on the dates we need to use it. One advantage of having several collaborating churches is that when one church lacks a piece of equipment, another can usually supply it. If coordination is not possible, the ministry has to be ready to rent or purchase the needed items, to ask that they be donated, or to go without.

Keys

You will need to consider what to do when access to the church is needed for after-hours counseling or training. Our board liaisons arranged for me to have church keys, but you could arrange to have someone open the church for you instead.

PERSONNEL NEEDS

Clerical support. From the first, BCM has relied upon its home and host churches for clerical support, which they provide at no charge to BCM.

Home office personnel. Staff duties at the home office require the most hours: making appointments, filing documents, collecting and depositing funds, preparing for seminars, answering calls, keeping our individual and student e-mail lists current, setting up online registration forms, and other similar tasks. The relationship between the home office staff and BCM is crucial for keeping things running smoothly, especially because I spend a lot of time at other churches so I am not always available to answer

---

"Having BCM join our church staff has been a blessing and a challenge. The blessing is having a biblical counselor as part of our staff. Her input and encouragement at weekly staff meetings benefits the whole staff. Also, for the three days per week that she spends with us, we have access to her wisdom and insight into various situations.

"The challenging part has been merging the extra workload in an already busy church office. The most hectic times involve seminar preparations, where eight to ten hours of work may be added to your schedule. The more typical addition is one to two hours per week that involve scheduling counselees, updating the counselor's calendar, printing and mailing information for counselees, and accounting for and depositing financial transactions.

"We found a good solution in an individual from the home church who was willing to donate her time to handle the clerical support of BCM. She adjusts her schedule and works around the current staff. This has taken a lot of pressure off the office staff."

Mrs. Kathy Parker, Office Administrator & BCM board member, Calvary Baptist Church, Wisconsin Rapids, WI

---

questions. We are highly indebted to the administrators at our home office; their cheerful assistance has been indispensable.

Training center personnel. The staff at our training center cares for class registrations, runs off handbooks, keeps our church e-mail list current, and helps with class preparations.

Resource center personnel. The office staff at our resource center maintains textbooks and counseling materials, prints brochures, and runs our book tables. Volunteers with professional technological experience maintain our Web site.

Support center personnel. The secretary at our support center does miscellaneous tasks such as mailings, copying, providing brochures, and helping with displays. Fundraiser arrangements are also the responsibility of our support center.

Written procedures. We have written procedures for office staff at our home office, training center, and resource center. These simple documents help to avoid confusion when we are not there to answer questions. They have been especially helpful during personnel changes. (See Appendix I for samples.)

To keep everything coordinated, regular communication is maintained via e-mail, phone, and personal contact with each church to be sure that needs are accommodated and everyone is on the same page.

OTHER SUPPORT STAFF VOLUNTEERS

We have been amazed and so grateful for the scores of people who have stepped up to help BCM. The Lord has laid our needs on many hearts at various points in our journey, and we are truly humbled at their generosity and selflessness.

Information technicians. Knowledgeable IT personnel from several locations have built and maintained our Web site, provided audio/visual assistance at seminars and other events, set up live streaming for classes, and helped with general computer troubleshooting and updating.

BCM Sunday teams. Once we had our ministry up and running for a few years, we brought in a team of our students to introduce churches to BCM on Sunday mornings. The team teaches Sunday Bible study lessons, gives their testimonies, and presents BCM's PowerPoint and video testimonials.

Literature publication help. Beyond her normal clerical duties, our resources coordinator has helped to edit and publish materials, including booklets and brochures.

Other help. Church groups (such as seniors and teens) assist with mailings, assemble handbooks, usher at seminars, and meet other needs. When kitchen or nursery help is needed at our seminars, volunteers have generously and willingly stepped up as well. In addition, we are extremely grateful for those many faithful believers who have reached out with discipleship after counselees have completed formal sessions.

Summary

Your resource counselor will lead your ministry, so you should set your standards carefully and conduct thorough interviews to select the right person. Be creative and realistic as you decide on the counselor's job description and roles for each church, prepare office and counseling space, and work out details with your staff. This process will yield a resource that can bless your church and your community in some very significant ways. It's worth the effort.

Notes

1   There are a number of good seminaries that offer advanced degrees in biblical counseling. We recommend these Baptist seminaries (but there are other reputable schools as well): Central Baptist Theological Seminary (www.centralseminary.edu); Shepherds Theological Seminary (www.shepherds.edu); Faith Bible Seminary (click on "Counseling" at www.fbclafayette.org).

2 We all live by what we believe. Even Marxists rest upon a theology—atheism. In particular, our worldview is shaped by our understanding of who God is (or is not) and how we relate to Him (or seek not to relate to Him). Theology has a profound effect upon the counselor's methods and goals (as well as the counselee's). For more information on this subject, see **Jay Adams,** *A Theology of Christian Counseling* (Grand Rapids, MI: Zondervan, 1979).

3 See Chapter 2 for more on integrationism. Any of the suggestions could be realistically carried out for candidates from outside the US. Thirty-six countries were represented at the BCTC in 2011 (www.faithlafayette.org). ACBC conferences are held all over the US, and they are working at developing international sites as well (https://biblicalcounseling.com). Biblical counseling classes are offered online from reputable schools such as the Christian Counseling and Education Foundation in Philadelphia, Pennsylvania (www.ccef.org). Thus, they are accessible from all over the globe. US ministries continue to expand to provide training in biblical counseling. Central Seminary has a campus in Romania. In addition, Dr. Jim Bearss, a ACBC-certified biblical counselor with On Target Ministries, is training pastors in places such as Haiti, Jamaica, Ukraine, Philippines, Lebanon, and Egypt with invitations open to minister in South Korea, Togo, and Jordan (www.OnTargetMinistry.org). I encourage readers from outside the US to contact these ministries to explore possibilities for training in their area. See also footnote 5 on page 80.

4 The BCM library consists of books owned by the ministry. I use these books for reference or occasionally to loan to counselees who cannot afford to purchase important learning materials for their sessions. When you loan books, I recommend asking for a reasonable deposit if you cannot afford to replace books that are not returned.

Pastor Paul scratched his head. Counselor selection had been a challenge. Several of the pastors had been pressured by people with family members who had had some training and wanted to see them plugged into the ministry position right away. At one point it seemed as though the board would not get past this hurdle. Much prayer had gone up about whom and when to call.

Eventually, the board recognized the importance of finding the right person for the job, and agreed to accept résumés and do some interviewing before making any decisions. A committee was appointed to contact a few Bible colleges for names of graduates who might be good candidates. State association representatives and BCM were also consulted. It wasn't long before they began to receive calls and résumés from interested parties.

While that process was ongoing, the board assessed which of their churches would initially house the ministry until incorporation was completed and they were ready officially to open their doors. Charity Baptist Church offered to put the new counselor on staff and set up a temporary office. The pastors would ask for mission support and then pool their resources to provide a modest salary. However, they soon discovered that initially their counselor would need supplementary work. One of the pastors offered to speak to a businessman in his congregation, but they would have to wait to discover the new counselor's skills before they could go further.

Pastor Paul was impressed at how church resources were dovetailing to bring the ministry together. Even while making difficult decisions, the pastors seemed in earnest about working as a team. He smiled as he realized what a blessing it was to pray together with those who understood the rigors of ministry. The others appeared to appreciate that, too. They actually cared about one another. How refreshing.

Their discussions were not without some challenges. Each of them had hoped to become the home office of the ministry. But they knew they had to assess realistically which of them could function best in that capacity. As they worked together, the choice was becoming obvious. Pastor Paul knew it would probably not be Glory Baptist, in spite of the fact that he had spearheaded the whole idea. Charity Baptist had two pastors and a large new building with an office area staffed by a full-time secretary. They were in a much better position to house the ministry. The other pastors seemed to be reluctantly coming to that conclusion as well.

As important as the home church was, they knew that teamwork and financial support would be necessary from each of the churches. Every contribution was valuable. Carole, for example, was a huge help with organizing resources and helping with brochures and posters for ministry events. City Baptist had an able technician who could maintain the ministry Web site. The Christian businessman from Shepherd Baptist was willing to serve as treasurer. Things were beginning to gel.

But the board knew that they needed a go-to person now, someone who could bring it all together and keep momentum rising. It was time to hire if they could possibly manage it.

BCM had been helpful as they walked through this process. The instructor there had answered questions and provided some feedback for their ideas. Grateful to God, Pastor Paul looked forward to the future.

Part 3

Help for the Biblical Counselor

Elizabeth Jensen's stomach was churning with excitement. That was the most unusual interview she had ever experienced. As she reached for the car door, she noticed that her hand was trembling. *Excitement or fear?* she wondered, and concluded it was probably a little of both. She coaxed the door open, relieved to have the interview over yet exhilarated at the possibilities that had been offered to her.

"Beth?" a voice called. She turned to see Pastor Paul with a folder in his hand. "I think you forgot something." He grinned as he handed it to her, then tilted his head and peered down at her. "You OK?" he asked.

Beth blushed, embarrassed and a little amused at what her expression must have been. She had probably looked like a scared rabbit. With a warm smile, she tried to keep her voice even as she assured him, "Oh, I'm fine, just a little dazed to think about what's involved in this job." She quickly added, "I mean, dazed in a positive sense. Your board's enthusiasm is contagious. I really like what you're trying to do here. But the concept is different from anything I've ever seen before. It's intriguing and unnerving at the same time. But I'm totally on board with the whole idea."

Pastor Paul liked her candor. "We've been praying for months," he said simply, "and we're sure it's what God wants for our area. But ours is not the first ministry group to do something like this." He told her about BCM and suggested that she call them.

As Beth left, his assurances rang in her ears: "You did a great job in there." She hoped that it was true. She had gone to the interview with some reservations about her age and position in life. Widowed four years ago after twenty-five years of marriage and raising three children, Beth had decided to leave her dead-end job and pursue her longtime dream of becoming a biblical counselor. She went back to school to finish her master's degree and was now ready to join the workforce.

Beth's years in seminary had taught her more than just how to counsel the Word. She was still struggling with grief when she started classes, but she was surprised and grateful to find comfort as she watched godly examples of faculty and other students in life-changing trials. Their faith seemed to stabilize them. Newly refreshed, Beth's study of Scripture became more to her than pursuit of a degree. She began to identify with the Man of Sorrows, who showed her that grief was not an enemy but a gift that equipped her to love people as He did. She learned to walk with her Savior more closely than she ever had before. But she knew that His purpose in comforting her was not to make her comfortable. She wanted to share what He was giving her.

At forty-seven, Beth knew that it would not be easy to find work in her field, but that didn't deter her. She had always been a go-getter, a risk taker who relished challenges. At first she had pursued this interview as merely one job possibility, but now she was deeply intrigued at the vision and the passion for developing local-church discipleship. For the next few days it was all she could think about. She shook her head sadly as she realized that one-on-one disciple-making had been missing in almost every church she had ever attended, with the exception of a few godly individuals who had reached out to her. Still, she knew Titus 2 ministry was in her blood. It was what the Lord wanted. It was what her interviewers wanted. And she wanted it, too, now more than ever.

Beth's fear had dissolved into determination. She didn't have to wait for a job offer. Her mind was full of possibilities, ideas, and hope for expanding her present discipleship efforts. Feeling more alive than she had in years, Beth prayed fervently, and purposefully bathed herself in Scripture. When the call came from the board for a second interview, she was ready.

To the Counselor: Gaining Perspective for the Next Chapters

So far, this book has spoken almost exclusively to pastors and ministry board directors. We will now turn to address the counselor.

Your job as a biblical counselor is complex, requiring diligence and balance, a willingness to give of self tirelessly, and an ability to be ready for anything. Therefore, your personal relationship with the Lord must be top priority. Your energy and perspective are not sustainable without consistent time in the Word, right worship, fellowship with the Lord and His people, and consistent prayer. God is your lifeline. Do not lose sight of Him. Your primary goal must be to glorify Him. Period. Biblical counseling can eat you alive otherwise.

Further, the demands of the job can easily crowd out your family and personal times. You can justify the loss for a while. But be warned: your family is your responsibility before God. Balancing work and home life is essential. You will need to set aside daily and weekly blocks of time for your family and your home, take your vacation time, and be content that God is honored when you do. One of the strengths of this model is the built-in support of the local church for each of your counselees. When they need help, they do not depend solely upon you. Therefore, you are realistically able to prioritize your personal relationships and devote appropriate time to your family.

When you are feeding on Christ's righteousness and sharing Him in sessions, the power of the Word will energize you even when you are scratching your head or weeping in prayer. Study the Word diligently and stay close to your Savior. You will encounter many "weights" (Heb. 12:1) as you come alongside others. You will be tempted either to center your study time on your counselee's needs or to get caught up in your own concerns. Do neither. Instead, center yourself in Christ. Read the Scriptures in order to meet with the Author, word by word and thought by thought drawing out His

> "When wisdom enters your heart,
> And knowledge is pleasant to your soul,
> Discretion will preserve you;
> Understanding will keep you …
> Keep sound wisdom and discretion;
> So they will be life to your soul
> And grace to your neck.
> Then you will walk safely in your way,
> And your foot will not stumble."
> (Proverbs 2:10–11; 3:21b–23)

intended meaning from the text and its application to your life. Then humbly follow through with what you learn. He will empower you to grow in your own life and thus prepare you to teach others. If you fail at this, you will ultimately fail to counsel biblically.

Stay in prayer, both in regular blocks of time and throughout the day. You do not know what a day may bring; you need His Word and prayer to prepare and protect you. Petition Him faithfully. Approach your life deliberately mindful of your utter dependence upon the Lord for the ability to carry out your responsibilities, and believe that He is faithful to complete the work He began in you (Phil. 1:6). You would also be wise to build a prayer team. Choose your team members carefully and share information without complaining, gossiping, or breaching confidentiality. You should have people praying for you while you are on the front lines.

Beware the temptation to presume upon God to keep you comfortable. He makes no such promise. When unexpected situations arise (and they often do), resist the urge to panic or bristle. Throw yourself upon the Lord, remembering that God is in control and will give you no more than you can handle in His grace (1 Cor. 10:13; 2 Cor. 12:9). Know what the

Word says, and skillfully show your counselees how Scripture—not your own wisdom—speaks to their true needs (see Appendices A and B). Be careful not to internalize the problems your counselees face. Remember, you are not their savior; you are called to point them to Him and help them as you are able, but not to assume responsibility for their lives.

Furthermore, remember that a disciplined working knowledge of the power and love of God will overcome any spirit of fear you may have, and free you to serve him well (2 Tim. 1:7). Finally, when you feel like quitting, refuse to indulge negativity. Instead, deliberately persevere by faith, trust God, and choose to grow in grace and knowledge of our Lord and Savior Jesus Christ. As your own faith is strengthened through your trials, you will find God opening doors to share your newfound growth with those He brings into your life.

The practical advice in the next few chapters rests upon the foundation of your close relationship with Christ and appropriate prioritizing of family responsibilities. Although we will not emphasize relationships with God and family in the coming pages, please do not think we are in any manner minimizing the necessity of Christ-centeredness at work and in your personal life. In the following pages, I will share some of the careful disciplines and preparatory steps that I exercise to help my job run more smoothly. They are all important for good stewardship. But none of these steps will build your ministry in lasting or meaningful ways unless you are centered in Christ.

"... I bow my knees to the Father of our Lord Jesus Christ, from whom the whole family in heaven and earth is named, that He would grant you, according to the riches of His glory, to be strengthened with might through His Spirit in the inner man, that Christ may dwell in your hearts through faith; that you, being rooted and grounded in love, may be able to comprehend with all the saints what is the width and length and depth and height—to know the love of Christ which passes knowledge; that you may be filled with all the fullness of God. Now to Him who is able to do exceedingly abundantly above all that we ask or think, according to the power that works in us, to Him be glory in the church by Christ Jesus to all generations, forever and ever. Amen." (Eph. 3:14–21)

Communication: Keeping Ministry Relationships Healthy

Biblical counselor, your interactions with pastors and other staff at each of the home and host churches are to be based on biblical love. These relationships are crucial to your ministry's health and must therefore be carefully nurtured through consistent prayer, biblically expressed care, and honest, open communication. Since good communication is essential, this chapter will cover some of the various approaches and the means through which I initiate and maintain consistent contact with my core churches.

> "It is crucial for a pastor to remember that he will be held accountable for the shepherding of his church. A certified counselor can greatly help in the pastoring ministry, but it can also become an excuse for a pastor to become overly 'hands-off.' Staying up-to-date with the progress of a counselee is the responsibility not only of the counselor, but also the pastor."
> **Corey Brookins, Senior Pastor, Berea Baptist Church, Stevens Point, WI**

Working with Pastors

One of the most important things you, the counselor, should remember is that you are there primarily for the purpose of supporting and helping the pastor to build up the local church, for the glory of God. The well-being of the local church, not of the counseling ministry, should be your target. Although the church will probably be a significant help and encouragement to you and your work, you must not seek affirmation from them, and you should consciously avoid making demands on the pastor's time, resources, and energies. Instead, diligently seek to bear his burden alongside him by faithfully praying, asking selflessly about his discipleship and counseling concerns, and offering whatever biblical help you are able to give.

> I write from the perspective of a female biblical counselor. Any gender-specific suggestions are based upon my experiences and are not meant to minimize a male counselor's value. My intent is to assist biblical counselors of either gender, not just women.

Carefully guard the pastor's reputation. A female counselor, especially, should take care to meet with a pastor only in honorable ways: with others in the building (if at all possible), always within sight and immediate access of anyone outside the room, and promoting godliness in every respect.

If you are a female counselor, you may be able to help the pastor in an important way by getting to know his wife. Offer her your friendship and respect, and provide positive help that will build trust and carefully uphold the pastor's reputation. Often the pastor's wife can use the confidential prayer support and discreet encouragement that a female counselor is in an excellent position to give.

You will also do well to remember that the churches you serve are not yours, but God's. God has given authority and care of the churches to the pastor, not to you. This truth impacts how you view yourself in relation to the church and moderates how you approach the pastor and the deacons or elders. Make your requests humbly, with deference and respect toward those God has put in authority, however flawed they may appear. Take biblical action in love by reflecting the glory of God and serving the good of His people. Your personal concerns should be left in the trust of our holy and faithful Lord, with acknowledgment of your sinfulness and His grace and gratitude for the opportunities you have been given to minister the Word.

When one of the churches in the home/host core experiences an internal struggle, the counseling ministry's role is to faithfully pray. Be willing to offer counsel only if asked. Wisely and discreetly seek the ministry board's advice if needed. Then patiently wait for God's will to be done. The church will probably not ask for your help. Be content with that.

REGULAR CONTACT WITH PASTORS

During regular visits to each church, I usually greet the pastor if he is available. I inquire about counseling-related concerns and frequently ask how I may be of service. E-mails may suffice if the pastor's schedule does not allow for personal interaction for a given period of time. However, verbal contact is preferable.

Communication with Pastors Outside the Core Group

Most of the pastors who call BCM are from churches that hold to the same (or very similar) beliefs as ours. They are grateful for our help, and we are happy to be there for them. Therefore, contact with them is natural and positive.

When referrals are made by pastors from outside our core group, we typically encourage them to accompany their counselees to sessions. There are two reasons for this request: (1) so that the pastors may have firsthand knowledge of the progress of their charges, and (2) to familiarize them with nouthetic counseling. When a pastor is reluctant or unable to come, I still accept the referral and ask the counselee to agree in writing to allow me to update the referring pastor about the progress being made in sessions. Updates may be provided to the referring pastor a few times during the course of counseling, provided written permission is granted by the counselee. The counselee is also encouraged to update his or her pastor directly.

As you counsel, remember that the pastor has entrusted one of his flock to you, one for whom he is accountable to God. Therefore, you are accountable for reporting progress and answering his questions as you are able. Your understanding of this responsibility mediates communication and places you in a humble state of mind, which pleases the Lord (1 Peter 5:5).

You are also wise to recognize when the pastor himself may need biblical encouragement. My objective is to communicate respect and appreciation for the work he is doing, even when disagreements occur. Any contact must be honorable and helpful, with the soul needs of the counselee and the pastor in mind.

Communication with the Home Church

BCM serves under the authority of the pastor and deacons of the home church. Our monthly e-newsletters keep our home church—and many other interested parties—apprised of events and prayer requests. Once per year, the home church deacons request a more detailed summary report of our annual activities and our plans for the upcoming fiscal year. Occasionally they will ask specific questions which I usually answer in written form. In addition, the senior pastor, who also serves as counseling supervisor, regularly meets with me to discuss cases, concerns, and ideas. Further, the staff includes me in its weekly meetings, where spiritual matters and ministry updates are shared. We have found this to be a good system of accountability and consistent communication with our home church.

Modes of Communication

Communication is an essential element in a multichurch ministry like ours. We rely on many modes, including phones, mailboxes, e-mail, voicemail, and personal contact. Each has strengths and weaknesses.

- *Mailboxes:* A church mailbox at each location can be helpful for general information exchange, but take care to safeguard confidential material. For that reason, we usually hold confidential mail in a locked compartment or in a secure location in the church office.

- *E-mail:* BCM has its own e-mail address, which I normally check daily. Return e-mails contain a confidentiality message. Generally, we do not counsel through e-mail, in part because of the danger of unauthorized discovery or misuse. Sometimes I may contact a church office via e-mail to reschedule sessions, but I use a counselee code rather than names. Our monthly and quarterly newsletters are e-mailed to churches, interested individuals, board members, and students. We also e-mail Web links and/or registration forms for our classes to churches and individuals who express interest in our training program.
- *Voicemail:* To avoid confusion, BCM has only one location for ministry voicemail, which I check regularly. When our core churches receive recorded messages for BCM, the secretary contacts me via e-mail or phone as soon as possible.
- *Phone access:* We request that our churches provide phone access in counseling rooms for safety and convenience, but we also ask that those phones be answered by someone outside the room when sessions are going on. Cell phones are acceptable, but please remember to silence your phone during sessions, and to ask your counselee to do so as well.

Communication Regarding Scheduling

COORDINATING SCHEDULING OF COUNSELING

Home office. Schedule coordination for five locations can be challenging. At BCM, counselees may schedule sessions in one of two ways: (1) through our home office, or, (2) more often, at the end of the previous session. While scheduling, I record upcoming appointments in my day planner and on payment record sheets that I deliver to home-church office personnel two or three times per week. I also maintain an online calendar that is always accessible to our home office staff. When the home office schedules a session, the office administrator calls or e-mails the information to me and changes the online calendar accordingly. I immediately add the information to my day planner (in pencil) to avoid missing appointments or double scheduling. Also, the office administrator and I personally exchange weekly and monthly schedules every Monday morning so we know our calendars are synchronized.

Host churches. I notify each host church of my weekly schedule on location as needed, via phone calls or e-mail (without using counselee names). After counseling, I usually stop in the office to greet the staff and let them know when I will return.

We have had very few problems with scheduling using this method.

SCHEDULING EVENTS AROUND CHURCH ACTIVITIES

Sometimes our core churches forget to inform me of church events that may impact BCM counseling sessions or training. Therefore, I read their newsletters. In addition to the scheduling benefits, their published prayer requests allow me to pray more specifically for each church.

I also watch core church calendars, provide them with our calendar, and consult with them as changes or additions are made. BCM classes and seminars are usually scheduled one to two years in advance, after seeking the approval of the church hosting the event.[1] Coordination can be difficult, so we try to set our events on the church calendar early so we do not conflict with their schedule.

We also consider the custodial needs associated with our events and provide as much support as we can.

SUNDAY VISITS TO CHURCHES

As needed, our BCM Sunday team travels to area churches to introduce our ministry. In addition, I periodically schedule Sunday visits with home and host churches, just as a missionary does when home on furlough. The primary purposes for these visits are (1) to keep communication lines open, (2) to express appreciation for their support, and (3) to challenge and encourage the churches to continue developing biblical counseling and discipleship. Through these visits, my face becomes more familiar to the congregation, and the people are given the opportunity to ask questions and receive information in a non-crisis environment. Sometimes BCM gains donors this way, too.

Ministry Board Communications

Regular communication with the board of directors is important. I write a monthly message exclusively to my board members and attach it to their copy of the ministry's e-newsletter. Thus, BCM directors are updated about the previous month's news, activities, and opportunities, the coming month's plans, and nonconfidential counseling information (e.g., how many counselees are currently in sessions). I also remind the directors of the date, time, and location of the next board meeting.

We hold our board meetings three to four times annually. As a meeting date approaches, I notify the BCM board of the agenda and assemble pertinent and supportive information for each director. We try to keep the agenda moving so that we can finish in about two hours. Soon after each meeting ends I follow up with e-mails and calls to express appreciation and provide follow-up information, if necessary.

Occasionally I will consult board members for advice between meetings, but I am careful to avoid decision-making about policies or activities that should be board-directed.

General Communication

Since BCM is not a church and does not have regular access to the congregations that we serve, I must communicate with churches in a creative variety of ways.

ANNUAL REPORTS

In December or January, I prepare an annual report to summarize ministry activities, plans for the coming year, prayer requests, and answers to prayer. I make it a point to thank the many people who have helped us throughout the year.

Periodically, the deacons at our home church will request a special annual report to answer their specific questions. I am happy to supply nonconfidential information like this because I consider it a privilege to work alongside these dear believers. And I enjoy opportunities to tell them so!

E-NEWSLETTERS

Every month I prepare and distribute a free e-newsletter to familiarize people with our ministry's philosophy and events. These one-page updates contain news and prayer requests, a brief article pertaining to biblical counseling, upcoming class and seminar information, and occasionally a book recommendation.

PROMOTIONAL MATERIALS

Upcoming events require me to produce new registration forms, brochures, posters, videos, handbooks, and other publications regularly. We design our literature not only to inform people of our events, but also to remind them of the ways we are ready to serve.

STUDENT COMMUNICATION

We invite BCM students to e-mail their instructors at any time. In addition, I communicate with students via a general student e-newsletter to encourage them and to keep them updated with class information. Advanced BCM students who are pursuing ACBC certification may join our exam blog for help with completion of ACBC entrance exams. We also invite our students to attend conferences and seminars that promote biblical counseling.

Web Site

Our Web site is a wonderful ministry tool originally created by Christian Web designer Wade Beavers. A highly skilled volunteer from our resource center has since taken over the site. He keeps it functioning and looking great, updates our monthly e-newsletter, and keeps our training information current. I don't have much administrative work to do on the site except to review it periodically and send new files for our technician to enter.

Keep in mind that a computer technician's time is in demand from just about every computer owner who knows him or her. We have found it expedient to get information to our technician early, to be as specific as possible, and to give him plenty of time for him to complete the tasks we request.

Biblically Addressing Ministry Conflict

CONFLICT IN GENERAL

Conflict management and resolution are important skills. You should avoid the temptation to personalize, ignore, accuse, or become aggressive when problems occur, even when a situation is painful. Biblically, in a spirit of Christian love, you should go to the source of conflict (Eph. 4:15, 25), seeking (1) to bring glory to God in the ways you respond (Col. 3:23); (2) to clarify the situation and related problems that need to be resolved (Prov. 18:13); (3) to identify your part in the problem and remove your "log" (Matt. 7:3–5); (4) to biblically restore your relationship as much as you can (Matt. 18:15; Rom. 12:18); and (5) to proactively seek to resolve troublesome problems (Matt. 5:23–24). These steps are more fully discussed in attorney Ken Sande's excellent book on conflict resolution, *The Peacemaker*.[2] You would be wise to become familiar with that book, and with the general principles of biblical conciliation and mediation.

Our BCM bylaws outline a biblically centered conflict-resolution method, based upon the Peacemakers Christian Conciliators plan. Our plan specifically identifies steps to be taken when conflict arises, so that God is glorified in our responses. Communication in line with Ephesians 4:29 is especially important during conflict. Moreover, each party should attempt to keep communication lines open by actively demonstrating a spirit of concern for the well-being of everyone involved, just as Christ would (see Luke 9:23; 2 Cor. 5:15).

Consult Peacemaker Ministries' Web site (www.hispeace.org) for help in writing a biblical conflict-management plan into your organizational documents.

WHEN A CHURCH FAILS A COUNSELEE

How should you deal with a church that fails to follow through with or mishandles a situation involving one of your counselees? For example, how should you respond if church leaders become aware that one of their men has been physically abusive toward his wife, but they do nothing?

- First, pray. Remember that the God who cares for your counselee is the one to whom the church answers. Appeal to God for wisdom, direction, and resolution of the matter. Keep praying (1 Thes. 5:17).
- Before addressing your concerns, make sure you have the facts. Would a friendly phone call help to clarify the situation? (See Prov. 18:13.)

- Honor church autonomy. Where you have no direct authority or responsibility, you must not undermine or interfere with decisions of the church (1 Thes. 5:12–15). Remember that you are not in charge, and take care to remain respectful.

- At the same time, you should help your counselee (in our example, the wife) to respond appropriately when the church fails to act biblically. Help her to know when and whom to call for help. Write a plan for escape to safety. Encourage her to talk to church leaders again. Lead her to forgive (Rom. 12:17–21).

- Give the benefit of the doubt (1 Cor. 13:7). Perhaps the church is failing because application of scriptural principles is difficult. In that case, be a team player. Write out specific suggestions for following Scripture and offer them with a humble, helpful spirit. For example, suggest that the church provide safe housing for the battered wife, assistance with decision-making, and accountability for her attitude toward her husband. Suggest that the church assign a disciple-maker with a tailor-made accountability plan for the husband. Offer to help write that plan.

- If necessary, explain the meaning and practice of Matthew 18:15–17 and respectfully request that the church begin the process with the situation at hand.

- If a matter is not life-threatening, ask yourself if it is wise and timely to address the issue at this time. Why or why not? What do you hope to accomplish? In what ways will God be glorified if you take action? How might you overcome evil with good? (See Prov. 16:20.)

- Seek counsel. Consult with your ministry board if you aren't sure how to proceed or if the situation is serious (Prov. 11:14).

- Watch your attitude. Be willing to do hard things, but do them kindly, wisely speaking truth in love (Eph. 4:29).

- Be reasonable. Who might be able to help resolve the problem? Set up a time to discuss your concerns and to explore biblical solutions (Prov. 11:14).

- In a case of escalating conflict, consult resources such as *The Peacemaker* by Ken Sande or contact Peacemaker Ministries (www.hispeace.org) for help with steps of conciliation or mediation.
- If the church's fundamental doctrines are unbiblical, or if the church is acting wickedly, help the counselee to evaluate whether or not to seek a more biblical church. (Rom. 6:17; Eph. 5:25–27; 1 Tim. 3:1–13; 2 Tim. 4:1–4; Heb. 10:25; 1 John 4:1–6).[3]

What should you do if the pastor (or another church leader) abuses his authority or sins against a counselee in other ways (Matt. 18:15–17; Gal. 6:1–3)? In addition to the steps above, you may need to consider the following:

- If a crime has been committed, you must obey the law. Do not help anyone to hide from his or her responsibilities or to continue to sin against others (Eph. 5:7–11).[4]
- Seek wise counsel from your ministry board. If you have legal concerns, consult your attorney. Your insurance company may also be able to offer legal advice.[5]
- Be an advocate for your counselee (Zech. 7:9–10).
- With an offending pastor or church leader, follow Matthew 18:15–17 (and help the counselee to follow it), to the degree that you are able. First, and biblically, the counselee should clarify the situation with the offender one-on-one (v. 15).[6] Depending upon the circumstances, consider whether it would be appropriate for you to accompany the counselee to speak with the offending person. (Do not try to carry out this step through electronic means.) Second, if you discover that the issue boils down to disagreement or misunderstanding rather than sin, defer to the pastor and respect the autonomy of the church. Seek to facilitate reconciliation

between your counselee and the offender.7 Third, if the issue constitutes more than a difference of opinion and the pastor or church leader is uncooperative, you should notify one or two of the church's deacons or elders and go to the offender together, in line with verse 16. Let the church carry out Matthew 18:16–17 from this point on, remembering that the authority of Matthew 18 is within the local church, not with ministries that serve that church. You should become involved only to the degree that the church leaders choose.

Regardless of the results of reconciliation efforts, lead your counselee to respond wisely, to forgive, and to seek forgiveness appropriately.

If the pastor or the church acts unbiblically but is within the law, there may be little more that you can do. For example, some churches are unwilling to follow Matthew 18 with a wayward member, even at a counselor's request. Alternatively, a believer may choose to stay in an unbiblical church. Be content that you have done all you can. Trust our sovereign God. It is His church. He sees.

Notes

1 Our home church hosts our seminars every year, and our training center houses all our classes.

2 *The Peacemaker: A Biblical Guide to Resolving Conflict* (Grand Rapids, MI: Baker, 1997).

3 See "Referrals from Churches outside the Core" in Chapter 9.

4 Governmental authorities have been appointed by God and should be engaged at appropriate times (Rom. 13:1–5).

5 When a crime is committed, the district attorney takes the criminal to court on behalf of the state. Therefore, it is biblically permissible to prosecute a criminal offender without violating 1 Cor. 6:1–8.

6 Consider safety issues, especially if you are a female counselor. Be sure that others are in the building and that you are both visible when you meet. If in doubt, ask a pastor from your ministry board to go with you.

Chapter 8

7   We recommend following the guidelines in *The Peacemaker* by **Ken Sande.**

Beth hurried up the church steps with a friendly greeting to the pastor's wife, who was just coming out the door. Somewhat breathlessly, Beth remembered how excited she had been to start her new position. The churches had been able to donate about half of her support. Beth's responsibilities, coupled with a part-time clerical job to supplement her income, were keeping her very busy, but the pastors had thoughtfully kept her counseling schedule light so that she was able to give a large portion of her time to completing administrative tasks, of which there were plenty.

Peg, office administrator at the home church, was highly experienced and had a great attitude. She often anticipated Beth's needs and provided feedback on paperwork, brochures, and ideas for the ministry. Even though Peg seemed to have boundless energy, Beth knew that she had a lot on her plate. The new counselor wanted to be a support person for the church, not a drain to them. So Beth was careful to voice appreciation and to limit her requests as much as possible.

As she settled into her office chair and glanced through her messages, Beth realized how much her communication efforts had proven to be her friend. Even when Beth thought that everyone knew what was happening and when, she made it a point to regularly talk to the office staff of her core churches and to e-mail or speak with the pastors on the board. As a result, miscommunication was rare, and the church staff seemed to understand that her heart was to serve, not to be served.

Beth's job was more complex than she had thought it would be, but it had helped to have BCM documents available as a model. Beth set up a schedule, worked with secretaries to clarify realistic expectations, and familiarized herself with the routines and people in the churches she served. Beth was glad that she had asked each of the core churches for their pictorial directories, so names and faces were becoming familiar. She found those directories to be very helpful in many respects.

Pastors at the core churches were protective and supportive, standing with her and helping to answer questions. Their introductions had raised church awareness of biblical counseling and of the ministry that would soon be opening to them. But Beth had not been surprised that there were some mild objections to starting a new ministry. After all, change is hard. Each pastor had his own style, some more direct than others at addressing opposition, but overall she knew that she was welcomed by each of the churches.

Once the ministry officially opened, the counseling load increased. Beth began to schedule sessions at each of the core churches on specific days of the week, with the smallest churches sharing a day. When she was directly approached by people who wanted biblical counseling, she resisted the urge to give them quick advice. Instead, she gently steered them (and sometimes brought them) to their pastor first for counsel and possible referral. She gave some of them Scripture to ponder as they considered how to proceed in God's will.

At first, the pastors on the board made most of the referrals from among their own people. They were also visited by unchurched individuals who wanted biblical counseling. The pastors shared the gospel and gave out Personal Data Inventory (PDI) forms, with an understanding that counselees were required to attend the referring church at least once per week while in counseling. Some of the referring churches set up funds to help counselees pay for sessions, sometimes through their deacon funds, some by special offerings or individual gifts, and some through their missionary budgets.

Working with six pastors had its challenges. Beth had known that she would have to balance her time carefully, but she was unprepared for the phone calls and interruptions that would challenge her careful preparations for counseling sessions. After a few months, things settled down a little. The pastors eventually chose to wait to speak with her when she stopped in after sessions at their churches. The secretaries became familiar with her schedule and what she needed from each of them. The written procedures helped to clear up confusion and answer questions.

Beth's weekly schedule called for her to travel alone to different locations every day. She might have felt somewhat isolated had not her home church welcomed her with open arms. She was warmly included in their weekly church staff meetings. Her counseling supervisor asked regularly about her spiritual health and allowed her to voice questions as she pioneered the unfamiliar world of a multichurch counseling ministry. This was a work in progress; she knew that it would take time before she felt comfortable with her responsibilities. But her determination remained strong as she became more and more convinced of the importance of her ministry.

Pastor Paul had wanted Beth to get started with Wendy right away. But he also wanted Beth to get her bearings, and he needed to be considerate of the other pastors on the board. Even as he waited, he was comforted by the fact that Beth was a valuable resource. He was able to ask how best to minister to Wendy even before Beth started to work with her. He also appreciated Beth's recommendations for books to use with Wendy and also in Bible studies and Sunday Bible classes. She had referred him to the BCM recommended reading list and had pointed out several resources she had found particularly valuable from that list. There he had found *The Christian Counselor's Casebook* by Jay Adams to help him build scenarios for his deacon board.

Pastor Paul was also encouraged by the bond that was growing among the ministry's directors. Whereas there had been an unspoken competitive spirit in the air when they had first begun to work together, now they were learning to see one another as friends. The pastors were sharing ideas, praying for one another, and offering help as they were able. To anyone else it might not have seemed like much. But to each of them, the growing camaraderie was refreshing and strengthening.

Pastor Paul was grateful that the men on the ministry board did not allow themselves to become comfortable with the initial temporary arrangement now that Beth was with them and working hard. Their goal was to provide a full-time position in a multichurch ministry, so they battled the urge toward complacency and moved forward to live up to their word.

Counseling

Biblical counseling is the bedrock of Biblical Counseling Ministries. However, a well-run ministry requires an organizational base within which counseling can function well. This chapter presents the underlying structure that keeps us local-church oriented, alleviates confusion and distractions, and allows us to focus on helping people.

Procedure for Referrals

All BCM counseling requires pastoral referral. If a potential counselee does not go to church, we provide names of BCM pastors who can be contacted for a referral.

When a pastor is asked to refer a counselee, we recommend that he evaluate whether the person might first benefit from pastoral counseling or lay discipleship through his local church. We also recommend that he share the gospel at that first meeting. A BCM pastor requires the person to attend at least one service per week at his church while in counseling or discipleship. BCM reinforces that requirement. We explain that the local church should be a permanent part of life, so we want people to be firmly established in a biblically sound church by the time counseling concludes.

If a pastor is new to BCM, he can call our home office to request a referral packet. The packet contains an instruction sheet for the referring pastor, a payment designation form, two informational brochures, and a Personal Data Inventory (PDI) form that serves as our intake form. Many pastors make a copy of our PDI form to use for future referrals.[1]

The referring pastor signs the PDI, and gives the signed PDI to the counselee to complete. (He can mail the payment form separately or can ask the counselee to return it with the completed PDI.) Once the counselee completes, signs, and returns the PDI, he or she may schedule an appointment. If we do not hear from the counselee within a few days after receiving the completed PDI, our home office secretary calls to schedule the first appointment.

Referrals from Churches outside the Core

We are happy to know that people from outside our core churches desire biblical help. We encourage each person to talk to his or her pastor about a referral and to have him call us for a referral packet. Often the pastor will call with questions, allowing us an opportunity to explain what nouthetic counseling is and to invite him to learn more.

Usually, referral calls come from believers in churches with doctrinal statements similar to ours. However, as a courtesy, we have prepared a letter to referring pastors whose doctrine is either unknown or thought to be unbiblical. The letter explains that our doctrinal statement (enclosed with the letter) is the basis for the counsel that will be given, and that if doctrinal error is exacerbating the counselee's problems, we may recommend a change of church. In so doing, we are carefully respecting pastoral authority in a counselee's life, within scriptural guidelines. We ask the counselee to personally give the letter to his or her pastor for signature. Usually the pastor signs the letter.

Counseling is generally more difficult with counselees whose doctrinal backgrounds differ from ours. Therefore, we must be prepared to answer other worldviews.[2] Some people reject such counsel. But because we share the Word, and because the gospel is central in Scripture, many counselees have received Christ through our counseling ministry (Isa. 55:11).

Preparation for Sessions

For time-management reasons, I seldom travel to more than one church per day. After carefully gathering session materials and locking them in my briefcase, I arrive at least thirty to forty-five minutes early to prepare the room and my heart for the session. Often our counseling rooms serve double or triple duty as Sunday Bible study classrooms, offices, or meeting rooms. Therefore, I plan adequate time to notify the office that I am in the building, tidy or rearrange furnishings, set out a sign, ready my files, refer to my Bible, and pray. If sessions involve co-counsel, I allow a few minutes to confer. After the session, I put everything back in order before leaving.

Preparations for sessions include prayer for wisdom and correct insight as well as intercession for the counselee. I review the file and seek God's specific direction for the session and my ability to discern what step of obedience the counselee should take next. As I gather data during the session, I note what homework may help this person to move forward, and I write assignments from those notes.

Inside the counselee's file I list some subjects to address before sessions conclude. Between sessions I check that list. Then I pray and search Scripture for principles and references to address the subject I want to cover in our next few sessions. Gospel-centeredness is essential, so I think through Christ's example and the implications of His gracious atonement in the life of this counselee. I also find it very helpful to consult the writings of other godly counselors, and occasionally to call one for assistance. (See the appendices for a general outline for sessions and a brief theology of biblical counseling to help you with session structure and content.)

Procedure for Payment, If Applicable

The BCM board determines the requested session donation. Our payment form asks the referring pastor to discuss payment options with the potential counselee. When the counselee is unable to pay the full amount, the referring church is asked to consider supplementing or paying it. When the church is unable to help, it may contact us about a reduction.

Payments are made at each appointment. Churches that supplement counselee payments usually send a check with the counselee or deliver payment to me ahead of time. BCM sends invoices, by written request, to churches paying in full for sessions. We do not invoice counselees.

At the end of each session, I note receipts on a payment form and a summary sheet. On each trip to my home church, I bring money and completed forms to the BCM office administrator, who records payments, deposits the money, and keeps the forms on file. She also prepares deposit slips in duplicate and supplies verification documentation for our treasurer.

Communication with Pastors Regarding Counseling Cases

Because we require a pastoral referral for every counselee, we routinely ask for written permission to communicate with the referring pastor regarding that counselee's progress.

Normally, when written permission has been granted, progress is reported verbally to the pastor only after significant sessions or when the pastor asks, unless problems arise that require the pastor's assistance, or if additional information is needed that he may be able to provide.

Informed pastoral care is important. Therefore, when permission is not granted, I usually inquire about the reasons for the person's reluctance and, after a few sessions, ask again for permission. The question is not usually revisited after that, except to request that the counselee let the pastor know how counseling is progressing.

Co-counsel

We require co-counsel for marriage counseling and for counseling of individuals of the opposite gender. The referring pastor or a male leader

Our goal is not to relieve pastors entirely of counseling. Pastors should be counseling their people, and should be increasing their own counseling skills. We lighten their load in several ways, including taking cases that they may find too time-consuming or challenging. But we want pastors to be involved as well, to have their finger on the pulse of the spiritual lives of the people with whom they serve, and to counsel the Word skillfully.

Pastors of smaller churches tend to know their people well and want to be involved in their lives. Co-counsel allows for that, but also provides input from a trained biblical counselor, which, in itself, lightens the load. We also provide consultations, counseling for women and children, and discipleship training, so that skilled male and female counselors are available for the pastor to draw upon. The pastors who have come to me are reluctant to send their people to counselors outside the church. I try to be sensitive to their challenging schedules, and may suggest that they ask another godly man from their church to serve as co-counsel.

But usually the pastor wants to come.

from the referring church usually serves as co-counsel. Other appropriate co-counsel may include a wise, godly parent or teacher.

Potential counselees are asked to request their referring pastor to provide co-counsel. If the pastor is unable or unwilling, or if a person objects to having his or her pastor as co-counsel, we provide a list of pastors on our board who may be asked to serve in that role. The counselee is normally required to attend the co-counseling pastor's church for a minimum of one service per week while in counseling, to reinforce what is being taught in sessions and to place the counselee under pastoral authority.

Before each session, the two co-counselors discuss plans and decide who will lead sessions. At BCM, it is not unusual for the pastor to have me lead sometimes. More often, though, counseling is give-and-take, with the lead being shared. To reinforce pastoral authority, the co-counseling pastor usually leads in prayer before and after each session.

After each session we take a few minutes to discuss the data, compare notes, and decide how to proceed next time. Typically, I prepare paperwork, recommend and gather materials, take notes, write reports, and provide a copy of my reports for the co-counselor if he so desires.

Co-counseling provides an indirect demonstration of nouthetic counseling. The pastors on our board have carefully discussed this arrangement and are in agreement with the biblical nature of informal training through co-counsel. Because BCM is not a church, and because we do not usurp the authority of our pastoral co-counselors, we are able to biblically train as we hold sessions.

Confidentiality is necessary for co-counseling and observation. If you are not reasonably certain that the person you have been asked to work with is trustworthy, sessions should not commence until co-counsel assures you that he or she will comply with the terms of biblical confidentiality. A signature on the document setting out the terms of counseling and/or the application form for counseling observation is best. See Appendix I for forms you may find helpful in counseling.

A co-counseling pastor serves in the capacity of his salaried position, so he usually does not ask counselees for compensation. His church's insurance company may, in fact, prohibit him from doing so. BCM leaves that decision entirely up to the referring pastor.

Requesting More Sessions
When a church pays in full for counseling sessions, we set a limit of twenty sessions. On the rare occasion when counseling is expected to last beyond twenty sessions, I submit a written request to the referring pastor, estimating the number of additional sessions that may be needed. The counselee usually previews the letter and may be asked to co-sign it to indicate his or her cooperation with the ongoing counseling process.

Coordinating with Church disciple-makers
After a counselee has completed formal sessions, the referring pastor

We have found that personal discipleship in the local church is a very effective way to help counselees maintain the changes that they have worked so hard to develop in sessions. We consult with the referring pastor to pair trained leaders with counselees who continue to need some extra support, teaching, or encouragement.

Counselees who are new in the Lord or new to the church tend to feel more accepted when they have a friendly, trustworthy person to greet them when they arrive, to sit with them and answer questions, to share a Bible study, and to introduce them to others. Most find this arrangement to be reassuring and comforting.

Friendships with godly church members often will spontaneously develop and move into discipleship by the time counseling sessions end. Other times, coordinated discipleship is arranged by the counselor through the pastor. Either way, the counselor remains available when questions and concerns arise. As the discipleship relationship runs its course, the counselee's circle of friends usually broadens, and he or she gets involved in serving and becomes established in the church.

may be asked to find an appropriate believer to exhort and encourage the person to continue moving forward. Often the pastor will choose a godly church member who has already been informally reaching out, especially if he or she has some discipleship training. I recommend materials and offer to meet occasionally with the pair if needed.

Counseling Supervision

The BCM board has appointed a counseling supervisor to ensure that I remain nouthetic in philosophy and practice and that I continue to follow BCM policies. Counseling supervision protects the ministry and me by preserving the integrity of nouthetic counseling and upholding ministry standards. I am grateful for the accountability.

Our counseling supervisor regularly meets with me to review cases and to test my spiritual health. He is careful to maintain counselee confidentiality, especially because he is evaluating me, not the counselee. His assessments are shared only with me, unless there is adequate reason for the board of directors to be made aware of a problem.

Skill Maintenance and Development

Because of the spiritual complexity and personal and intellectual demands of biblical counseling, I attend seminary classes and conferences regularly to keep my skills sharp and to meet up with other counselors. I usually invite advanced BCM students to come with me to ACBC conferences and to the Biblical Counseling Training Conference (BCTC) to build teamwork and accountability, to continue skill development, and to make acquaintances in the field. BCM pays my expenses when possible, but usually I must cover my costs for classes and conferences.

HERE'S MORE FOR YOU:

Appendix A: A Brief Theology of Biblical Counseling
A concise outline of some of the foundational beliefs behind biblical counseling. Compare this with the counseling and discipleship offered by you and your church.

Appendix B: A General Outline for Offering Biblical Counsel
Guidelines to help you with biblical content and thoroughness in each of your sessions.

Appendix I: Helpful Forms for Ministry Use
A variety of counseling forms to help you keep your records organized and thorough.

Notes

1 Our PDI was adapted from **Jay Adams'** form in *Competent to Counsel: Introduction to Nouthetic Counseling* (Grand Rapids, MI: Zondervan, 1970), 171–174.

2 This underscores the need for a solid theological education. See 1 Peter 3:15 and Col. 4:6.

Wendy's grief is as fresh as the day Jordan died, Beth realized with compassion as her counselee's head dropped into her arms and she dissolved into choking sobs. Beth blinked back hot tears and dabbed at her eyes. She was not surprised that the women at Glory Baptist had found Wendy hard to counsel. Reaching for the distraught mother's hands, she prayed silently, then aloud, asking the Lord to calm Wendy's heart so that they could continue.

Beth had found her counseling load to be challenging, to say the least. She scheduled her time carefully to adequately prepare

"Sue never gave up on us ... She stood strong in the promise of God's Word, that He wants His children restored in Him. There were some difficult times. Sue was always patient and always reflected Christlike character in every session. We grew to love her and her godly counsel early on. There was always such a sense of peace as we sat across the table from her. Christ's love was always reflected in her ways. There were times she'd need to go over the very same things time and again, yet she always respected our child and used God's unfailing example of love and patience.

"The very fact that between our meetings I knew without a doubt that Sue was thinking of us and praying and always looking for the Holy Spirit to guide her to new info that would help shed light on our situation, I found so comforting and at some very low times it helped me to know I wasn't the only mom on her knees.

"I can't thank Sue with BCM enough for her ministry ... "
BCM counselee

her heart and her paperwork before sessions, and to write her reports afterward. She had a lot to learn, but she was also encouraged to find that God had faithfully equipped her each day for the work she had to do.

Beth's time with the Lord was more important to her than ever. But every morning as she sat with her open Bible, she found her mind easily moved to relate to counselee needs instead of focusing on her own relationship with God. Prayer time was precious and necessary, but Beth had to fight to discipline her wandering thoughts. It was worth the effort, though, she firmly decided. She would not let that slip.

Beth was recognizing some warning signs in herself. As she rejoiced when counselees grew and changed, she detected pride raising its ugly head and she was tempted to coast a little. Beth found it easy to let her schedule crowd out her personal time with God. When that happened, she soon found herself floundering inside when unforeseen challenges presented themselves.

Beth acknowledged that difficulties would arise even when she was carefully attending to the Word and prayer. *But,* she remembered, *the quality and consistency of my walk with God makes a difference when storms hit.* She thought of Matthew 7:24–27.

Wendy's grip loosened and she looked up, grateful that Beth wasn't taken aback at the intensity of her

> "I finally know and can stand on a firm foundation of faith. With this firm foundation and God's strength I have learned to overcome depression and loneliness.
>
> "God's Word (Truth) is the only real thing by which we can measure who we are or where we are in life and is the founding principle to base all our decisions on.
>
> "Biblical counseling helps one to look at God's truth and enables one to move toward that truth. Knowing God's truth and having His direction for our lives gives us hope and peace."
>
> **BCM counselee**

tears. Rather than consoling her with platitudes or telling her to get herself together, Wendy's counselor had taken her to the Psalms to learn about David's responses to grief. Wendy knew, even in this second session, that Beth would teach her how to grieve with hope. She deeply longed to be rid of the aching hole in her soul. As she reached for another tissue, she wondered how many years it had been since she had known hope. Could it be that God was still with her, that He was going to help her? How could He possibly mean this heartache for her good? She was flooded this time not with grief, but with a desire to know God through the eyes of her counselor, a woman whose faith had survived tragic loss.

Beth was grateful for the opportunity to work with people like Wendy. The Lord had been good to her when her husband died. She was able to connect the Word with personal experience to reach out meaningfully to this distraught mother. She also appreciated the skill set provided by her training, so that she could present Scripture more effectively, using her experiences to illustrate the clear principles of God's Word and the importance of following Christ. Beth was grateful for the resources that she had discovered while in college, too, and for the colleagues to whom she could go for further help when she needed another perspective.

As she had begun to work with her counselees, Beth appreciated the many ways in which the core church pastors had watched out for her. They had carefully decided to limit the number of sessions until the ministry was established. Beth thought about how her energies had been taxed as she had finalized ministry documents with their attorney, counseled, set up the offices and trained staff, developed a Web site with their IT volunteer, and learned a routine. The directors were mindful of her schedule. They provided help by asking qualified volunteers from their congregations to care for the needs that Beth did not have to handle personally. Volunteer work became a refreshing way for Beth to get to know people at each of her core churches.

Beth had met Laura and was impressed by the woman's love for Wendy. BCM was coming back to present its seminar in a few weeks, and Beth was happy to discover that Laura would be there. She decided to talk to Pastor Paul about arranging some time with Laura and Wendy after the seminar to work at a discipleship plan.

She and the ministry board planned to follow the seminar with a few evening classes to encourage church discipleship development. People were already asking for help with outreach to friends and family. Beth was encouraged by their growing interest. But she realized, now that she was traveling from church to church, that she would have to be careful not to over-schedule herself. She didn't want fatigue to compromise her effectiveness or to dull her compassion.

Wendy leaned a tear-stained cheek over Beth's Bible as the counselor read Psalm 55:4–6: "My heart is severely pained within me, and the terrors of death have fallen upon me. Fearfulness and trembling have come upon me, and horror has overwhelmed me. So I said, 'Oh, that I had wings like a dove! I would fly away and be at rest …'" Slowly Wendy sat up. Maybe God wasn't angry with her. Maybe He wasn't doling out punishment. Could it be that He understood her pain and cared about her struggle? She listened to the psalmist's mournful words: his close companion had betrayed him. She knew that kind of betrayal, but whereas the psalmist had answered his pain with a declaration of faith in God, she had nursed doubts. A hundred questions popped into Wendy's mind, but, strangely, she did not feel overwhelmed. A bond of understanding had budded. Wendy knew she could trust this counselor to help her find the truth.

Training

Biblical Counseling Ministries seminars and classes introduce nouthetic counseling to area churches in a friendly non-crisis format, inviting believers from all walks of life to become involved with biblical discipleship. Whether across a kitchen table or a desk, in a coffee shop or a pastor's office, the Word of God should be the basis for any advice that is offered. People need to be trained to handle Scripture well as they face the challenges of life in a fallen world.

Seminars/Conferences

BCM seminars and conferences are held annually at our home church, usually in the fall. We invite special speakers to present topics of general interest for everyday discipleship. Our seminar expenses are covered through registration money.

> "BCM's training has been a blessing not only to me and those whom I disciple, but also to my church. I now work with my pastors to help ladies in need. It is not always appropriate for a pastor to meet with a lady, so God is providing opportunities for me to minister to women under the supervision of my pastoral staff. I have the benefit of the godly experience, wisdom, and spiritual protection of my pastors, and they have the benefit of BCM's training in my life so that I am more competent and equipped for the task at hand. I highly recommend BCM's training to any believer wishing to grow and glorify God better in the way that he or she lives and ministers in Jesus's name."
>
> **Amy Knoll, ACBC counselor, BCM student**

Every other year we offer a three-track choice. Participants choose from among an everyday discipleship track with a special speaker or a series of workshops, our ACBC-certified "Basic Skills for Giving Wise Counsel" track, or our "Pastor's Toolbox" track for developing church leadership. Consult our Web site for current information on each of these tracks.

As BCM executive director, I coordinate these events with the help of home and host churches who each provide resources and manpower. We divide autumn seminar responsibilities at our summer board meetings. I carry out some tasks and delegate others, staying in contact with volunteers and core churches to discern where help is needed, to provide necessary materials, and to assist with problem solving.

Class Curriculum Development or Purchase

The BCM "Basic Skills" curriculum was developed to meet the educational requirements for ACBC certification, but our classes are useful for discipleship at any level. Basic Skills classes include an introduction to biblical counseling that describes the differences between nouthetic counseling and secular or Christian psychology, and teaches the basic elements of biblical discipleship. Our Case Studies class views and discusses a series of biblical counseling sessions. Skill-Building class utilizes role playing to help students apply what they have learned in the first two classes. Then we go on to learn about theology's connection to discipleship, followed by a study of ten themes commonly faced in counseling sessions, with biblical marriage and parenting constituting our final course. Check our Web site for current class information and a more detailed description of our curriculum plan.

We are careful to stay theologically consistent. For example, at one point when considering another ministry's curriculum, our board asked a retired theologian to evaluate the lesson materials and offer suggestions. We followed his suggestions as we taught the lessons.

At first, we kept lesson materials on hand at our resource center, along with textbooks and counseling materials. This required some initial expense that we did not always recover. Eventually, we came to a logistical and financial decision to require students to purchase required textbooks for themselves. We continue to supply course handbooks.

Class schedules for our Basic Skills classes are set up on a two-year rotating basis, with three or four classes being offered each year. This schedule is subject to change, based upon demand. We print a master schedule for office use, and we distribute registration forms for each class to students and churches via e-mail, information centers, worship folders, conferences, mailings, poster displays at churches, and personal contacts. Posters and brochures are printed to announce special training events.

Instructors

At first, I taught most of our seminars and classes, but now we have area pastors and professionals from churches of like faith and practice to do some team teaching as well. We try to be considerate and accommodating regarding the amount of time and energy our instructors can devote. They may be asked to teach a weekend class, for a week or two, every other week, on a substitute basis, or by subject area. Our two-year class rotation means that our instructors are not obligated to teach every year.

Finding Students

Potential students are made aware of our classes through a variety of means:

- BCM e-newsletters
- Information centers at home and host churches[1]
- Newspaper articles
- Community calendars
- Church conferences
- Direct mailings
- BCM speaking and Sunday visits
- Announcements from the pulpit
- Posters and brochures supplied by BCM to all churches and camps who have contacted us in the past

- Student e-mail notices
- Counselees

Administrative Organization

Classes. I have a ring binder for each class we offer. Inside each binder I keep a student form to track attendance and assignment completion, student contact information, a master class schedule, a course syllabus marked with a schedule of guest instructors, a list of recommended books to bring to class each week, a few extra registration forms, an envelope for completed forms and checks, a folder containing additional handout sheets, assignment due dates, and my lesson plans and content for each week.

Our training center secretary receives registrations and compiles the student contact list for each class. She also arranges for room preparation. I touch base with her frequently during the two or three weeks before classes begin to clarify expectations and answer questions so that we are fully prepared.

> "Make sure that you communicate expectations ahead of time for room setup, etc., so everything can be ready to go on time, and to avoid last-minute scrambles as people are arriving. Also, make sure that you plan and communicate appropriately with those who need to assist in getting things set up."
> **Kristen Akright, Office Administrator and pastor's wife, Grace Baptist Church, Plover, WI, and BCM Training Center**

Seminars. My administrative seminar binder contains a time line/checklist of preparatory tasks and designated areas of responsibility, including board meeting decisions, people to contact, budget projections, and actual costs. Pocket dividers keep notes, receipts, brochures, and other items organized and easily retrievable. Everything from e-mails to travel preparations, meeting notes, and personal reminders is recorded in that binder. It goes everywhere with me for the six to eight weeks leading up to the seminar.

Follow-up with Students

Class follow-up can be very important. We recommend that you give your students an e-mail address at which they can reach their instructors after classes are finished. Students can become discouraged as they attempt to complete their assignments and exams amid the demands of everyday life. Contact with their instructors can keep them going, particularly when they have sincerely tried to keep up with the work but are falling behind. We instructors can communicate compassion and understanding, encouragement, and assurance of the significance of their efforts, as well as answering questions, exhorting them to persevere, and clearing up misconceptions.

Students are given assignment instructions and deadlines for which they are held accountable. However, sometimes a kind word or an extended deadline can encourage a budding disciple-maker to endure and finish well. These efforts all take time, which is in short supply for instructors just as it is for the students. But the effort is well worth it as disciples grow in grace and knowledge of the Word.

Discipling Disciple-Makers

We have already discussed the importance of developing disciple-makers. As a biblical counselor, you should model discipleship, teaching and mentoring your students through classes, counseling observations, and (if they so choose) the process of certification. Our instructors periodically send student e-mail messages to keep our disciple-makers aware of BCM training and to encourage them in their walk with the Lord within the local church. We encourage our students to go to ACBC conferences and the Biblical Counseling Training Conference (BCTC) to gain further training, and often I go along to offer additional

> "Now we exhort you, brethren, warn those who are unruly, comfort the fainthearted, uphold the weak, be patient with all."
> 1 Thessalonians 5:14

encouragement and instruction. These conferences energize discipleship and offer a source of help beyond that which BCM can provide. In addition to these formal ministries, I also offer informal discipleship through my local church, as well as with family and friends.

Counseling Observation

Advanced BCM students may apply for permission to observe counseling sessions as part of their training. They must fill out and sign an application form that includes a behavior contract and references. Then they are personally interviewed by the BCM board of directors. The board determines if it will grant permission to observe live counseling sessions, and, if so, for what period of time. Participating counselees must give written consent before any observations take place.

The lead counselor contacts the student with the time and place of observations. The student silently observes the session and keeps notes on a form provided by BCM. After the session, if time allows, the student and the counselor may confer for instructive purposes. Before leaving the room, the student completes and submits the observation form, which is kept in the counselee's file. The student is not allowed to take notes away with him or her, or to discuss the case outside sessions, not even with the counselee.

HERE'S MORE FOR YOU:

Appendix I: Helpful Forms for Ministry Use
Offers a variety of student record forms to help you keep your class records organized and thorough.

Note

1   Handsome oak information centers were built for BCM by the Men for Missions group at our home church. The centers can be mounted on the wall or on a stand and located in convenient spots for people to have access to brochures, posters, and registration forms for BCM counseling, classes, and seminars.

Wendy listened intently as Beth opened her Bible and read, "Blessed be the God and Father of our Lord Jesus Christ, the Father of mercies and God of all comfort, who comforts us in all our tribulation, that we may be able to comfort those who are in any trouble, with the comfort with which we ourselves are comforted by God" (2 Cor. 1:3–4).

During the past few weeks, as Beth had shared her experience of faith-driven grief, Wendy's heart had warmed and stirred. She had always been told that Christ was sufficient, but those words had seemed hollow in the face of her sorrow. However, her faith had flickered again as she became familiar with David's laments. She had read, memorized, and reviewed those psalms daily, as her counselor had assigned her, until they resonated within her and she learned to cling to them. The strength of David's trust in God urged her to recognize God's compassion and power in her life. As she had written in her journal about the grace of God toward David, she began to recognize the undeniable evidence of His enduring presence and intervention during her own painful journey. Now, hearing Beth's steady voice, she was pierced by Scripture. A new measure of understanding broke her heart and she realized with alarm how hardened she had become.

A renewed thirst for Christ awakened in Wendy's parched soul. As

Interlude

His Word penetrated the bitter crust of her doubts, she began to drink deeply of His mercy. God had shown His sufficiency to David and to Beth through their grief, and Wendy could now see that He was doing the same for her. By faith she again allowed herself to believe the Bible was true, and Christ became deliciously sweet and desirable.

Wonder flooded her, and words poured from her heart in prayer: "Lord, I thought You had turned against me. I thought You hated me! I let myself think You were cruel and unfair … heartless … stomping me down when I needed You most. But Lord, I was wrong! My own doubts were what crushed me. You didn't push me away at all, did You?" Her tears flowed freely. She did not wipe them away.

"How could I have doubted You like that?" Wendy cried. "I thought You had rejected me, but I was the one who turned away. If only I had turned to You! Please forgive me, Lord, for judging You to be unfaithful, for not believing You. I didn't understand—there's still so much I don't understand—but that's no excuse …" She paused, trembling, and drew a deep breath. Then in a hushed tone she whispered, "Thank You for loving me enough to stay with me … I'll never turn away again. I need You so much! Help my unbelief!"

After that prayer, Wendy's grief changed. Although she continued to face difficult challenges, she learned to replace her doubtful thoughts with the Word of truth. The reality of the gospel caused her faith to steady and grow. Through ensuing encounters with loneliness, fear, resentment, forgiveness, daily responsibilities, and changing relationships, Beth helped Wendy to locate passages that disciplined and guided her thoughts, actions, and motives in Christlike ways. Wendy was learning how to trust Jesus Christ and follow His example. For the first time in years she felt springs of newfound joy in her soul.

As she counseled with Beth and met with Laura, Wendy was increasingly strengthened by the Word and comforted by the presence of the Lord. She became aware that other grievers needed this kind of help and she asked Beth what she might do. Her counselor was pleased to see the change from introspection to outreach. She suggested that Wendy attend a discipleship seminar to learn more. Wendy was excited at the idea. When she told Laura about her plans, Laura offered to go with her.

Pastor Paul and Beth were delighted to see Laura and Wendy walking into the BCM seminar together. The pastor had noticed the improvement in Wendy's outlook. She was gaining hope, coming out of isolation, and learning to express concern for those around her.

Pastor Paul appreciated that Beth had worked with Laura to disciple Wendy in ways that reinforced their counseling sessions. Early on, Beth had written a contingency plan for Wendy that outlined what to do when she began to feel overwhelmed. The plan included immediate steps that she could take to identify and solve problems, plus several phone numbers that she could call when she needed assistance. At first Laura had to repeatedly help Wendy walk through the plan. But lately Wendy had not needed to use it, having gained a sustaining hope in Christ and having trained her mind to think as David did in the psalms. And now she was actively learning to share her growing faith with others.

Pastor Paul smiled widely and shook Wendy's hand as she stepped into the foyer.

Chapter 11

Resources

Church Resources

Each of our home and host churches has purchased a small library to help its pastors and other church leaders increase their understanding of biblical discipleship. (See Appendix H for a list of titles from which they chose.) We often direct counselees and students to those church libraries to find assignment materials and extra reading in specific areas of interest or need.

Our core churches have added materials to their libraries over the years, in part through my verbal recommendation, our recommended reading list, and book reviews in the BCM e-newsletter. Pastors, disciple-makers, students, and counselees have become more aware of BCM and nouthetic counseling because of the reliable relevant literature we recommend.

Relationships with Bookstores

BCM has a friendly relationship with an area Christian bookstore owner. We send him the names of books that we would like to have on our seminar

"Our space for textbooks and booklets is limited, so when BCM came on board we had to carefully consider how to accommodate the materials. Since textbooks are used only once per year, we try to order fairly close to class dates (or when books are on sale) and keep any extras in boxes on a top shelf in our storeroom. Counseling booklets are alphabetized and stored accessibly in plastic boxes to optimize shelf space. We have a sign-out sheet for Sue to record materials she takes from stock so I can keep track of inventory."

Julie Landowski, Resource Center Secretary, Faith Baptist Church, Wisconsin Rapids, WI

tables and the bookstore supplies the books as it is able. We man the tables, record sales, and return the books and money after the seminar ends. The bookstore takes an inventory of returned items and donates a percentage of the sales to BCM.

Textbooks and Counseling Resources

We require students to read one or more textbooks for most BCM classes. If we supply a textbook for a class, our resource center is responsible for purchasing and storing those books until they are needed.

Counselees are usually asked to read a book that is related to their area of concern. Usually they can find the literature online, new or used. We carry a few titles to loan, and we keep a supply of materials to give away when we can afford them. Our home and host churches also have booklets and brochures available for use in counseling and discipleship.

Many of the brochures and booklets we like to use are out of print. Therefore, we usually choose to loan our materials rather than give them. Counselees are instructed to record reading notes and responses to questions in their journals so that they have reminders available after they return the materials. BCM's DVD and CD resources are not allowed to be taken out of the building by individual counselees, but we encourage people to watch them on site before or after sessions. Sometimes we watch them together as a basis for session discussion.

Other Resources

In addition to arranging for counseling resources, seminar books, and textbooks, our resource center helps to produce brochures, booklets, and other ministry materials for BCM. It prints our general brochures and

> **HERE'S MORE FOR YOU:**
>
> **Appendix H: Further Resources**
> A list of reliable books to build libraries for the counselor and the church, for use in teaching and discipleship.

discipleship development booklets, and it assists with materials for special events, such as seminar brochures and posters. BCM loans our DVDs or video series to core churches for use in their Sunday Bible classes or midweek Bible study groups, which saves them money and gives us a broader scope for training.

The ministry was purchasing textbooks and counseling materials as funds became available, in anticipation of the classes that Beth would teach following the seminar. She smiled. The resource center was a small church with a big heart. A volunteer had stepped up to keep track of counseling literature, set up a counseling library, help with promotional literature, and manage textbooks for classes. They had a plan to replace textbooks after classes were held, using the portion of the registration monies that were designated for literature.

The resource center had graciously set up a Sunday Bible class room for her counseling, and had placed a cabinet in the room to house resource center ministry materials, including the counseling library. Although Beth had plans to move the library to the home church office soon, the resource center offered to continue to maintain a record of the books in the library.

Beth felt blessed. The ministry's resources were eagerly received by pastors, church staff, students, and counselees. Pastors regularly asked her to recommend literature they could use in counseling and church ministries. She tried to stay on top of materials and books that came out so she could narrow down some choices and save them time. They seemed to appreciate her efforts. Staff and students asked about resources they could use for discipleship. Beth's past experiences and education helped her to suggest appropriate books and study guides for them. In addition, she gave out brochures and loaned booklets to counselees to reinforce session points and to encourage them to keep moving forward between meetings.

Beth's first choice was to ask counselees to purchase any books they would use in session so they would have the materials for future reference and reminders. But some counselees were not able to afford the materials she wanted to use with them. Beth tried loaning books from the ministry's counseling library, but she found that frequently a book would be missing when she needed access to it. Some books were never returned. Now she was sending counselees to church lending libraries when they needed to borrow books, and she typically used the ministry library for her counseling reference needs. She also purchased duplicate copies of the books she used most frequently, so she could loan out a copy when necessary but still have one on hand. Beth liked that arrangement better.

Administration and Office

Working with Church Office Staff

Biblical Counseling Ministries' home and host churches generously supply clerical help at no cost to us, usually through the church office administrator or a volunteer. Each core church decides who will be responsible for its BCM clerical support. See Chapter 8 for more information about clerical arrangements.

We try to be sensitive to the needs of office staff in several ways:

- Respecting the complex nature of the office administrator's work
- Asking for help rather than assuming or demanding
- Communicating regularly so staff is aware of my schedule and whereabouts, class dates/times, project dates, and help needed
- Regularly expressing appreciation
- Offering to help (or staying out of the way) when the office is very busy

"I have found the training center procedures guide to be extremely beneficial. When coming on as a new office administrator, you have a lot of information given to you, but it's hard to remember all the details until you're doing that 'actual' work. The procedure guide is something that I can turn to at any point as the source of what I need to be doing. It's also very valuable in helping to understand what others' roles are in the different locations. Since there are several sites that may not interact very much with one another, this is extremely valuable to know. It is very clear what each part of the organization is supposed to do."

Kristen Akright, Office Administrator and pastor's wife, BCM Training Center, Grace Baptist Church, Plover, WI

- Doing as much of our own record-keeping as possible
- Acknowledging special events, including birthdays, office professionals days, and Christmas
- Being aware of prayer concerns, and being faithful in prayer
- Reviewing office needs and resources to determine when changes are expedient or more help is necessary

Working with the Ministry's Treasurer

BCM works with a pool of human resources from five churches, with our treasurer coming from one of our host churches and our financial secretary being at our home church. Therefore, we have had to create a reliable means of communication and transfer of money and materials. Since I go to each BCM location regularly, lots of information is carried by hand from church to church. My briefcase contains color-coded folders—one for each location—into which I put materials that should be dropped off on my next visit.

We chose a bank with branches in the cities where we serve, to make it easier for our treasurer and financial secretary to make deposits and carry out other bank transactions. In addition, we bought QuickBooks financial software, which our treasurer has installed on her computer to assist with record-keeping.

A dedicated lock box is kept in a secluded spot at the treasurer's church. When I come to that host church for sessions, I bring bank statements, mail, vouchers, and other paperwork from the financial secretary and lock those documents in the box. In turn, the treasurer may choose to mail checks and notes or to leave them in the lock box to be picked up. Occasionally we schedule a meeting and exchange materials at that time.

When counselees give me their session donations, I record the amount and give the money to the home office with a completed per-session payment record form. I also keep a summary sheet that lists all the money that I receive. That list is cross-checked by the home office secretary and a copy is sent to the BCM treasurer along with cross-checked bank statements (see Appendix I for the forms that we use). The BCM office administrator makes copies of bank deposit slips and bank statements to be filed at the home office before delivering originals to the treasurer.

Our treasurer is on the BCM board and is held accountable through financial secretary cross-checking and regular treasurer reports at board meetings.[1] We also have our books audited annually by a qualified volunteer from another of our host churches.

MILEAGE

As executive director, I keep a record of mileage for BCM work, noting work-related miles, destination cities and purpose for the trip. Mileage records are signed and submitted to the treasurer every quarter for reimbursement, and I keep a copy for my files.

REPORTS

Our treasurer is responsible for preparing and filing nonprofit reports at the state and federal levels, and for planning for quarterly payroll taxes. (Yes, payroll taxes are required for nonprofit corporations.) Electronic filing is required at the US federal level, but state requirements may vary. You will receive filing instructions when your articles of incorporation are filed with your state, and when your 501(c)(3) federal status is approved. Be sure to carefully prepare and file every required report on or before the due date.

VOUCHERS

We have three kinds of vouchers to help our treasurer keep accurate records.[2]

- A disbursement (expense) voucher, used for expense reimbursement. After each purchase, this voucher is completed and submitted to the treasurer with the original receipt(s) attached. This is the voucher I use most.

- A deposit voucher, used to record monies that are deposited in the bank. The deposit voucher designates the source of the money (e.g., counseling donations, church support, individual donations, class registrations) as well as who handled it. Our financial secretary uses this voucher to make deposits, and a copy of the deposit voucher is submitted to the treasurer with the bank receipt(s) attached.

- A non-cash donation voucher, for materials such as books or other gifts that have been purchased by a donor and given to the ministry. When such a donation is received, this voucher is filled out by the appropriate recipient and given to the home office secretary to record and file, with a photocopy supplied to our treasurer. The secretary sends a letter of receipt to the donor.

General Record-keeping[3]

COUNSELING RECORDS

BCM counseling records are filed by counselee number rather than name, to guard confidentiality. In each folder are placed the completed PDI, consent forms, phone records, weekly reports and notes, correspondence, session plans, observation forms, and contact information. File compartments are locked when not in use.

To help with organization, consistency, and thoroughness, counseling session notes are recorded on a form. During sessions, I jot by hand on the front of the form. After the counselee leaves, I fill out the back of the form as I analyze the session and make future plans. Weekly record forms include counselee name, file number, number of sessions held so far, today's date, time, location, counselor name, and the next appointment date. Each form has space for information on homework assignment completion, agenda, history, and halo data.[4] At the bottom I record the assignment given at this session as well as some ideas for future sessions. On the back, I answer a list of questions to assist with reflection on the session, discernment of heart issues, thorough recording of session content, and plans for our next meeting. I note what data should be gathered during future sessions, which subjects to cover, some Scripture and possible illustrations to use, and resources to bring with me. To the back of my completed form I staple any additional session notes and a copy of the homework assignment sheet. Session reports are stored in the counselee's file with the most recent session on top.

You should store counseling files for the length of time required by your state law (anywhere from three to ten years), and then destroy them.

DATA TRACKING

We purchased a software program called ServantKeeper to document students, churches, counselees, and donors. ServantKeeper has granted us permission to use the program in two of our churches, allowing for data entry to be made by more than one person and shared via zip files. This is especially helpful with class and seminar registrations and mass mailings.

E-Mail Lists

E-newsletters are converted to PDF format and e-mailed monthly for distribution in church worship folders, on bulletin boards, on Web sites, and in handouts. We send our official e-newsletter to two groups each month: individuals and churches. Our training center maintains our church e-mail list, and our home office maintains our individuals e-mail list. The appropriate office is informed of any mail list changes as we become aware of them.

Personal and Vacation Days

The board of directors sets the number of vacation and personal days for

BCM staff. Vacation days are not carried year to year if they are not used. Personal days may be taken for sickness, funerals, emergencies, or other personal needs, and, if not used, are carried over year to year. I keep an annual record of all personal and vacation dates and file those with my year-end hours report.

Student Records

If you provide discipleship training, you will need to keep student records, especially for students who intend to pursue a Bible college or seminary degree program or certification with ACBC. We have developed a record form for each individual who enrolls in a class. At the top of the form we record student name, address, e-mail, phone number, name of church of membership, and other basic information. Below the personal data is a list of the classes that we offer, so I simply mark the classes the student has taken, the dates completed, earned grade, and any comments.

When a class begins, I create a class roster to record attendance for each student each week, along with assignments and reading that the student has handed in. Once class is done and all assignments have been submitted, the final grade is entered onto each student's record and class rosters are filed chronologically. We create a separate folder for each of our advanced students, where we file some of their assignments for future reference.

Our ACBC exam blog is available for advanced students who want help to complete their certification entrance exams. On the blog, each student records answers to exam questions, and his or her BCM coach or instructor supplies helpful comments and suggestions for improvement. ACBC-certified BCM students help with our blog.

Time Management

I keep a daily record of my hours in categories of administration, counseling (with the number of sessions also recorded), training, travel, and miscellaneous work. There's no doubt about it: this job takes time and effort. Time management and balance are a constant challenge.

Our organizational documents outline the ideal breakdown of my weekly hours for administration, counseling, training, and other duties. To stay as close as possible to that guideline, I must guard my time as carefully as possible.

It helps to set aside blocks of time to fulfill each area of responsibility, including personal time with the Lord. I pull out my day planner (an electronic calendar is another good alternative) to record special events, personal tasks or notes, phone calls to make, and session times as soon as I become aware of them. I consult my day planner several times per day and review my plans at least once or twice per week, especially when I am writing down my schedule for the home office secretary.

Counseling sessions take priority, so my weekly schedule is built around those. After prayer, I may squeeze in some training preparation, writing, reading, or studying before or after sessions. I try to schedule appointments so that one day per week can be devoted to administrative work (communication with board members, students, secretaries, volunteers, and others), as well as clerical work, writing, general record-keeping, reports, preparation for speaking/seminars/classes, and miscellaneous tasks. But my plans must remain flexible for unforeseen interruptions. I often remind myself to willingly allow God's agenda to override mine.

Because I have an office at home, it can be difficult to set apart time for personal life and family. After-hours phone calls, reading, planning, and even informal counseling or teaching are all part of reality in the life of a counselor, much as for doctors, attorneys, and pastors.[5] Home and family time can quickly be swallowed up unless I deliberately prioritize time with them. In addition, finding one day per week to rest is a challenge. Originally, we had planned to offer Saturday counseling.

However, in reality, Saturday is my only day for rest and family time, because Sundays frequently involve counseling, teaching, BCM visits to churches, and afternoon phone calls, as well as ministry in my own church. Even certain Saturdays are taken up with seminars, conferences, and other weekend training events. Therefore, we chose not to offer Saturday sessions while we have just one counselor on staff.

> **HERE'S MORE FOR YOU:**
> **Appendix I: Helpful Forms for Ministry Use**
> A wide variety of administrative and financial forms to help you stay organized and thorough.

Notes

1 At one point we had an assistant treasurer do most of our accounting. Although she was not on the board, she was answerable to the treasurer and the ministry board three to four times per year. Her work was also audited regularly. We greatly appreciate the high-quality financial research and record-keeping that she did for us.
2 These vouchers are included with the forms in Appendix I.
3 See Appendix I for copies of all forms described in this chapter.
4 Halo data includes relevant nonverbal information usually gathered by observation rather than through verbal communication (e.g., posture, timeliness, attitude, clammy handshake, eye contact).
5 Once you are someone's counselor, in that person's mind you remain his or her counselor. So when that person sees you, he or she will often ask for advice.

Beth pulled an expense voucher out of her drawer. It was already 6:30 p.m. and she would rather have been home sitting down to supper than filling out another form. There was no doubt about it: record-keeping was work. Beth was grateful for BCM's forms, which meant that she did not have to develop her own. Counseling—not record-keeping—was her passion. She had to discipline herself to record her mileage, hours, expenditures, session reports, and student and class information every day. It was worth it, though, especially when year-end reports were due or nonprofit records had to be filed.

Beth was learning which records she should manage and which she could delegate to the office administrator. She asked Peg to file important papers, make deposits, and arrange counseling appointments when people called. In addition, Peg printed labels and other routine papers. Otherwise, Beth kept her own records. She supplied her directors with reports of her hours, vacation days, and personal days. She delivered expenditure vouchers and mileage records to the treasurer. In addition, Beth's session reports, student files, and class information were filed at the home office, where her counseling supervisor had access to them.

Beth thought about her afternoon session with Wendy, who was blossoming in her walk with Christ and making good progress in everyday challenges. She decided that her administrative tasks were worth the privilege of counseling the Word.

After her session with Wendy, Beth had stopped to greet Pastor Paul. He was excited about students from Beth's evening classes, who were getting other people interested in discipleship. He had shared a few ideas for making other churches aware of courses that Beth was offering. They had talked for a half hour about some possibilities, and prayed together before she left. Refreshed by his encouragement, Beth prayed for her directors all the way back to the office.

All in all, Beth was satisfied with the ministry's organization and progress. Things were coming together, and she felt privileged and humbled to be part of it. There were days when she couldn't see how everything would get done. Beth did her best to manage her time and balance the complexities of traveling between the churches, as well as trying to keep track of which church was handling what. She was encouraged when she recognized that God's finger was on the thermostat. He had unexpectedly cleared two hours for her yesterday when a counselee called with the flu. She knew the joy of living in His care, and found it a privilege to help others grow closer to Him, too. Beth rejoiced in the blessings of ministry, but also in its challenges, as she witnessed a growing unity within and among local churches.

Paperwork was easier to face when her perspective was in the right place. With a smile, she picked up her pen.

The Model at Work

Relationships Among BCM Churches

We are grateful for the relationships that exist among the churches served by Biblical Counseling Ministries.

- *We pray for one another.* Our bonds are strengthened largely because the members of our board care about one another and pray for one another. BCM board meetings start with a full round of prayer, recognizing that this is our Lord's work and that He is providing both the ability and the means to accomplish His will. We offer ourselves as His tools and enjoy the working of God among us in lots of ways, even beyond counseling and discipleship training.

> "Throughout the Book of Acts and the Epistles, the benefit of like-minded churches working in cooperation is clearly seen. This cooperation can be applied in some counseling situations. One example is to encourage a counselee to attend a 'sister church' if attending your church is not possible or not advantageous. You can then be confident that the counseling that that person is receiving from the sister church's pulpit will complement what he or she receives in the biblical counseling sessions."
>
> **Corey Brookins, Senior Pastor, Berea Baptist Church, Stevens Point, WI**

- *We evaluate together.* No ministry is perfect. Therefore, we constantly seek ways to improve BCM. Counselee evaluations, seminar feedback, pastor surveys, and board input all help us to see where change is needed. Our strategic planning is carried out with these responses in mind.

- *We enjoy one another.* Our five churches are from two different Baptist associations, and we have differing personalities and methods, but we stand together as brothers and sisters, rejoicing in one another's victories and reaching out to support one another during hard times.
- *We help one another.* Our churches reach out to one another by praying, opening our doors to one another's prodigals, assisting with events such as vacation Bible school, coming together for church conferences, sharing building repair work, and discipling one another, including pastoral mentoring among board members. As a result, we have a growing fellowship.

HOW IS THIS RELATIONSHIP POSSIBLE?

- *Our doctrinal statement* has been a big help. The statement was built in a scripturally defensible way, and the result is acceptable for everyone. We're glad we took the time to work through that process.
- *Our vision statement* has also been important to us. As individuals, we do not always agree. Our efforts are imperfect. Sometimes we fail. But we work for the cause of Christ and respect what God is doing in each of our churches. Our vision statement serves to remind us of our mutual goals.
- *Our teamwork.* We see ourselves as a team. We build on our churches' differing abilities and perspectives rather than criticizing or ignoring them, because each church is valuable. As a result, God has been gracious in keeping church politics out of our boardroom. Instead, we share ideas and we keep our eyes on our vision, because we want one another to succeed. That is occurring now even in contexts unrelated to BCM.

We want to see other churches outside our core group succeed, too, when their work is Christ-centered and true to the gospel of grace alone through faith alone in Christ alone. This book was born out of that desire.

Relationships Between the Counselor and Each Church

Although I am far from perfect, my heart's desire is to honor God by being a wise counselor. With that goal in mind, I purposefully view myself as a member of a team. Christ is my Head and the ministry board is the God-appointed authority under which BCM serves our Lord in the local church. I regularly remind myself that I am not the center of the ministry. It is God's work. As a counselor, you will need to keep that approach as well.

When counseling at each local church, be respectful of the pastor's authority. Carefully keep the doctrinal statement in mind and act within ministry policies on behalf of the churches in which you serve. Consistently speak of (and to) each pastor and each church with respect and deference, maintaining diligence in your work ethic and sincerity in your walk with Christ. Conduct yourself in such a way that pastors can have confidence in your counseling and can trust you elsewhere as well.

Work hard to maintain appropriate communication with each of your core

> "The help that I received from BCM was invaluable. At the time, I was experiencing problems with my son and husband that were affecting my relationships with them. My work with Sue Nicewander not only helped me understand my role with each of these family members … but, more importantly, my personal relationship with Christ was improved. I realized that He loved my family members more than I did, and that their relationship to Him was up to each of them. My role was to embrace my relationship with Christ and let that relationship be an example for them. I received the knowledge and guidance from BCM to not only work through these issues, but also to deal with other stressful or emotional issues that have come my way. God promises that life will be tough, but He is always with me, and He always will provide the best for me."
> **BCM counselee**

churches, bearing in mind the time demands upon each pastor and his staff. When you make a mistake, seek God's wisdom to correct it as soon as possible, out of concern for the well-being of the offended party.

When you are misunderstood or criticized, deliberately avoid a defensive posture (Prov. 15:1–3, 18). Knowing that you work for the Lord, who is sovereign over His churches and His counselor, submit your desires to Him, asking Him to conform your will to His. When you feel troubled or when conflict arises, purposefully give thanks for what God is doing through the adversity. Seek to glorify God and consider how to accomplish His goals.

> "The ear that hears the rebukes of life
> Will abide among the wise.
> He who disdains instruction despises his own soul
> But he who heeds rebuke gets understanding.
> The fear of the LORD is the instruction of wisdom,
> And before honor is humility."
> Proverbs 15:31–33

Ask for godly counsel when you need help. Listen to correction (Prov. 9:8–9; 10:17–19). Then submit to authority, fulfill your biblical responsibilities, speak respectfully (when it is appropriate to speak— Prov. 10:19), and leave the rest in God's hands.

These principles are difficult to follow. Therefore, you will need to seek to identify and abide with Christ in every setting, whether inside the counseling room, at a board meeting, on the phone, or in the church office (John 15:4–5). Christ-centered living is the basis for strong church alliances that will keep relationships intact when unexpected conflicts or challenging events occur.

An Important Note

Expect to have to work hard, especially spiritually. Human beings are sinful at heart, without exception. You will have to deal with flawed people in flawed churches. Examine yourself and don't be shocked to find that you are at least partially at fault when problems arise. Resist the urge to complain and criticize (Phil. 2:14–15). Remember, Christians are at war, but not with one another. You will do well to remember who your true enemy is. Fight the Lord's battles in His strength, alongside your brothers and sisters rather than against them. Christian unity is a beautiful, powerful, and effective weapon that your adversary wants to destroy. Don't be part of his treachery.

Ministry is challenging work, but there is no better way to spend your life. Although the demands of the job are many and spiritual opposition is fierce, you walk with the Victor. When you diligently emulate Christ's character and minister His love in your relationships with churches and individuals, you win.

May God richly bless the faithful ministry of His Word and, through you, transform many lives for His glory through biblical counseling and discipleship.

Testimonials: The Benefits of the BCM Model for Biblical Counseling and Discipleship Training in Local Churches

"It seems that we live in unprecedented times when it comes to the spiritual needs of people. It is not that people have any more or fewer needs than before, but it seems that people are turning from God and seeking help in all the wrong places.

"As a pastor, I appreciate the purpose, goals, and direction of Biblical Counseling Ministries. BCM has personally helped me in three ways. First, it has opened doors for our church family to become equipped to help others. BCM seminars and discipleship training provide a wealth of opportunities for God's people to get the right tools for guiding others through their needs, using the Word of God. Second, BCM has also been a help to me personally in my counseling load. It has been especially helpful in counseling women and children. Sue Nicewander has been very helpful to several women who have deep-seated needs. Many of those women relate to her in a way in which they would not relate to a male counselor. BCM always uses the Scriptures as the only format to help individuals with their emotional and spiritual needs. Third, I have benefited much personally as a pastor from BCM in becoming more compassionate and skillful in the use of Scripture.

"I heartily recommend the ministry of BCM."

Larry G. Gross, Senior Pastor, First Baptist Church, Waupaca, WI, and BCM Charter and current member of BCM board of directors

"We are thankful beyond words for what God has done in raising up BCM and allowing us to be part of it from the very beginning. It has been work, to be sure, but the benefits

to the ministry of our church are evident. It has been a wonderful help to me as a pastor. First, I have utilized the resources recommended by BCM in my own counseling. People have always had problems, but it seems that the number, complexity, and intensity of the counseling issues have increased. I'm glad to have solid help available that will define the issues and direct me to the appropriate Scriptures. Beyond the printed reading recommendation list, which is valuable in itself, BCM's director has given excellent personal suggestions based on a thorough knowledge of a wide range of resources. Second, a number of our people have taken BCM training and it is no coincidence that we have seen a surge in personal discipleship, with believers more confident to reach out to others. As He often graciously does, God allowed the discipleship relationships to develop in step with the training, so that the disciple-makers were hungry for direction and received it as needed. Third, when we have directed people to BCM for counseling, it has been everything we would want it to be— biblical, compassionate, direct, concise, informed, well researched and applied, and most importantly to us, consistent with the doctrines and purposes of our church. When it is not a co-counsel, I have always been kept well informed of the counsel being given and the progress of the counselee.

"Our situation is unique in many ways, but every situation is unique in some ways. Rather than duplicating our experience, perhaps the Lord would use the seeds of what He has done here to give a vision to other small churches of what could be done in their area. It is a possibility well worth pursuing."

Stephen Steinmetz, Senior Pastor, Faith Baptist Church, Wisconsin Rapids, WI, and BCM Charter and current member of the BCM board of directors

"BCM has been a catalyst that has helped our church to grow by impacting our leadership, our body life, our equipping, our outreach, and the outward expression of our grace. Because of God's command, we were striving in each of these areas, as I am sure your church seeks to do. BCM helped us to focus and pursue this obedience in a greater way. We pastors are to present our members as instruments of righteousness, and, as leaders, we are to foster this within our life and in our church body. Allow me to *suggest seven areas in which BCM helps to present our members and my life as an instrument of righteousness:*

1. Equipping the saints. *BCM impacts this area directly by training people to think biblically about problems and by helping them to build healthy life patterns. You can use the seminars to introduce people to the big picture of how to address problems through biblical discipleship, as well as to great books. We encourage all of our leaders to take some of the seminars as a refresher and as a way to whet their appetites for more training. The greatest thing that people tend to take away from the seminars is something for them to personally resolve with God. Don't forget, leaders at peace produce.*

2. Discipling counselees. *Obviously, a biblical counseling ministry brings impact in the lives of counselees. Biblical counseling is beginning discipleship that readies counselees for more discipleship in their lives, and they naturally then bring it to others in their homes and church families because their worldviews and proficiencies have changed. Some of our former counselees are now our best counselors, mentors, and confronters in our church, which has deepened the health of our church, stopped disunity, and removed burden from our pastors. Remember, though, they will want solid training and regular discipleship, so be ready to provide this.*

3. Thanksgiving. *Because God is faithful and stunning in His work, we are seeing growth in biblical reliance on Him. BCM and the influence of the curriculum, the counselor, and the trials that have come with working in this area of ministry have helped our church to develop a more biblical way of life. One way that this is reflected is in the increase of thanksgiving by individuals, our staff, and our entire body.*

4. Increasing holiness and accountability within our body. *In addition, the BCM training and counseling of our church members causes them to be more sensitive to sin, the truth of the Word, and care for one another. Accountability has grown stronger and more consistent between friends and ministry partners because hope has become part of their way of life as they learn that change is possible and commanded. This means that as a pastor you need to be ready for some hard questions that may get personal. But the return from this sharpening is beautiful. The steps of church discipline happen naturally, many are restored before public destruction, and who knows how many are*

protected from evil altogether?

5.   Sharpening our leadership. *Whenever the body gets serious with God's Word, it will require and desire strong biblical leadership that helps it to obey the commands of outreach, discipleship, and holiness. Members will want order, because God is orderly. They will love a gracious, gentle leadership unmovable in the truth. They will hold you accountable to this. They will listen to your preaching in a better way and be expecting sound biblical application for life.*

6.   Living in grace. *Biblical counseling expects failure, change, and the capacity for both to function together. This is the grace of the gospel. Your church will have public sinners changed and wanting to serve. Without strong grace teaching, those being changed will have a hard time productively mainstreaming into your church. But when this path of grace happens, they then add to the wave of impact.*

7.   Reaching and reclaiming the lost. *About half of the adults saved at our church in the last few years have come out of the counseling ministry. Many other families that would have left our church, or that have left other non-gospel-preaching churches in disarray, have been salvaged and have become productive body members. Jesus reached those who knew that they were lost—the desperate. This ministry targets those 'readied' by God."*

Jonathan Jenks, Senior Pastor, Calvary Baptist Church, Wisconsin Rapids, WI, and BCM Charter and current member of the BCM board of directors

"I benefited greatly from the ministry of BCM before I even knew what BCM was about. When I stepped in as pastor, I learned that a number of the key people in our church were in such a position because of the impact that God had made on them through BCM. The ministry of BCM goes far beyond helping someone 'work through' his or her problems—it equips such a person to become an integral part of God's church.

"There is not enough that could be said about the power of the Word to change people's lives. When it comes to my pastoral counseling, there are times when I simply get stuck regarding the direction to go with a counselee. I have been so blessed to be able to talk through some of these issues with our BCM counselor and to receive solid,

biblical advice for a 'plan of attack.' It is priceless to be able to receive this kind of advice without wondering if it is watered down by a worldly philosophy."

Corey Brookins, Senior Pastor, Berea Baptist Church, Stevens Point, WI, and member of the BCM board of directors

"Taking the biblical counseling training classes from BCM has been life-changing for me. These classes, from start to finish, have helped me to better 'know God and know people.' For many years, I considered myself to be a biblical thinker, and that was partly true. But BCM's training helped me to see that some of the world's dangerous, deceptive, and God-less psychological philosophies had infiltrated my thinking! BCM taught me that God's Word is sufficient for all matters of spiritual life and practice (2 Peter 1:3), because it claims to be (2 Tim. 3:16–17; Heb. 4:12)! Our problems do not stem from outside us but rather from inside us—our sinful hearts (James 4:1)—and this brings hope because of the gospel! I learned that God's Word is not an encyclopedia for problems, a rule book, or something to make one feel good about oneself, but rather the very words of the God of the universe so that we may know Him personally and be changed into His Son's likeness through the power of the gospel. Over and over again I was helped to see how God's Word is practical for every situation in life (Ps. 19:7–11; 119:105). It is sufficient for all inorganic problems! Through BCM I learned that God-glorifying change can therefore only come as I see my sinful heart desires and confess and put off sins of the heart and behavior and put on righteousness from the heart that then extends to my behavior. I have been helped to see where the gospel connects to all of life—my thoughts, actions and emotions—and that problems are redemptive opportunities to apply the gospel of God's grace to put off sin and put on righteousness. I also learned that sanctification is progressive, not instantaneous. For this reason, we can enjoy the journey as we take steps of obedience to grow in Christlikeness.

"These truths have been so life-changing for me that I am excited to share them by discipling others in my church. Instead of relying on my own wisdom to help another, BCM has helped me to be much more competent in relying on the power of God's Word

(Heb. 4:12). I can see myself as having the same needs as those I minister to, but I can point them to the same gospel of God's grace—the same Savior Jesus Christ! In discipling others, BCM has also helped me tremendously in being able to use God's Word more as a laser than as a shot gun—to shine it better on the specific area of need at the moment, by listening, asking questions to draw out heart desires, and implementing helpful teaching and homework.

"BCM's training has been a blessing not only to me personally and those I disciple, but also to my church. I now work with my pastors to help ladies in need. It is not always appropriate for a pastor to meet with a lady, so God is providing opportunities for me to minister to women under the supervision of my pastoral staff. I have the benefit of the godly experience, wisdom, and spiritual protection of my pastors, and they have the benefit of BCM's training in my life, so that I am more competent and equipped for the task at hand. I highly recommend BCM's training to any believer wishing to grow and glorify God better in the way that he or she lives and ministers in Jesus's name."

Amy Knoll, BCM student (now a ACBC-certified biblical counselor), Calvary Baptist Church, Wisconsin Rapids, WI

"The more that I work with pastors, the more respect I have for their position as undershepherds, the grace with which they must do their jobs, the dedication of their hearts to the Lord and His people, and the diligence with which they must tackle the myriad challenges they are called to undertake. They are examples of God's faithfulness. It is my privilege to walk alongside them with counseling resources that are firmly founded in Scripture, and to know the joy of seeing God changing lives through His Word. By His power and grace, souls are coming to Christ and learning to walk with Him victoriously. Some are now taking discipleship classes. Others are simply sharing what they have learned in sessions. Their lives have been changed, and they have responded by reaching out to others who are struggling (2 Cor. 1:3–4). What a privilege to be His tool in that process!

"I am also excited about the development of discipleship in each of our churches, especially now that our students are becoming ACBC-certified and are able to take over *some of the counseling that I would otherwise do for their churches. This is encouraging for two reasons. First, my time demands are shifting so that I have more opportunities to teach and write. But, more importantly, it means that their local churches are being internally strengthened to do the work of ministry with more biblical skill and direction. As people at church see our disciples growing and serving effectively among them, interest in biblical counseling and discipleship is growing.*

"Our model is not the only way that biblical counseling and church discipleship can be developed. However, to our knowledge it is the only one that encourages ordinary churches to work collaboratively to provide biblical counseling and discipleship resources for themselves and their communities. Whether you decide to base your counseling ministry in one church or through a group of churches, we think you may benefit from our experiences, build upon them, and adapt them to fit your particular situation.

"BCM is a work in progress, requiring patience, flexibility, and faith as we press on. God has encouraged us with slow but steady growth as we have pioneered this plan, encouraging friendships and discipleship among pastors, strengthening church unity, increasing development of one-on-one evangelism and discipleship in churches, and holding out biblical counseling as a viable and essential tool for the local church. The results we've experienced in changed lives, in building up church unity and community, and in enthusiasm for the Word all point to the value of this multichurch effort. We are grateful to God for the opportunity to serve him through BCM."

Sue Nicewander, MABC, ACBC, Executive Director and Biblical Counselor, Biblical Counseling Ministries, Inc.

Appendix A. A Brief Theology of Biblical Counseling

I. General Philosophy

A. Suffering and chaos exist because sin exists in and around every individual (Rom. 7:15–25; 8:20–23).

B. Man is culpable for the choices he makes (Rom. 3:10–12).

C. Jesus Christ and His provision through the gospel make victory possible (Rom. 6:1–23; 8:1–4, 28–39).

II. View of Man

A. MAN

1. Man is created by God as His image-bearer (Gen. 1:26–27).
2. Man has purpose:
   - Fellowship with God (Heb. 10:22; 1 John 1:3)
   - Worship of God (John 4:23–24)
   - Ministry to mankind (Matt. 22:39; John 4:34)
3. Man has rebelled against God by nature and by choice (Rom. 3:23).
4. Man is accountable to God (Rom. 14:12).

B. SIN

1. Sin is committed by all people (Rom. 3:10–12, 23).
2. Sin severs relationship with God (Rom. 3:10–18).
3. Sin causes spiritual death and eternal separation from God for every individual (Eph. 2:1–3; Rev. 20:10–15).
4. Sin distorts personality, heart, and mind (Jer. 17:9).
5. Sin corrupts all social and physical environments (Rom. 8:22).

III. Basic Problem

A. Every human being is a sinner by nature and by choice, living in a fallen world where bad things happen (Rom. 3:10–23).

Although we are not as bad as we could be, sin negatively impacts every aspect of our lives. Therefore, a counselor must discern where sin may be causing or otherwise impacting the problem the counselee wants to solve (Rom. 8:23; Gal. 6:7–8).

Because sin is real, guilt is real and must be biblically addressed (Rom. 3:19–20; 4:7–8).

Because we live in a fallen world, suffering occurs and must be biblically addressed (1 Cor. 10:13; 2 Cor. 4:7–18).

B. Jesus Christ

1. Christ provides redemption and hope through His divine sacrifice for mankind (1 Peter 2:24–25; 2 Cor. 5:21).

2. All who place their faith in Christ, apart from works (Eph. 2:8–9; Titus 3:5),

- Are completely forgiven (1 John 1:9–2:2)
- Have eternal spiritual life (John 3:16; 5:24)
- Have been adopted into the family of God (Rom. 8:14–17)
- Have a progressively restored personality (2 Cor. 5:17; Rom. 6:12–22)—are being changed into His image (Rom. 8:28–29; 2 Cor. 3:18)—as they cooperate with God's will (Phil. 2:12–13)
- Can overcome sinful tendencies (Eph. 4:22–24)
- Can endure adverse circumstances victoriously (Rom. 8:31–39; 2 Cor. 2:14)

IV. Function of the Counselor

A. *Nouthetic* biblical counseling uses a compassionate approach, careful listening, and appropriate confrontation through Scripture out of concern for the glory of God and the good of the individual (Rom. 15:14; Matt. 22:37–39). The nouthetic biblical counselor takes into account that suffering is not always due to the sin of the sufferer, and proceeds accordingly (Job 1:1; 42:8).

B. The counselor is like a *coach*, not a savior or a fixer. As a coach, the counselor listens, evangelizes, teaches, encourages, exhorts, and admonishes the counselee to live wisely in God's will according to Scripture (Prov. 18:13; Matt. 28:19–20; 1 Thes. 5:14; Col. 3:16).

- The biblical counselor does not take a "holier than thou" attitude, but walks alongside to offer help (Gal. 6:1–3).
- The biblical counselor points to Christ—not to self or to other people—as the One who is to be followed and worshiped (Luke 9:23–24; John 4:23–24).
- The biblical counselor cannot cause anyone to change. Transformation comes from God through the renewing of the mind and the willing biblical obedience of the counselee (Rom. 12:1–2; Eph. 4:22–24; Phil. 2:12–13).

V. Avenue for Change

A. JUSTIFICATION

A person is justified (declared righteous by God) by grace alone through faith alone in Christ alone, when he or she willingly believes—sincerely admits his or her sin and personally receives Christ (places his or her trust in the provision of God in Christ's sacrifice and resurrection alone) (John 1:12; Rom. 3:19–20, 28; 4:5; 5:1–2; Gal. 2:21; Eph. 2:8–9; Titus 3:5–7).

1. Therefore, the counselor should present the true gospel and ask about the counselee's relationship with God, specifically through personal faith in the substitutionary sacrificial death and resurrection of Jesus Christ (John 3:16–21; Rom. 4:5).

- Does this person believe that we receive eternal life through faith alone by grace alone in Christ alone (Eph. 2:8–9; Titus 3:5)?
- Does this person rely on any kind of human effort to merit acceptance by God (Gal. 2:20; Eph. 1)?

2. The counselor should learn how the counselee views and interprets Scripture. Establish a biblical view of Scripture. This is essential because it is the basis upon which you will work together. Such a view of Scripture includes its:

- Authority (2 Tim. 3:15–17)
- Sufficiency (Ps. 19:7–11; 119; 2 Peter 1:3)
- Applicability (James 1:22–25; 1 Peter 1:3–10)
- Relevance (Ps. 19:7–14)
- Accuracy (John 17:17)

3. The counselor should ask and answer questions to discover the counselee's theological basis. Include questions about the roles of Scripture, the definition of the gospel, his or her view of God and self, and the role of prayer in his or her life. How does the person's life match up with his or her theology? People live what they truly believe (2 Cor. 3:2).
4. The counselor should sensitively answer error with Scripture (Col. 4:5–6).

B. PROGRESSIVE SANCTIFICATION

A believer learns to become more like Christ day by day by obediently living according to God's Word in the power of the indwelling Holy Spirit with the goal of pleasing God (Rom. 8:1–17, 28–29).
1. Believers cannot be perfect this side of heaven, but they should be growing more and more like Christ every day (Rom. 8:29; 2 Cor. 3:18).
2. Believers cannot experience heaven on earth, but they are to live for Christ through the power of the Holy Spirit in the midst of trials (2 Cor. 3:5–6; 4:7–18).
3. How a person responds to situations—whether or not they are of his or her own making—reveals (but does not cause) the desires of the heart. This is of primary importance to God (Prov. 4:23; 23:7).
4. The counselor should, to the best of his or her ability, discern to what extent this person's suffering is a result of living in a fallen world

(disease/illness, tragedies, etc.), and to what extent the counselee has contributed to the suffering (Prov. 12:15; Gal. 6:7; Matt. 7:24–27).

5. The counselor should explore how this person's sin impacts upon the problem:

- Personal sin against God and other people (Ps. 139:23–24; Matt. 7:3–5)
- Sinful responses when sinned against by other people (Ps. 141:4; 1 Peter 3:9; Rom. 12:21)

6. The counselor should address sin by pointing to Christ through the gospel (Eph. 2:1–10):

- Define what it means to repent (2 Cor. 7:9–11).
- Exhort the counselee to exercise sincere repentance and faith (1 John 1:8–2:2; Heb. 11:6).
- Teach him or her to receive Christ's forgiveness, not to wallow or doubt (1 John 1:9–2:2).
- Teach him or her to extend Christlike forgiveness to others, not to stew in anger (Eph. 4:31–32; James 1:19–25).

VI. Man's Responsibility

Man is responsible to God for his thoughts, behaviors, and motives (Rom. 1–3).

A. Every believer is responsible before God for thinking and acting with an ultimate desire to please God (2 Cor. 5:9; Eph. 2:10).

1. The counselor should explore what drives the counselee's responses. Is it love for God? If not, why not? What does this person need to learn or believe about God, self, and others?

2. The counselor should lead the person to respond to life in a way that brings God glory and honor (Isa. 43:7; 1 Cor. 10:31; 2 Cor. 5:7):

- Thanksgiving (1 Thes. 5:17–18)
- Sacrificial love for God and other people (Matt. 22:37–39; 1 Cor. 13:1–8)

- Forgiveness (Eph. 4:32)
- Wisdom (Prov. 9:1–11)

3. The counselor should point out that God cannot be bullied, manipulated, or coerced into action (Eph. 1:11). Good works do not earn personal merit with God or more love from God, but are to be motivated by awe for God and gratitude to Jesus Christ (John 4:23–24; Phil. 4:6–8; 1 Thes. 5:18).

4. The counselee's responsibility is his or her own. The counselor should not coerce or attempt to run the counselee's life, but should respect the fact that each person is free to make choices and is personally accountable to God for them (Matt. 7:24–27; Gal. 6:7–9; Rom. 14:12; Phil. 2:12–13).

5. God will bring some predictable consequences for a person's actions. The counselor should point those out to help the counselee to acknowledge his or her part in the problem, the need for personal forgiveness and transformation in Christ, and the responsibility and ability to change (Gal. 6:7–9; Matt. 7:24–27).

- God is always good, and His ongoing purpose is to build Christlikeness into His children, not to punish (Rom. 8:28–29).
- Even God's discipline, though difficult to bear, is beneficial to those who are trained by it (Prov. 3:11–13; Heb. 12:5–13).

B. We should think and act according to the truth (Phil. 4:8; John 14:6).

1. The counselor should study Scripture faithfully using a literal–grammatical–historical method (1 Tim. 1:15–16; 2 Tim. 2:15).

2. The counselor should open the Word at every session and present it in a manner that lets Scripture do the counseling.

- Apply Scripture carefully and specifically (2 Tim. 3:16–17). Who is God? Who am I? What are my responsibilities toward God and others?
- Check the counselee's comprehension (Prov. 2:2–5).

- Where specifically does the passage touch the person's life (Ps. 19:7–14; 2 Peter 1:3)?
- How might biblical changes be made in the person's thoughts, behaviors, and motives related to the problem he or she wants to address (Eph. 4:22–24; Col. 3:1–25)?
- How will you teach the person to biblically evaluate the changes he or she makes (Ps. 19:12–14; 139:23–24)?

C. The role of the local church is critical (Rom. 12:1–16; Eph. 3:1–4:16; Heb. 10:25–26), through

- Regular attendance and membership
- Hearing the preaching/teaching of the Word for spiritual growth into godliness
- Service to others in love (edifying)
- Accountability
- Purposeful fellowship and outreach
- Friendship/godly examples
- Practical assistance (prayer, help with daily concerns)
- Discipleship received and shared

Appendix B. A General Outline for Offering Biblical Counsel

I. Remember Your Goal

A. The first goal of biblical counseling is to bring glory to God (Isa. 42:8; 43:7). This may be accomplished whether or not the counselee's circumstances improve.

B. Consider Christ, and point to Him.

- *His suffering.* Although He was perfectly sinless, Christ's suffering led to a humiliating death on a cross (Isa. 53:10–11).
- *His sinless example.* Throughout His life, He glorified God in His goals in and responses to every situation (Heb. 4:15).
- *His purpose,* which was fulfilled. He demonstrated His deity, His justice, and His love, and God brought salvation to mankind through Him (Phil. 2:7–11).

II. Prepare

A. PREPARE YOUR HEART

1. Pray for God's will for the counselee.

2. Pray for yourself in your role as counselor (Col. 1:9–12):

- Wisdom and knowledge of God's will
- Accurate discernment of problems
- Scriptural perspective
- A worthy walk with this person, that you may be a good example and a godly teacher
- Effective expression of the knowledge of God through His Word
- Strength according to His glorious power

- A spirit of compassion and patience as you stand on the Word
- Gratitude toward God for using you as His tool in this person's life

B. PREPARE YOUR MIND

1. Carefully read the PDI and/or notes on your previous session and write down questions to ask during the session.
2. Consider which biblical categories you are likely to face.
3. Study applicable Scripture.
4. Consult reliable literature.
5. If necessary, ask another godly counselor for help.

C. PREPARE YOUR ENVIRONMENT

1. Be on time.
2. Make sure that paperwork and files are accessible.
3. Have your Bible open.
4. Ensure that the room is uncluttered and comfortable.
5. Place a sign on the door indicating that you are in session.
6. Confer with your co-counsel.
7. After the session, return the room to the church's preferred setup.

III. Gather Pertinent Information

A. Greet the counselee warmly and invite him or her into the room, noticing nonverbal information such as body language, personal hygiene, facial expression, vocal inflection, punctuality, etc.

B. Pray together.

C. Explain what biblical counseling is, how the hour will be spent, your pleasure in serving him or her, and your confidence in God and Scripture.

D. Give the person time to tell his or her story. Ask good questions and listen carefully (Prov. 18:13). You can't act according to the truth unless you know the truth.

- Discern the facts about the situation: who, what, where, when, why, how. Ask about health, available resources (in the family, church, work, education, etc.), and how the past relates to the person's present problems.

- Draw out the person's thoughts, actions, and feelings regarding the problem, and his or her beliefs about God, him- or herself, and his or her responsibility toward others. You will hear how others are causing distress or harm; ask the person to turn the "camera" on self, too. How does he or she respond when others do wrong?
- Discern what the person wants most—what he or she lives for. A willingness to sin indicates a heart that is living for something other than God. But be careful not to pre-judge. Just because a person needs help does not mean that his or her heart desires are wrong (Luke 6:45).
- Continue to gather information at each session.

E. Demonstrate compassion and care, and try to understand the person's anguish (Mark 10:21; 2 Tim. 2:24–26).

- Build an appropriate relationship out of sincere concern, pointing to a relationship with Christ as the person's primary need (1 Tim. 1:5).
- Acknowledge that we are all sinners. You are neither an expert nor a savior. Come alongside to help as a sinner saved by grace (1 John 1:7–9; 4:7–12).

F. Other considerations when gathering information:

- Keep your body language open and receptive.
- Observe the counselee's body language and voice inflections throughout the session; you will gain lots of additional information from this.
- Gently maintain control of the session when the counselee gets off track or tries to lead.
- Establish accountability, point to current godly examples, and suggest or assign additional discipleship with a mature believer in the person's local church (Gal. 6:1–2).

IV. Give Hope

Your first session will be largely for the purpose of gathering information, but stop to give hope whenever you think the counselee is feeling hopeless.

A. Definition: Biblical hope is not the fulfillment of my expectations, but a daily decision to place my faith in a sovereign God, based on the truth presented in His Word, confident that His plan will prevail both for me and for all of His creation (1 Chr. 29:11; Rom. 8:28–29).

B. Rejoice with those who rejoice, and weep with those who weep (Rom. 12:15).

C. As you gather information, point out specific ways in which God has faithfully cared for the counselee, and encourage him or her to acknowledge Him as well (1 Thes. 5:18).

D. Comfort the sufferer without indulging self-pity or excusing sin (Ps. 42:11; 1 Thes. 5:14).

E. Explain God's good purposes for suffering (Rom. 5:3–6; 8:28–29; James 1:2–4; 1 Peter 5:10).

F. Present the four promises from God for believers who are experiencing trials. The promises are contained in 1 Corinthians 10:13: (1) *No temptation has overtaken you except such as is common to man;* (2) *but God is faithful,* (3) *who will not allow you to be tempted beyond what you are able,* (4) *but with the temptation will also make the way of escape, that you may be able to bear it.* (Note: The word translated "tempt" means "test" or" tempt.")

V. Assess and Interpret Information

After each session, scripturally assess what you learned and what instruction and action steps are probably needed next (2 Tim. 3:16–17).

A. Pray (Eph. 1:15–21).

B. Interpret your data using biblical categories and terms.

1. SPIRITUAL CONDITION

- Is the person a believer or an unbeliever (1 Cor. 2:14–15; 1 Thes. 5:14)?
- If a believer, is he or she carnal or spiritually mature (1 Cor. 3:1–2; Heb. 5:11–14)?

2. SITUATION

- What is the situation?
- How do situations and responses in the person's past and present life relate to one another?
- How are others impacting this situation?
- What physical/health factors may be affecting this problem? What medical referrals may address these factors appropriately?
- What is hindering change (Phil. 2:12–13)?

3. THOUGHTS

- What does the person think about the problem, God's role, and his or her responsibilities?
- What does this person believe about him- or herself?
- What does this person think of God?
- What specific thoughts or beliefs usually lead this person to lose hope, act sinfully, and/or experience powerful emotions of fear, anger, or despair?
- How does Scripture address those thoughts (Phil. 2:5; Eph. 4:23)?
- How might you help this person to apply scriptural commands, principles, wisdom, examples, or models?

4. ACTIONS

- How has the person typically acted in response to the problem situation?
- How does this person handle personal and professional relationships?
- How does this person deal with conflict?
- What does Scripture say about such actions?

- What undesirable consequences might this person be experiencing as a direct result of his or her actions? In other words, how might this person be causing trouble in his or her own life (Matt. 7:24–27; Gal. 6:7–8)?
- Which biblical characters might be used to illustrate a scriptural principle or command? In particular, how did Christ handle similar problems, and how were His responses received by others? By God?

5. EMOTIONS

- How does the person feel?
- According to Scripture, how might those feelings reflect the need for specific changes in thought and action (Gal. 5:16–25)?
- To what extent does this person allow feelings to rule him or her? Does the person understand that emotions are like thermometers (not thermostats) indicating that a "fever" (his or her thoughts, actions, and motives) needs to be "treated" (biblically addressed)?

6. MOTIVES

a. Do this person's responses reflect gospel truth (John 1:12–13; 5:24; Rom. 15:12–13; Eph. 2:1–10; 4:31–32)?

- I am totally depraved (Rom. 3:10–12, 23).
- I am deeply loved by God because of His great love, not because of my worth or value to Him (Eph. 2:1–10).
- Jesus Christ paid the full price for my sin in His death and resurrection, apart from any merit or works I might contribute (Titus 3:5–6).
- When I receive(d) Him, I receive(d) eternal life and new identity (John 1:12; 10:27–29).
- Because of Christ, I can treat others as He treats me (1 John 4:20–21).
- When I receive(d) Him, my hope becomes secure in Him, both now and for all eternity (John 1:12; 10:27–29; 1 John 5:13).

- If I reject Him, I reject eternal life and hope (John 3:16–18, 36; 1 John 5:11–12).

b. Does the person's life reflect, first, a strong desire to bring God the glory and, second, to love his or her neighbor (Matt. 22:37–39)?

c. If not, what may be motivating the person's responses to this situation (e.g., love of money, fear of man, desire for power, pleasure, acceptance, peace, or security)?

d. Anything that takes precedence over God is an idol. How does Scripture address the idols you have observed in this person's life (Isa. 42:8; James 4:1–3)?

e. Remember, the biblical goal is to bring glory to God by addressing the person's heart—not necessarily by resolving the situation (which may be impossible)(Prov. 4:23; Matt. 12:35).

VI. Test Your Interpretations When You See the Counselee Again

A. Continue to gather information until you are reasonably certain you have a correct perspective (Prov. 18:13).

B. When appropriate, gently present one or two of your observations (2 Tim. 2:24; 4:2; Heb. 3:13), using Scripture. This is a delicate but critical moment. You may gently say something like, "Based upon this passage and what you have already told me [use the person's words], what do you see in your motives, thoughts, and actions that needs to change? [Pause for his or her response.] I see some things God wants you to learn and some ways He wants you to change. I'd like to help you make those changes. Will you let me help you?" In my experience, people usually feel relieved to hear the truth when it is accompanied by a sincere offer of help (rather than condemnation). But allow the person to discuss objections to your observations: remember that you are not omniscient, so you may not have come to correct interpretations.

C. Express hope in Christ and confidence in Scripture (Rom. 15:13; Eph. 3:14–21; Phil. 4:13). The Word offers the only truly lasting solution!
D. Express your desire to help by discussing some specific ways you will use Scripture to guide and direct the person to address the problem God's way (Eph. 4:22–24; 2 Tim. 3:16–17; 2 Peter 1:3–10).

VII. Encourage and Oversee Biblical Change

A. Learn more about the biblical way to address the specific problem(s) you have discovered.

- Study Scripture to find applicable commands, examples, and principles.
- Consult reliable literature for particular areas to address and biblical ways to proceed.

B. God's solution for mankind is centered in the gospel of Jesus Christ.

- 1. Therefore, to be biblical, your counsel must be centered in the gospel as well. Be sure you understand how the sinfulness of man (Rom. 3:10–12), the everlasting love and grace of God (John 3:16; Eph. 2:1–10), the sacrifice of Christ that offers complete forgiveness for sin (Eph. 1:7–14; 1 John 1:7–2:2), the effectual faith of the believer (Eph. 2:8–9; Heb. 11:6), and the enduring promises of justification (Rom. 3:28), adoption (Eph. 1:5, 11, 14), progressive sanctification (Phil. 2:12–13), and glorification (Rom. 8:18) apply to this person in this situation.
- 2. Sincere repentance is necessary if the person's sin is part of the problem.
- 3. Your motive must not be simply to solve the issue at hand, but to lead the person to a right relationship with God. Encourage him or her to exercise sincere faith in the forgiveness and grace of our wonderful Savior Christ Jesus (2 Cor. 7:9–11; Eph. 2:1–10; 4:32).
- 4. Jesus Christ offers mercy and grace to help in time of need (Heb. 4:14–16). The person must be in right relationship with Christ to

cooperate with the helping ministry of the Holy Spirit (James 4:6). Prayerfully consider how you might encourage this person to draw near to the Savior (James 4:8).

- 5. The gospel means that a believer's identity is in Christ, not in the past, other people's opinions, earthly family, or anything else that distracts us from fulfilling God's purposes for us (Eph. 1:1–14).
- 6. Faith is the key without which no one can please God (Heb. 11:6). Changed behavior is not enough.
- 7. Nonetheless, new thoughts and behaviors *are* necessary and will require diligent effort (Rom. 12:9–16; 1 Tim. 4:7–8). Change is not easy, especially because it involves denying self and surrendering completely to God's ways (Luke 9:23–24).

C. Set biblical goals and build a plan for change based on 2 Timothy 3:16–17. It is essential to be relevant.

1. DOCTRINE

Teach the counselee about God, him- or herself, and his or her responsibilities toward others *in the context of this problem.*

- Correct wrong theology.
- Reinforce right theology.
- Nurture learning: through your commitment to Scripture and practical application of Scripture; through assignments that get the person regularly into the Word; through assignments in Scripture that directly connect to the person's real life.

2. REPROOF

- Help the person to see where he or she can contribute to the problem and what changes are needed in his or her thoughts, actions, and motives.
- Lead the person to repent of his or her sin and to forgive others, but not to take responsibility for the sins of others (2 Cor. 7:9–11; Eph. 4:32).
- Assure the person that feelings will eventually improve as he or she deals biblically with sinful thoughts, actions, and motives (Ps. 139:23–24).

3. CORRECTION

In the context of the current problem, teach the person to actively put off sin by deliberately correcting thinking, actions, and motives according to God's Word.

- Correct thinking about personal responsibility, past and present circumstances, fear of the future, God's character and role, obedience and disobedience, expectations, attitude toward others, etc. (Phil. 4:8–9).
- Correct actions that are disobedient, foolish, dangerous, unloving, etc. (Proverbs; Phil. 1:27–29).
- Correct motives that dishonor God and perpetuate fear, anger, doubt, and despair (1 Tim. 1:7).

4. INSTRUCTION IN RIGHTEOUSNESS

- 1. Teach the person to put on righteousness in thoughts, actions, and motives that consistently glorify God, *especially in the context of the problem situation.* Be relevant.
- 2. Teach thoughts that reflect the mind of Christ: to be consistent in faith when trials come, and not to lose heart while the person's relationship with Christ matures. It takes time and effort for new biblical behaviors, thoughts, and motives to become established (Phil. 2:5; Eph. 4:22–24; Heb. 10:35–39).
- 3. Teach behaviors that consistently follow Christ in wisdom, love, kindness, forgiveness, integrity, and grace in all circumstances (Eph. 4:22–32).
- 4. Teach motives that consistently honor Christ and perpetuate faith, hope, and love toward God and man (Matt. 22:37–39; 1 Cor. 13:13).

VIII. Ask for Commitment to the Process of Biblical Counseling

A. Get the counselee to count the cost. Be real. Commitment costs time, effort, strength, humility, and faith (Luke 14:25–34). Have you presented Christ such that the person recognizes the cost is worth it?

B. Encourage perseverance by teaching the person the nature of progressive sanctification
(Phil. 3:13–14).
C. Ask the person to commit to completing the homework assignment and to come to the next session as an act of faith in Christ.

IX. Assign Homework
This homework should:
A. Be appropriate to the counselee's abilities and limitations, so your assignments are truly helpful rather than frustrating. Give specific written instructions for manageable tasks to be accomplished between sessions. The intent is to teach the counselee specifically how he or she can become a doer of the Word, not just hear Scripture in session or read it to finish an assignment (James 1:22).
B. Build relationship with God (James 4:6–10):
- Contributing to a fuller understanding of the gospel's relevance to life today (Eph. 1:3–2:11)
- Growing the person's overall practical knowledge of Scripture (James 1:22–25)
- Increasing his or her trust in God's character (Prov. 3:5–7)
- Practicing praise and thanksgiving (1 Thes. 5:18)
- Building a consistent prayer life (1 Thes. 5:17).

C. Reinforce what you discuss in session and help the person to take the next step of biblical obedience with a right motive (1 John 2:3–6).
D. Establish personal accountability that leads to dependence upon God more than the counselor (Heb. 10:19–23).
E. Increase appropriate involvement in the local church (Heb. 10:23–25).[1]

Note

1 For more on the subject of biblical counseling, see **John MacArthur and The Master's College Faculty,** *Counseling: How to Counsel Biblically* (Nashville: Thomas Nelson, 2005).

Appendix C. Questions to Help Church Leaders Assess Church Health and Direction

1. What are my personal goals for spiritual growth and ministry?

2. What is the goal of our church?

3. Are those goals in line with Scripture's goals for a local church: to glorify God, make disciples, baptize them into the body, and teach them to live life in Christ? (See Matt. 28:19–20 and the book of Ephesians.)

4. Do our people know and share the gospel? If so, are new believers coming into the church? If not, why not?

5. Do our people understand the big picture of redemption and grace? Is Christ relevant to them during good times, in trials, and in the mundane? Do they deliberately choose to respond as He would, out of gratitude and love for Him and their neighbors, rather than responding with works righteousness or emotionalism?

6. What particular struggles are our people experiencing, and what questions are they asking? What themes are resonating from those trials and questions (e.g., difficulties with conflict resolution, parenting, marriage, or basic doctrines)?

7. How might those themes be prioritized and addressed so that the church becomes more scriptural in practice, following Christlike motives and biblical responses to everyday questions and challenges?

8. Which relevant fundamental doctrines and responses could be emphasized to help people meet their challenges and questions from a biblical worldview?

9. Where and how should church discipline be exercised?[1]

10. Which gifts, disciplines, and skills are evident in our people, and how are they being used?

11. Which spiritual disciplines (e.g., evangelism, prayer, Scripture study, journaling, discipleship, service) are in need of development among our leaders?

12. Which spiritual disciplines are in need of development in the rest of the body?

13. How might the identified disciplines and skills be developed?

14. What relevant resources are necessary to develop disciplines and skills throughout the church, through worship services, Bible studies, children's programs, music, etc.?

15. Which human and material resources do we have right now?

16. Which church resources should be developed? For example, should a church library be started and stocked with biblical resources? Should the books in the present church library be weeded? Which present lesson materials are valuable, and which should be discarded?

17. How might Sunday Bible study materials be chosen to harmonize themes among age groups?

18. Which of our Bible study materials are helpful, and which are harmful or functionally useless?

19. What other methods of study might be helpful? For example, could teachers be sent to training conferences? Would a Sunday evening regimen of training DVDs be a good choice?

20. Which of our programs/activities build up our church? Which of our programs/activities are draining resources? Write a plan to eliminate nonessentials and to replace them with resources that will build up the church.

Note

1 Consult **Jay Adams,** *Handbook of Church Discipline: A Right and Privilege of Every Church Member* (Grand Rapids, MI: Zondervan, 1986) for an evenhanded approach to this sensitive subject.

Appendix D. Key Components for Pastors Developing Disciple-Makers

Contributed by Pastor Jonathan Jenks

A pastor with God-given, grace-driven courage can be used of God to guide people to maturity for the formation of a New Testament disciple-making church. Six key components are necessary: Scripture-directed prayer, preaching, prompting, personalizing, planning, and protecting.

I. Pray

Prayer is essential for a growing relationship with God that brings Holy Spirit wisdom and Christlike courage along with unity among the saints. Plan to pray. Lead in prayer. Confess often. Pray in private and in public. Pray as leaders and pray with the people. Seek Him together.

II. Preach and Teach the Biblical Mandate of Disciple-Making

A. Disciple-making is what God has intended, according to many passages such as Ephesians 4, 2 Timothy 2:2, and Titus 2.

B. Preach the "one another" passages.[1] Start looking for all the commands given to the body to do together.

- When, where, and how should those commands be followed in your church?
- Point out ways in which discipleship relationships are ideal for carrying out God's "one another" mandates.

C. Provide practical pictures. What does it mean to be a disciple-maker and to be discipled by someone? Be ready with a plan to help people move into those roles (see Appendices D and E).

III. Prompt Individuals

Pastor, take the initiative to prompt people personally. Push deacons to lead the way, prompt friends to get on board, tell new believers that this is normal, and emphasize this expectation to all new members. Personally take Scripture to people with an expectation that they will obey and, as they grow, that they will develop the desire and ability to "disciple others also" (see 2 Tim. 2:2).

IV. Personalize Your Discipleship Plan

A. Because of your position as pastor, and because you are personally exhorting and discipling individuals, you will need to be accountable and obedient to a greater degree than the average church member.

B. As a pastor, you should be seeking always to be discipling a new believer, a "level 2" type person or small group, and a "top end" leader or small group as well (see chart at end of this appendix). Always expect your discipled individuals to reproduce what you have given them. In other words, as you help them to move to their next spiritual level, they in turn should be discipling others.

C. You may need to start slowly, probably with only one person or group level at first, to give yourself the time to find and/or write the materials that you are going to use. I have had to adapt and prioritize my work schedule as a pastor to accomplish this. For instance, I wrote material and taught it on Sunday nights or in deacons' meetings in order to get this done. I have since used my written materials over and over in other small groups and personal discipleship relationships.

V. Plan Bigger with Synthesis

Now that you are thinking about how and what to do with individuals, you need to think about how to systematize this training throughout your current church life. Here are a few suggestions.

A. Always seek to lead leaders (or potential leaders) to lead other leaders, who themselves then lead (see chart at end of appendix) (2 Tim. 2:2). Otherwise, your sphere of influence will be very limited.

B. Commit your energies to the core ministries of discipling and shepherding. (Note: Other ministries that expand your church's influence for Christ should be left in the hands of those you have trained. Provide the most limited pastoral oversight necessary for those ministries to flourish.)

1. Systematize the shepherding processes.

- Who is keeping track of the families of the church and their spiritual and practical needs? If you as a pastor are basically doing this alone right now, form and train a godly team to work at this together.
- Assign responsibilities. For example, decide who will contact a man or woman who comes to church but does not serve and is not being trained.

2. Systematize the training processes. Publish a plan, no matter how simple, and put it in front of your people as you preach, to cast vision for discipleship training and to make applications effectively.

VI. Protect Your Disciples

A. Plan how, when, and in what instructive setting your people will be taught each of the following:

- The ten areas of theology (shown here alphabetically): Angelology (study of angelic beings), Anthropology (study of man), Bibliology (study of Scripture), Christology (study of Christ), Ecclesiology (study of the church), Eschatology (study of things to come), Hamartiology (study of sin), Pneumatology (study of the Holy

Spirit), Soteriology (study of salvation), and Theology Proper (study of God)

- Core spiritual disciplines
- Relationship building
- Practical living applications
- Ministry skills

B. Plan to hold leaders accountable and teach them how to hold others accountable.

C. Practice biblical church discipline (restoration).

D. Teach people how to build relationships through discipleship (see Appendix E).

VII. Additional Ways to Lead Leaders[2]

A. Affirm and compliment people (especially leaders or potential leaders) when you see growth and faithfulness, even just in small ways.

B. Train people to do what you ask them to do by providing positive accountability and consistent helpful feedback.

C. Emphasize that every setting is sacred and offers opportunities to minister for Christ. Help people learn how to find a place that fits their skills, and teach them how to minister in their settings (including home, work, school, and church).

D. Expect excellence, and set people up to succeed. Don't just assign tasks or positions and leave people to figure it out on their own.

E. Plan before an event, and evaluate afterward.

F. Allow time for people to make new ideas theirs.

Spiritual Development Strategy
People and Ministry / Training Overview

A leader is a worker, and a trainer is both a worker and a leader.

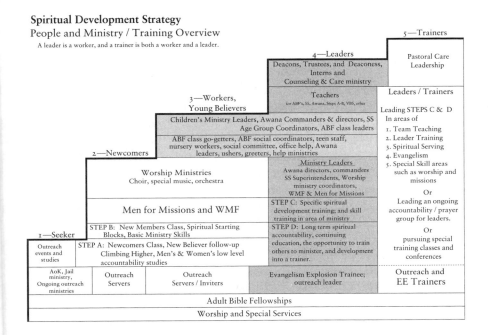

ADDITIONAL RESOURCES FOR CHURCH LEADER DEVELOPMENT

BCM Seminar *Pastor's Toolbox: Developing Leaders in Your Church.* Click on the "Resources" tab at www.bcmin.org. Phone: 715–423–7190 weekdays 9–12 and 1–4.

Biblical Counseling Training Conference, Faith Baptist Church, Lafayette, IN, www.fbcmlafayette.org

Bixby, Dr. Howard, ChristWay Ministries: Website: www.christwayministries.us/ E-mail: hlbixby@comcast.net.

Alan Nelson, *Me to We: A Pastor's Discovery of The Power of Partnership* (Loveland, CO: Group, 2007)

Mark Shaw, *Strength in Numbers: The Team Approach to Biblical Counseling* (Bemidji, MN: Focus, 2010). See his blog www.histruthinlove.org.

Appendix D

Notes

1 "One another" passages include (1) Love one another (John 15:12, 17; 1 Thes. 3:12; 1 John 3:11); (2) Be kind to one another (Rom. 12:10a; Eph. 4:32); (3) In honor give preference to one another (Rom. 12:10b; Phil. 2:3); (4) Be like-minded (of the same mind) toward one another (Rom. 12:16; 15:5–6); (5) Do not judge one another (Rom. 14:13); (6) Edify one another (Rom. 14:19); (7) Receive one another (Rom. 15:7); (8) Admonish one another (Rom. 15:14); (9) Minister to one another materially (Rom. 15:27); (10) Greet one another (Rom. 16:16); (11) Wait for one another (1 Cor. 11:33); (12) Have the same care for one another (1 Cor. 12:25); (13) Serve one another in love (Gal. 5:13); (14) Beware lest you be consumed by one another (Gal. 5:15); (15) Do not provoke or envy one another (Gal. 5:26); (16) Bear one another's burdens (Gal. 6:2); (17) Bear with (forbear) one another in love (Eph. 4:2; Col. 3:13); (18) Forgive one another (Eph. 4:32); (19) Submit to one another (Eph. 5:21; 1 Peter 5:5); (20) Do not lie to one another (Col. 3:9); (21) Comfort one another (1 Thes. 4:18; 5:11); (22) Consider one another (Heb. 10:24); (23) Do not speak evil of one another (James 4:11); (24) Do not grumble against one another (James 5:9); (25) Confess to one another (James 5:16); (26) Pray for one another (James 5:16); (27) Be hospitable to one another (1 Peter 4:9).

2 Section VII was adapted from **Alan Nelson,** *Me to We: A Pastor's Discovery of The Power of Partnership* (Loveland, CO: Group, 2007), 144–168.

Appendix E. The Disciple-Maker's Task: Building Christ-Centered Relationships

Contributed by Pastor Jonathan Jenks

I. The Key to Your Christian Walk

A. Build your personal relationship with our God and Savior Jesus Christ (Matt. 22:37–38). Evaluate yourself in the following areas and seek accountability when needed:

- Scripture reading and memorization
- Prayer
- Struggles and victories over sin
- Service to those at home, church, and work

B. Build godly relationships with one another (Matt. 22:39).

- Use the points from **A** (above) with another person. Ask these questions of one another.
- See point **III** below for the ingredients of relationship. Seek to build a discipleship relationship by weighing these ingredients and keeping them in an appropriate balance.

C. Learn to follow the "one another" commands in Scripture, with accountability to one another (see note in Appendix D).

II. Identifying the Absence of Relationship Skills

A. Spend some time observing relationships around you and in your life. How spiritually deep and resilient are those relationships?

B. Ask people, "How do you build a relationship?" You will probably find much silence and some stuttering. Relationship-building skills are mostly caught from parents and mentoring relationships. Most people come from relationally starved homes where they have been offered little or no mentoring. Therefore, they have no basis for knowing what good biblical relationships look like or how to develop them.

C. Be prepared to help people to develop better relationship skills.

III. Five Key Ingredients for Building Relationships

The more prominently these ingredients are present in both parties, based upon sincere belief in the true gospel of Jesus Christ and the Scriptures, the stronger the human relationship will be. Evaluate how these ingredients are manifested in a given relationship to determine where repentance, exhortation, or teaching may be needed. Examples here refer to you and a disciple, but this model can be used to evaluate any relationship.

A. SHARED VALUES

People in growing relationships have a set of values that they continually rehearse or "share" with one another. Even an evil gang can have close relationships because they share evil values (however, when the sharing is based upon error, it eventually ruins the relationship). People in relationship must continue to speak their affirmation of the other when they agree. Matthew, Mark, Luke, and John all record Jesus repeatedly speaking the truth that binds us together, beginning with the gospel. The following questions are based upon Scripture passages that demonstrate the importance of shared biblical values. Asking these questions will help you to recognize the extent of your shared values and where you should work at development.

- To what extent do you and your disciple share moral character and moral values, such as views regarding anger and lustful thoughts (Matt. 5:21–30)? To what extent does each of you minimize sin?
- What are your positions on law vs. grace (Exod. 20:1–17)? Are you

both believers in the true gospel of Jesus Christ? To what extent does each of you understand grace? To what extent do you and your disciple live as if you are still under the law (Gal. 2:20–21)?

- In what ways do you each tend to be led or influenced by the flesh rather than the Holy Spirit (Gal. 5:16–25) (e.g., when do you become sinfully angry, fearful, discouraged, or depressed)? To what extent does each of you live according to fleshly wisdom, heeding earthly philosophies rather than following Christ (Col. 2:8) (e.g., what confuses or distracts you)? What evidence is there of spiritual hunger and thirst for God (Matt. 5:6) (e.g., what excites or motivates you)?

B. TRUST

Out of the power and gift of the gospel in our lives, we sinners choose to trust other sinners. Trust is given as a part of loving one another, in line with 1 Corinthians 13 (love hopes and believes all things). God, as our authority, recognizes the dangers inherent in trusting people, and He protects us via the use of human authorities such as government, church, and family. These human authorities limit the trust that can be extended to those who are living in open evil.

Forgiveness gives us a starting place to nurture trust. The more that trust is valued and kept by both parties, the deeper the relationship can go. Again, the Gospels reveal Jesus teaching and living this out (e.g., John 3:16).

- How strongly does each of you trust in God for salvation, provision, protection, sanctification, guidance, and wisdom (John 3:16)?
- To what extent does each of you manifest trustworthy character in thought, speech, action, and motivation according to the biblical standards of love for God and neighbor (1 Cor. 13; Matt. 22:37–39)? Specifically, how are you living this out in your everyday lives? In what ways are you seeking to grow?

C. UNDERSTANDING EACH OTHER

Jesus perfectly understood those around Him, and on that basis He could relate to them, care for them, correct them, and serve them well. The command to understand is given to husbands in 1 Peter 3:7, but it extends to every relationship. God expects us to learn the relevant facts and their impact upon the other person in the relationship. Therefore, it is important not to assume what someone thinks, or to judge a person by his or her actions alone. The leader who wants to understand others will ask people what they mean, what they love, and what they intend, and then will trust their answers and live accordingly.

- To what extent does each of you know and follow God (Luke 9:23–24; 2 Peter 1:3–9)?
- To what extent does each of you seek to emulate the mind of Christ (Phil. 2:5)?
- To what extent does each of you seek to know the other well? To know your spouses well (1 Peter 3:7–9)?
- In what ways do you struggle with a decision you need to make or with a recent puzzling event? Discuss your dilemma. Practice asking the following questions: (a) What do you mean (clarify statements or words)? (b) What do you love or desire? What would you like to see happen? (c) What do you intend when you say/do that?

D. GIVING TO/SERVING EACH OTHER

Jesus taught us to serve. He served while on earth, and He continues to give to us constantly today. We are commanded to follow His example, which means we must give and be willing to receive. The more this takes place between people, the deeper the relationship becomes. The relationship is stunted unless both parties are giving and receiving.

- In what ways does each of you serve God sincerely (2 Cor. 2:17)?
- In what ways does each of you willingly serve others with humility (John 13:3–7)?

- In what ways does each of you treat others kindly and tenderly under persecution, as God has done through Christ (Eph. 4:32)?
- What qualities of love, if any, are demonstrated toward others, especially during conflict or hardship (Rom. 12:7–15)?

E. PEACEMAKING: PRACTICING A BIBLICAL PLAN DURING CONFLICT

In the Gospels, Jesus taught us the basic peacemaking skills: trusting and glorifying the sovereign God (Prov. 3:5–6; Eph. 1:12); removing the log from our own eye before trying to remove the splinter from someone else's eye (Matt. 7:3–5); and following a biblical restorative plan that appropriately involves the church (Matt. 18:15–17).

- Do you both know how to solve conflict biblically?
- In what ways does the example of Christ's forgiveness govern the responses of you and your disciple when someone has wronged you (Eph. 4:30–32)?
- To what extent does each of you understand and submit to the principles of restoration through church discipline (Matt. 18:15–17)?
- When you sin, in what ways does each of you manifest humble confession and repentance toward God and toward those you have offended (Matt. 5:23–24; 1 John 1:8–10; 2 Cor. 7:9–11)?
- To what extent, and in what manner, does each of you forgive others (Matt. 18:21–35)?

IV. The Necessity of Modeling

A. Modeling must be built into your spiritual development plan.

- Demonstrate your commitment to God and to the relationship by being considerate. Prioritize discipleship, be on time, follow through with promises, solve conflicts biblically, serve others, remember prayer requests, etc.
- Personally challenge yourself to grow in spiritual disciplines,

discipleship efforts, and serving in ministry. Share your journey. What is God doing in your life?

B. Accountability must be fostered in every step of your plan.

- Ask others to keep you accountable in various ways (e.g., Internet guards, phone calls, permission to ask you questions about what you are reading, doing, memorizing, and how you are spending your time, growing in your marriage, etc.).
- Ask your disciples how they are progressing spiritually in their homes, churches, and work settings. Follow up with prayer, questions, care, and exhortation when concerns are made known.
- Challenge your disciples with scenarios that will prompt them to locate and apply biblical principles.

C. Teach and model the skill of asking heart-probing questions. Use these principles in many settings. For example, speak these questions and principles from the pulpit, when teaching classes, and during one-on-one discipleship.

I. Move superficial conversations or topics to spiritual depth by asking questions such as the following:

- "What does God think about that?"
- "What did you hope to accomplish when you said/did that?"
- "How did that action or thought impact your walk with Christ and your relationships with others?"
- "What is your goal? What do you live for, and how is that showing up in your life?"
- "Where do you find support for that perspective in Scripture? Show me how Scripture addresses that action or thought."
- "How does your response reflect a Christ–church relationship with your spouse?"
- "In what ways is the gospel driving your life right now?"

2. Increase the substance and focus of prayer by praying Scripture together. For example, pray Colossians 1:9–12 and Ephesians 1:15–21.

3. Teach people to think bigger than the task at hand, to connect their everyday lives to a vibrant walk with Christ and meaningful ministry goals (Eph. 3:8–21). For example, accomplish tasks such as roofing a house or washing a car with the purpose of talking to fellow workers about Christ, demonstrating His character, sharing His perspectives from Scripture, and challenging others to follow Him. Provide proactive ideas for walking with Christ in their circumstances to accomplish spiritual goals using their particular gifts and abilities.

4. Faithfully press on, even during difficulty, and encourage others to do the same, for the glory of God (Phil. 3:7–14).

5. Walk wisely alongside those who are struggling, and help them to trust God and bring Him glory in the process (1 Cor. 5:9; Gal. 6:1–2).

Appendix F. A Checklist for Setting Up Your Ministry Model

First Step: Assess Need

I. PERSONAL ASSESSMENT

A. Am I the godly leader I should be?

- In what ways should I improve my relationship with God?
- What steps will I take to lead my home and my church more biblically?
- Whom could I ask for scriptural ideas and accountability?

B. How might I more actively and realistically disciple godly leaders in my church? (See Appendices B, C, and D.)

C. In what ways would my pastoral effectiveness be scripturally and practically enhanced if we had a biblical counselor as a resource?

- Personal growth in the Word through more study time
- Personal growth in biblical counseling and discipleship through co-counseling
- Time management through appropriate delegation of responsibilities
- Reliable help for difficult situations
- Encouragement for my family
- Cooperative relationships with like-minded pastors in the area

D. In what ways would my church's ministries be enhanced if we had a biblical counselor as a resource?

- Additional teaching resources
- Biblical counseling resources

- Women's ministry enhancement
- Friendly, collaborative relationships with like-minded churches in the area to make group outreach efforts possible

II. LEADERSHIP ASSESSMENT

What do our church leaders (church staff, deacons, teachers) think about the value of developing discipleship resources here?

A. Personal Value

Do they see the need

- For personal spiritual growth?
- To become better disciple-makers?
- To increase ministry skills?

B. Value to the Church

In what areas do they see deficits that could be answered in full or in part by the resources of a biblical counselor?

C. Value to the Community

What outreach possibilities could be started and/or enhanced through the ministries of a biblical counselor (e.g., seminars, classes, residential care, pregnancy center)?

III. CHURCH ASSESSMENT

A. Do our people recognize the need for gospel-centeredness in our marriages, parenting, work ethics and relationships, service, and relationship with God?

B. Are our people interested in a biblical approach to counseling and discipleship? If so, how can we enhance training and nurture growth? If not, how can we foster biblical growth

- Through mentoring/discipleship relationships?
- Through preaching?
- Through targeted biblical training?
- Through hands-on experiences?

(See also Appendices B, C, and D.)

IV. REGIONAL ASSESSMENT

How might a biblical counselor help in our area?

A. Evaluate regional advantages and disadvantages.

B. How might counseling be extended to this community, by pastoral referral, to evangelize and to bring people into the local church?

C. Offer biblical training through seminars on topics of interest to the community

- To increase awareness of scriptural relevance and comprehensiveness
- To increase effectiveness in church discipleship

D. Make biblical consultations and resources to encourage the growth of biblical counseling available in the area.

Second Step: Organize

I. ASSEMBLE AN ADVISORY BOARD

A. Identify area pastors with similar doctrinal beliefs within a reasonable radius to optimize time and mileage.

- Contact each pastor for his assessment of need (see above).
- Once you have four or more like-minded pastors, meet as a group to discuss how you might pool resources for additional counseling and training help.

B. Designate duties:

1. Secretary to take minutes

2. Someone to draft documents

3. Someone to do clerical work:

- Mailings
- Creating brochures and other ministry information
- Preparing a logo

4. Someone to do the IT: Web-site creation and maintenance

C. Discuss when and how to bring in a resource counselor.

II. ESTABLISH THE FOUR PILLARS

Pillar 1: Doctrinal Unity

Write your doctrinal statement.

Pillar 2: Unity in Purpose and Philosophy

Together, learn more about biblical counseling (see Appendices A and B).

- Read books on biblical counseling[1]
- Attend BCM seminars and classes[2]
- Attend BCTC at Faith Baptist Church in Lafayette, Indiana[3]
- Attend classes online or at reputable Bible colleges or seminaries

Pillar 3: Commitment to Method

A. Develop a vision/mission statement.

B. Work out the division of labor among home and host churches, including volunteers who will take care of ministry tasks at each church.

C. Choose your board of directors.

D. Complete your incorporation papers:

- Get secure help from a knowledgeable attorney.
- Write and file your articles of incorporation with your state government. (Your board of directors must be named in that document.)
- Once the articles are filed, you will receive your filing number and a list of other paperwork that must be submitted. Keep that list and carefully file every required document.
- Write your bylaws, with the help of your attorney.

E. Trouble-shooting: anticipate problem situations and think through procedures.

F. Complete your policies and organizational manuals.

Pillar 4: Sharing Ministry Needs
A. Finances

1. Write a budget, estimating both income and expenditures.
2. Choose a treasurer.

(a) Set up your accounting software and procedures. Consult an experienced accountant for help to set up your books correctly if your treasurer is not able to do so.

(b) Obtain a checking account/savings account/credit card in a bank with branches in the cities in which your ministry operates, so your financial secretary can make deposits and your treasurer can do disbursements conveniently.

(c) Create a voucher system so each person knows what has been done, when, by whom, where, and why. Keep vouchers up-to-date, accurate, and thorough.

(d) Set up a system to move deposit slips, bank statements, etc., from the ministry's financial secretary into the hands of your treasurer regularly.

(e) Arrange to have your books audited annually.

(f) Keep up with federal and state requirements for nonprofit reporting.

3. Purchase insurance.
4. Raise support.

(a) Donations: How much will each home/host/helper church donate, and when?

(b) Counseling:
- Will you charge for counseling? If so, how much?
- What discounts, if any, will apply to home/host church referrals?
- How will you handle counselees who are unable to pay?

(c) Training events:
- Will you charge for classes? If so, how much?
- Will you provide discounts for your home/host church students?

(d) Resources:
- Will you sell books and other resources? How and where?
- Look into licensing and tax requirements in your state.
- Consider personnel hours and space needs.

(e) Grants and endowments:
- Who will research and write grants?
- Who will seek endowments and how will you find sources?

(f) Fundraisers:
- Will you have fundraisers?
- If so, who, how, where, and when will you run them?

B. Introducing the Ministry

1. Literature:

(a) Design a logo and use it in your correspondence and on all your literature.

(b) Develop brochure(s) and business cards.

2. Prepare an introductory PowerPoint presentation.

3. Pastors in home and host churches should:

(a) Keep the church family aware of the preparation process.

(b) Point out the need for biblical counseling resources.

(c) Provide general leadership training in discipleship.

(d) Deliberately disciple key church leaders, especially deacons.

- Discuss ministry possibilities and plans in deacons' meetings. Be prepared to answer questions and concerns about ministry development and the church's involvement.
- Have the resource counselor and a board representative come to a deacons' meeting to introduce the ministry and answer questions.

4. Home and host churches at large should:

(a) Host a seminar or class to introduce biblical counseling to awaken interest and understanding.

(b) Teach a series featuring the fundamentals of biblical counseling.

(c) Have the resource counselor bring a presentation to introduce the ministry and get to know people.

C. Community Outreach

1. Mail introductory letters and brochures to area churches and Christian-owned businesses.

2. Invite area churches to seminars and classes.

3. Get board members to call colleagues:

- Introduce the ministry and answer questions.
- Encourage consultations and referrals.
- Encourage attendance at seminars and classes.

Third Step: Prepare for Your Counselor

I. CHOOSE A COUNSELOR

A. Appoint a search-and-interview committee.

1. Prepare paperwork: application, interview questions.

2. Release notices of job openings and deadlines to seminaries, ACBC, and other reliable sources of qualified biblical counselors.

3. With your attorney, write contracts or hiring agreements, if desired.

B. Receive and review applications/résumés.

C. Screen candidates for:

- Educational qualifications
- Personal qualifications

D. Conduct interviews in line with board policy.

E. Bring recommendations to the board for vote.

II. PREPARE TO RECEIVE THE RESOURCE COUNSELOR

A. Temporary arrangements:

1. Set up a temporary church staff position until the ministry opens its doors.

2. Arrange for finances.

3. Provide for housing, if necessary.

4. Help with supplementary income or interviews for jobs.

B. Provide keys as necessary.

C. Prepare the buildings.

1. Set up administrative office space at the home church:

- Furnishings: desk (with room for computer and printer), chair, phone and phone book, file cabinets, book case, appropriate storage space
- Office supplies: appropriate lighting, stapler, tape dispenser, pens, etc.
- Counseling space: table and chairs, door with a window, phone access, waiting area (if possible).

2. Set up counseling rooms:

- Uncluttered and clean
- Table and chairs (adult size)
- Phone access
- Door with a window
- Reasonably soundproof
- Comfortable temperature
- Accessibility outside church hours

D. Training needs. Provide or arrange for:

1. Appropriate classroom space for training events

2. Whiteboards and markers.

3. Technological needs, including computers, PowerPoint, pointers, etc.

4. Refreshments: coffeemaker, water, etc.

5. Teaching materials, including textbooks

6. Instruction for staff in how to handle registrations and run off materials

E. Resource needs:

- Provide bookshelves for resources, including textbooks and counseling materials.
- Inform your staff about materials to order and book table needs at seminars.

F. Technological needs:
- Set up an informative, user-friendly Web site with contact information.
- Arrange for audio and video help as needed.
- Provide computer and printer for the counselor, if needed.
- Clarify expectations for copier use.
- Provide for the printing of brochures and other ministry literature.

Fourth Step: Equip Your Counselor

The following checklist will help your biblical counselor to function well in his or her administrative and relational roles.

I. COMMUNICATION

A. Ensure regular contact with pastors at home and host sites.

B. Visit churches regularly.

C. Coordinate and communicate your schedule.

D. Arrange for mailboxes, e-mail, voice mail, and phones.

E. Schedule around church activities.

F. Written communication:

1. Write monthly newsletters or e-newsletters.
- Arrange to keep mail and e-mail distribution lists up-to-date.
- Arrange for regular distribution of the newsletter or e-newsletter.

2. Write reports to the ministry board and home office deacons.

3. Develop and maintain promotional materials.

4. Communicate with students.

G. Develop a conflict-resolution plan.

II. COUNSELING

A. Set up your procedure for referrals
- In core churches
- Outside core churches

B. Implement your payment procedures and accountability for funds.

C. Set up procedure and personnel availability for co-counseling.

D. Develop a plan to work with church disciple-makers.

E. Implement counseling supervision.

F. Continue your skill development.

III. TRAINING CENTER

A. Plan seminars and conferences.

B. Develop class curriculum.

C. Choose instructors.

D. Engage students.

E. Follow up with students.

F. Keep accurate student records.

G. Offer student counseling observation opportunities.

IV. RESOURCE CENTER

A. Make recommendations for church resource libraries.

B. Develop relationships with area Christian bookstores.

C. Plan for purchase, storage, and check-out of textbooks and counseling resources.

V. ADMINISTRATION AND OFFICE

A. Train church office staff in each building.

B. Keep accurate job-related personal records.

- Scheduling
- Hours
- Vacation/personal days
- Mileage
- Counselor skill maintenance and development
- Speaking schedule and topics

C. Communicate, communicate, communicate!

VI. FINALLY

- Stay true to Scripture.
- Pray for one another.
- Work as a team.
- Deal biblically with conflicts as they arise.

- Rejoice in what God does through you!

Notes

1 See our recommended reading list in Appendix H.
2 Click on the "Training" tab at www.bcmin.org or call BCM at 715-423-7190.
3 www.fbcmlafayette.org.

Appendix G. An Outline of Information to Include in Your Incorporation Papers

Articles of Incorporation

Article 1:   Name
Article 2:   Organization
Article 3:   Initial Registered Agent
Article 4:   Street Address
Article 5:   Mailing Address
Article 6:   Members and Election
Article 7:   Directors
Article 8:   Purpose
Article 9:   Earnings
Article 10:   Limitations of Activities
Article 11:   Non-discrimination
Article 12:   Dissolution
Article 13:   Activities
Article 14:   Incorporator

Bylaws

Article I: Description
                Section 1: Mission
                Section 2: Philosophy
Article II: Board of Directors
                Section 1: General Powers and Functions
                Section 2: Number and Tenure

Policies

Preamble

I. General

II.   Standards of Employment
    A. Qualifications, General
    B. Counselor Qualifications
    C. Executive Director Qualifications
    D. Application
    E. Job Description
    F. First Day
    G. Reference Check
    H. Irregular Duties
    I. Initiative
    J. Status Changes
    K. Annual Tax Forms
    L. Personnel File

III.   Counseling Relationship
    A. Primary Goal
    B. Standard of Conduct
    C. Explanations to Counselee
    D. Required Forms
    E. Counselor Forms
    F. Objectivity
    G. Inadvisable Counseling Relationships
    H. Gender Considerations
    I. Procedure in Dangerous Situations
    J. Crime
    K. Abuse or Neglect

IV.   Consultation and Confidentiality
    A. Protecting Confidences
    B. Recommendation for Referral
    C. Unrepented Sin
    D. Overhearing
    E. Legal Advice

F. Group Counseling

G. Record-keeping

V. Financial Policy

    A. Nonprofit Organization

    B. Fee Arrangements

    C. Contracts and Indebtedness

    D. Checks

    E. Deposits

    F. Fundraising

    G. Donations

    H. Personal Possessions

    I. Resource Center Sales

    J. Monetary Gifts

    K. Revenue and Rights for Books/Materials Produced

VI. Communication

    A. Questions

    B. Calendar of Events

    C. Telephone Etiquette

    D. Inter-office Communications

    E. Mail

    F. Emergencies

    G. Scheduling

    H. Receiving Counselees

VII. Personnel and Discipline

    A. Hiring and Dismissal

      1. Executive Director

      2. Other Personnel

    B. Interviews

    C. Standards for Personal Conduct

      1. Unto the Lord

      2. Dress

3. Solicitations
4. Purchases

D. Salaries, Benefits, and Raises
E. Hourly Employees
F. Full-time Counselor Hours
G. Expenses
H. Vacation, Hourly Employees
I. Vacation, Salaried Employees
J. Vacation Year
K. Extended Leave
L. Sick Days
M. Deaths
N. Jury Duty
O. Contribution to BCM Mission
P. Reporting Damaging or Disruptive Conditions
Q. Evaluations
R. Goals and Program Reporting
S. Rescheduling Sessions
T. Holidays
U. Pre-excused Absence or Tardiness
V. Un-excused Absence or Tardiness
W. Discipline
X. Termination of Employment
  1. Cause for Termination
  2. Code of Discipline
  3. Termination

Doctrinal Statement
The Scriptures
The True God
The Deity of Christ

The Holy Spirit
The Creation
The Devil or Satan
The Fall of Man
Salvation by Grace
Sanctification
Baptism and the Lord's Supper
The Church
Civil Government
The Second Coming of Christ

Organizational Manual

I.   Description
II.   Reasoning
        A. Legal Considerations
        B. Local-Church Involvement
        C. Financial support
        D. Ministry Considerations
III.   BCM Home Church, Host Churches, and Helpers
        A. Home Church
           Clerical Support
        B. Host Churches
           1. Training Center
           2. Resource Center
           3. Support Center
        C. Fewer Than Three Qualified Host Churches
        D. BCM Helper
IV.   Compensation for Counseling
        A. Pastoral Referral
        B. Host and Helper Churches
        C. Referring Churches

D. Mileage
V. Duration of Counseling
VI. BCM Seminars
VII. BCM Training Classes
VIII. Resource Center and Bookstore
IX. Counseling
    A. Pastoral Referral
    B. Fee
    C. Adjustment of Fee
    D. Training of Referring Church Leaders
X. Fundraising
XI. Relationship of the Counselor to the Church
XII. Relationship of BCM to the Church
XIII. Financial Accountability
XIV. Financial Responsibilities of the Host Churches
XV. Continuing Education and Skills Development

Job Description: Executive Director

I. Position Title
II. Qualifications
III. Line of Responsibility
IV. Relationship to the Churches
V. Duties and Responsibilities
    A. ACBC Certification
    B. Counseling
    C. Teaching
    D. Administration
    E. Writing and Research
    F. Work Schedule
    G. Seminars
VI. Salary and Benefits

Appendix G

Terms of Counseling[1]

Annual Agreement

Budget

Note

1 See Appendix I "Counseling Forms" for terms of counseling, annual agreement, and budget forms.

Appendix H. Further Resources

Other worthy titles may be found at the "Resources" tab at our Web site, www.bcmin.org. Our recommended resources list is updated periodically and may be printed out for your personal use.

Books

Adams, Jay E., *The Biblical View of Self-Esteem, Self-Love, and Self-Image* (Eugene, OR: Harvest House, 1986). A biblical examination of the rise of the self-esteem movement and its effect on self-image in our society and our churches. Useful for counselors.

——*The Christian Counselor's Casebook: Applying the Principles of Nouthetic Counseling* (Grand Rapids, MI: Zondervan, 1974). Presents a variety of counseling scenarios and questions to stimulate thought. Useful for development of discipleship skills.

——*The Christian Counselor's Manual: The Practice of Nouthetic Counseling* (Grand Rapids, MI: Zondervan, 1986). The sequel to *Competent to Counsel* (see below), this volume biblically addresses specific issues often faced by counselors. One of the first books to promote the growth of practical skills in the discipline of biblical counseling. Useful for counselors.

——*Competent to Counsel: Introduction to Nouthetic Counseling* (Grand Rapids, MI: Zondervan, 1970). This early classic how-to book is Dr. Adams' groundbreaker for a basic understanding of the discipline of biblical counseling. Useful for counselors.

——*Handbook of Church Discipline: A Right and Privilege of Every Church Member* (Grand Rapids, MI: Zondervan, 1986). A biblical examination of Matthew 18:15–17 and the church's responsibility for restoring wayward members. Useful for counselors.

——*Ready to Restore: The Layman's Guide to Christian Counseling* (Phillipsburg, NJ: P&R, 1981). An entry-level book, slim and concise, for those who want to offer biblical advice but don't know where to start.

——*A Theology of Christian Counseling: More Than Redemption* (Grand Rapids, MI: Zondervan, 1979). All Christians should think through the practical outworking of their beliefs. Because every person lives what he or she truly believes, a counselor always observes a counselee's theology in action. Are those beliefs in line with Scripture? This book will help counselors to discern which spiritual and behavioral issues to address.

Appendix H

Barthel, Tara, *The Peacemaking Church Women's Study: Living the Gospel in Relationships* (Billings, MT: Peacemaker Ministries, 2007). This Peacemaker series deals with the experience of conflict from a woman's perspective, using biblical principles to reconcile those involved in the conflict itself and the personal difficulties of doing so. Useful for counselor and counselee.

Berg, Jim, *Changed into His Image: God's Plan for Transforming Your Life* (Greenville, SC: Bob Jones University Press, 2000). Based upon Ephesians 4:22–24, this is an in-depth exhortation using practical "put off/renew/put on" examples to encourage biblical change. An excellent format, and memorably presented. Workbook and textbook formats are also available. Useful for counselor and counselee.

Bridges, Jerry, *Trusting God: Even When Life Hurts* (Colorado Springs: NavPress, 1988). The book and study guide present God as completely wise, fully loving, and all-powerful, and therefore worthy to be trusted with all our cares. Useful for counselees.

——**and Bevington, Bob,** *The Bookends of the Christian Life* (Wheaton, IL: Crossway, 2009). Two aspects of belief about the gospel are central to victorious living: that Christ's righteousness is sufficient to save (utter dependence), and that the power of the Holy Spirit is sufficient to guide and keep us (Christian responsibility). If the human life is a set of books, both bookends are necessary for stability. Useful for counselees.

Broger, John C., *Self-Confrontation: A Manual for In-Depth Discipleship* (Nashville: Thomas Nelson, 1994). A Scripture-packed presentation of the elements of biblical discipleship, covering many issues and providing a wealth of helpful tools. Useful for developing biblically directed counselors.

Custis James, Carolyn, *When Life and Beliefs Collide: How Knowing God Makes a Difference* (Grand Rapids, MI: Zondervan, 2001). An engaging walk alongside Mary of Bethany to exhort women to move from emotionalism to sound theological belief in Christ, who sustains the soul during trials. Useful for counselors and counselees.

Fitzpatrick, Elyse, *Overcoming Fear, Worry, and Anxiety* (Eugene, OR: Harvest House, 2001). An extremely effective examination of the heart issues that fuel fear, and God's hope-filled solution. Useful for counselees.

——**and Cornish, Carol,** *Women Helping Women: A Biblical Guide to Major Issues Women Face* (Chicago: Harvest House, 1997). A helpful tool dealing with women's issues such as abortion, marriage to an unbeliever, learning disabilities, parenting, abuse, divorce, eating disorders, aging, and physical questions. Useful for counselors.

Ganz, Richard, *PsychoBabble: The Failure of Modern Psychology—and the Biblical Alternative* (Wheaton, IL: Crossway, 1993). A comparison of integrationism and biblical counseling. Useful for pastors and counselors.

Halla, James, *Pain: The Plight of Fallen Man: God's Prescription for the Persevering* (Stanley, NC: Timeless Texts, 2000). Hope for those who suffer from chronic pain or life-changing illness or injury. A theology of suffering—useful for counselees.

Harvey, Dave, *When Sinners Say "I Do": Discovering the Power of the Gospel for Marriage* (Wapwallopen, PA: Shepherd Press, 2007). An excellent application of the gospel in the marriage relationship. The chapter on mercy is alone worth the price of the book. Useful for counselees.

Hendrickson, Laura, M.D., and Fitzpatrick, Elyse, *Can Medicine Stop the Pain? Finding God's Healing for Depression, Anxiety, and Other Troubling Emotions* (Chicago: Moody Press, 2006). The impact of spiritual problems in physiology. Examines the appropriate use of psychotropic medications, and when they can do more harm than good. Useful for counselor and counselee.

Hindson, Ed, and Eyrich, Howard, *Totally Sufficient: The Bible and Christian Counseling* (Eugene, OR: Harvest House, 1997). The authority, relevance, and sufficiency of Scripture. Useful for counselors.

Kellemen, Robert, *Equipping Counselors for Your Church: The 4E Ministry Training Strategy* (Phillipsburg, NJ: P&R, 2011). A detailed reference book for development of discipleship ministry in a local church. Useful for pastors and counselors.

Kruis, John G., *Quick Scripture Reference for Counseling* (Grand Rapids, MI: Baker, 2000). A topical reference book of Scripture passages that address common themes faced in counseling. Useful for counselors.[1]

Levicoff, Steve, *Christian Counseling and the Law* (Chicago: Moody Press, 1991). Examines relevant legal considerations for counseling ministries. Useful for counselors.

Lloyd-Jones, Dr. Martyn, *Spiritual Depression: Its Causes and Cures* (Grand Rapids, MI: Eerdmans, 1965). A timeless look at depression and the spiritual dimensions that are keys to overcoming it. Useful for counselors and important for depressed counselees.

MacArthur, John F., Jr., and Mack, Wayne A., *Introduction to Biblical Counseling: A Basic Guide to the Principles and Practice of Counseling* (Dallas: Word, 1994). Although currently out of print, this is a classic introduction to the philosophy and form of biblical counseling. Chapter 4 should be read by every biblical counselor.

MacArthur, John, and The Master's College Faculty, *Counseling: How to Counsel Biblically* (Nashville: Thomas Nelson, 2005).[2] An updated version of *Introduction to Biblical Counseling* (see above). Learn how to structure a counseling session. Also addresses why biblical counseling is superior to psychology. Useful for counselors.

Mack, Wayne, *A Homework Manual for Biblical Living, Vol. 1: Personal and Interpersonal Problems*; and *Vol. 2: Family and Marital Problems* (Philipsburg, NJ: P&R 1979–1980). A variety of thoughtful homework assignments on many topics. Each of the volumes contains a different set of assignments. Useful for counselors.

——**and Johnston, Wayne Erick,** *A Christian Growth and discipleship Manual, Vol. 3: A Homework Manual for Biblical Living* (Bemidji, MN: Focus, 2005). A variety of thoughtful homework assignments on many topics. Useful for counselors.

McMillan, S. I., M.D., and Stern, David E., M.D., *None of These Diseases: The Bible's Health Secrets for the 21st Century* (Grand Rapids, MI: Revell, 2000). A classic enlightening discussion of physical and spiritual interconnections that demonstrate the relevance of Scripture during times of physical suffering. Useful for counselees.

Nelson, Alan, *Me to We: A Pastor's Discovery of the Power of Partnership* (Loveland, CO: Group, 2007). Today's church tends to rely upon the pastor to disciple, rather than upon the whole body of Christ. In conversational style, this book discusses how a pastor can build a team. Useful for pastors.

Newman, Jeff, *Conflict Under Control* (Schaumburg, IL: Regular Baptist Press, 2007). How to systematically seek reconciliation during times of conflict, according to the mind of Christ. A workbook useful for counselees or small-group Bible classes.

Peace, Martha, *The Excellent Wife: A Biblical Perspective* (Bemidji, MN: Focus, 1995). A classic to help wives understand and undertake their biblical roles, even in difficult marriages. Useful for counselees.

Powlison, David, *Seeing with New Eyes: Counseling and the Human Condition through the Lens of Scripture* (Phillipsburg, NJ: P&R, 2003). Learn to see Scripture more robustly and to think more biblically. This thoughtful book will help to stretch your mind and awaken your desire to drink deeply of the Living Water and to share effectively what you learn. Useful for counselors.

Priolo, Lou, *The Heart of Anger: Practical Help for the Prevention and Cure of Anger in Children* (Merrick, NY: Calvary Press, 1997). Packed with biblical information to help those ruled by anger (adults as well as children). Useful for counselees.

Pryde, Debi, *A Biblical Approach to What to do When You Are Abused by Your Husband* (Newberry Springs, CA: Iron Sharpeneth Iron, 2004). Practical and easy to read, this little book helps battered women to respond biblically in extremely difficult situations. Useful for counselees.

Sande, Ken, *The Peacemaker: A Biblical Guide to Resolving Personal Conflict* (Grand Rapids, MI: Baker, 1997). The classic volume on reconciling conflict biblically. A must for every Christian.

Scott, Stuart, *The Exemplary Husband: A Biblical Perspective* (Bemidji, MN: Focus, 2000). Strong assistance for men to become the husbands God wants them to be. Especially useful for mature counselees.

Shaw, Mark E., *Strength in Numbers: The Team Approach to Biblical Counseling* (Bemidji, MN: Focus, 2010). Another approach to building a counseling ministry, in which counselors travel from church to church. Useful for counselors and pastors.

Smith, Robert D., M.D., *The Christian Counselor's Medical Desk Reference* (Stanley, NC: Timeless Texts, 2000). A reference book helpful for developing a biblical perspective regarding specific physical and mental problems often seen in counseling sessions. Useful for counselees.

Tripp, Paul David, *Age of Opportunity: A Biblical Guide to Parenting Teens* (Phillipsburg, NJ: P&R, 1997). An excellent approach to parenting teens by reaching their hearts through the gospel. Useful for counselees.

——*Instruments in the Redeemer's Hands: People in Need of Change Helping People in Need of Change* (Phillipsburg, NJ: P&R, 2002). A well-rounded approach to biblical counseling. Required reading for most biblical counseling degrees. Highly recommended for all counselors.

——*War of Words: Getting to the Heart of Your Communication Struggles* (Philipsburg, PA: P&R, 2000). How to develop biblical communication that springs from a right heart. Useful for counselees in conflict situations, especially in marriage and family.

Tripp, Tedd, *Shepherding a Child's Heart* (Wapwallopen, PA: Shepherd Press, 1995). Biblical parenting does not simply seek to manipulate behavior, but to reach the heart of the child. Study guide available. Useful for counselees.

Vernick, Leslie, *How to Act Right When Your Spouse Acts Wrong* (Colorado Springs, CO: Waterbrook Press, 2003). Identifies the attitudes that fuel sinful responses in marriage, and offers practical ways to change biblically. Useful for counselees.

Viars, Steve, *Putting Your Past in Its Place: Moving Forward in Freedom and Forgiveness* (Eugene, OR: Harvest House, 2011). An essential read for those struggling with events of the past. Addresses four categories, how and when to forgive, and how to move on biblically. Useful for counselees.

Welch, Edward T., *Blame It on the Brain: Distinguishing Chemical Imbalances, Brain Disorders, and Disobedience* (Phillipsburg, NJ: P&R, 1998). An even-handed look at the impact of a person's spiritual life/thinking upon his or her physiology. Useful for counselors.

——*When People Are Big and God Is Small: Overcoming Peer Pressure, Codependency, and the Fear of Man* (Phillipsburg, NJ: P&R, 1997). Addresses the universal problems of peer pressure, shame, and fear of man. A must-read for any counselor. Useful for counselees, too.

Wheat, Ed, and Perkins, Gloria Okes, *Love Life for Every Married Couple: How to Fall in Love, Stay in Love, Rekindle Love* (Grand Rapids, MI: Zondervan, 1984). How to keep love alive in marriage through B.E.S.T. (Bless, Edify, Share, Touch). Excellent chapters on saving your marriage alone, based upon the book of Hosea. Useful for counselees.

Booklets

Most counselees are more likely to read a small booklet than a full-size book. Booklets suitable for counselee homework are available on a wide number of topics, including ADD, addictions, anger, depression, forgiveness, grief, marriage, miscarriage, parenting, sexual sin, shame, pain, suffering and many more.

Adams, Jay, *What Do You Do When* … A series of pamphlets regarding anger, addiction, fear, marriage, worry, and depression (Phillipsburg, NJ: P&R, 1975). Help your counselees to learn a biblical approach by giving them one of these pamphlets to think through. Packs a biblical perspective into a folded sheet of paper. Useful for counselees.

Consult the Web sites below for additional booklets on the subjects mentioned above and a growing number of others:

Christian Counseling and Education Foundation: www.ccef.org—"Resources for Personal Change" series

Day One Publications: www.dayone.co.uk—"Living in a Fallen World" series

Faith Resources: www.frlafayette.org—"The Biblical Counselor's Toolbox" series

Focus Publishing: www.focuspublishing.com—"Hope & Help Through Biblical Counseling" series

P&R Publishing: www.prpbooks.com—"Resources for Biblical Living" series

Shepherd Press: www.shepherdpress.com "Lifeline"series

Timeless Christian Books (formerly Timeless Texts): www.timelesschristianbooks.com— distributor of the Jay Adams booklets mentioned above

Workbooks and Other Resources

The following series of three books by **Paul David Tripp and Timothy S. Lane** is produced by the Christian Counseling & Educational Foundation. Each book comprises twelve lessons and equips people in local churches to help others. Easy to understand and apply, they are useful for discipleship development. DVDs are now available, but the lessons may be taught without the DVD sets. We have also listed Garrett

Higbee's excellent *Soul Care* DVD series for discipleship development in the local church. A study guide is available.

How People Change (Winston-Salem, NC: Punch Press for the, 2005)

Helping Others Change (Winston-Salem, NC: Punch Press, 2005)

Change and Your Relationships (Greensboro, NC: New Growth Press, 2009)

Biblical Soul Care for The Local Church produced by Twelve Stones Ministries and Harvest Bible Chapel (see www.biblicalsoulcare.com). A DVD series teaching the foundations of biblical discipleship in the church. Includes reproducible study notes. Study guide available.

Notes

1 Also available are *Quick Scripture Reference for Counseling Women* (Grand Rapids, MI: Baker, 2002) and *Quick Scripture Reference for Counseling Youth* (Grand Rapids, MI: Baker, 2006).

2 Formerly *Introduction to Biblical Counseling* by **John MacArthur and Wayne Mack**.

Appendix I. Helpful Forms for Ministry Use

We share the following forms as examples, not to serve as legal advice. Biblical Counseling Ministries assumes no responsibility for the use or adaptation of these forms. We encourage you to receive competent legal counsel to determine if these forms comply with the laws that apply to you.

For a Personal Data Inventory form (PDI) that may be adapted to meet your needs, consult the appendices in *Competent to Counsel: Introduction to Nouthetic Counseling* by **Jay Adams** (Grand Rapids, MI: Zondervan, 1970), 171–174.

BCM organizational documents are available only by application and approval of the BCM board of directors. Some restrictions apply. Call our home office (715–423–7190 weekdays 9–12 and 1–4) or email BCM at info@bcmin.org for more information.

These forms in this appendix may be reproduced by the owner of this book for his or her use in good faith in a biblical counseling ministry. They are also available for download and modification from www.bcmin.org.

HOME OFFICE PROCEDURES

A. Contact information (list counselor and appropriate liaison board members contact information):

B. Keep the counselor's schedule so you can contact him/her when needed.

1. New Counselees and Appointments
   a. *New Counselees.* Counseling is available by pastoral referral only. When a pastor wants to make a referral, he will call the home office (you). Mail him the referral packet, which includes a PDI form, a payment form, our brochures, and a cover letter.

   When the PDI is completed, it will be returned to you. It contains confidential information. Please keep it in a secure spot and give it to the counselor as soon as possible. The counselor will process the information, make the file, and provide you with counselee data to enter into ServantKeeper. The counselor will also give you some appointment dates and times so you can call to arrange for the first counseling session if the counselee does not contact you in a few days.

   b. *Counseling appointment* times will usually be set by the counselor at the end of a given session, but occasionally a counselee will call to set up a session time. The counselor will give you an updated schedule once per week, usually on (day) _____ morning, or via an electronic calendar (calendar site and password: _____). When someone calls for an appointment, <u>first look at that schedule</u> and find out what dates/times would work for the session. Then <u>confirm with the counselor the best date/time</u> and finalize with the counselee.

   c. When a counselee arrives, they usually go right into session. However, if they come into the office, just ask them to wait in the _____ room, and then notify the counselor that they have arrived.

C. Financial Secretary: Enter payments and make bank deposits. When at the home church (usually two to three times per week), the counselor will give you the money collected from sessions and classes, along with payment vouchers or registration forms. Keep in a secure place until ready to deposit. Keep the ministry credit card in a safe place and allow only authorized users access to it.

   All cash and checks are deposited at _____ Bank.
   Account numbers: _____

   1. Enter counseling payments into ServantKeeper. Mark the counseling voucher to signify that you have entered it into ServantKeeper. File vouchers.
   2. Enter support checks into ServantKeeper.
   3. Update any address/phone info.
   4. Prepare and mail invoices to churches who pay for sessions and request monthly invoicing. Use only counselee numbers, not names. Send one copy to the church and keep one with counseling vouchers.
   5. When the checks are received, enter into ServantKeeper, deposit money, and file

vouchers.

<u>Fill out deposit form,</u> numbering sequentially. Note donations from individuals, counseling money, support from churches, class or seminar money.

<u>Make the deposit.</u> Staple the bank receipt to your copy of the deposit form. Make a copy to file with vouchers, then give the originals to the ministry's treasurer.

6.   Send out year-end financial statements,

   a.   Fill out a yellow donation voucher if something other than money is donated (e.g.books). Make a copy for the person donating.

   b.   The first or second week of January each year, do a contribution statement for each church, plus each person who made a tax-deductible contribution.

D. Classes

Held throughout the year at _____. You aren't responsible for classes, but you will probably get questions. Consult the master class schedule and/or class registration forms provided by your counselor. _____ Church (training center) is responsible for mailings, registrations, books distributed to students at their church, and running off class materials. Refer questions to: _____.

E. Resources

Ministry brochures, booklets, library, and textbooks are located at _____, our resource center. Contact information:

F. Seminars

   1.   Keep registration information current. Registrations will come in by mail and online.

   2.   Advertising: Mail seminar information to:

   3.   Prepare and man registration tables.

   4.   Prepare seminar handbooks.

   5.   Organize additional staff, as needed, and supply staff nametags

   6.   Prepare and put up signs indicating where to register, etc.

   7.   On the day of the seminar, keep a count of individuals and churches represented.

G. General

   1.   *Filing*

Insurance papers, referral packets, pastor packets and other documents are kept by the church office. Keep several copies of PDI packets in folder at all times. Assemble new packets as needed. Lock up all confidential information and valuables.

   2.   *Mailing*

Mail pastor referral packets (intake forms), invoices, year-end financial statements and seminar advertising letters as needed. Keep address list up to date.

Home Office Procedures, page 2

RESOURCE CENTER PROCEDURES

A. Book Table
    1. Inform book store owner of upcoming events where we would like to sell their books.
    2. Provide a list of books requested, per counselor's suggestions.
    3. Arrange for book table personnel at the event, as needed.
    4. Make arrangements to pick up and return books to book store.
    5. Keep records of sales as provided by book store.

B. Class Textbooks
    1. If you have not been given a copy of the master class schedule and textbook list for each class that will be offered, please ask.
    2. Order textbooks for classes as requested.
    3. Watch for sales of textbooks normally used for classes and contact _____ for permission to order if request has not already been made.
    4. Maintain inventory.

C. Booklets and Brochures for Counseling
    1. Provide written documentation of booklet inventory.
    2. Order as requested.
    3. Store any unused stock and make available to counselor.

D. Other
    1. Maintain the recommended reading list by adding titles supplied by the counselor.
    2. Keep a list of books in the ministry's library.
    3. Make copies as requested.
    4. Keep inventory records up to date. Maintain the resource sign-out sheet as needed. Check with the training center periodically to verify inventory they may have on hand.

RESOURCE CENTER BOOK SIGN-OUT SHEET
(Ministry Name)_____

BOOKS MAY BE SIGNED OUT BY AUTHORIZED PERSONS ONLY.
Please check in the office for assistance.

Date	Qty OUT	Qty IN	Title	Person Taking Book, and Phone Number	To What Location	Reason

TRAINING CENTER PROCEDURES

Contact information:

A. Class Schedule and Textbooks
(Instructor: Give the training center a master schedule of classes and textbooks for each class. Confirm dates before finalizing the master schedule.)
  1. You are responsible for mailings, registrations, some book distribution to students, and running off class materials including posters and registration forms.
  2. Contact the Resource Center to be sure we have textbooks in stock. Contact information:

B. Class registrations
  1. Record student information for each class. Include name, address, church, email and phone, class, and payment. Supply this information to class instructor(s) before classes commence.
  2. Send checks to home office.
  3. Run student handbooks.

C. Seminars
  1. You are responsible for seminar mailings, and for running off brochures and designated handbooks.
  2. You are not responsible to record seminar registrations. Send seminar registrations to home office. Contact information:

D. General
  The training center provides a place for classes and for counseling. Please have tables and chairs set up for classes. If possible, beverages such as coffee or tea and water should be available for students.

HOURS TALLY SHEET for (Employee)_____

Month_____, 20___.

20___	DAILY TALLY					TOTALS		
DATE	Counsel	Admin	Training	Other Driving	Misc	Day	Week	Home Hours
1								
2								
3								
4								
5								
6								
7								
8								
9								
10								
11								
12								
13								
14								
15								
16								
17								
18								
19								
20								
21								
22								
23								
24								
25								
26								
27								
28								
29								
30								
31								
Totals								

Appointments:	Vacation/Personal Days:
Workdays This Month:	Hours Per Workday:

ANNUAL BREAKDOWN OF HOURS

Employee: _____ Year: _____

Month	Counsel Session Hours	Number of Appoint-ments	Admin-istrative	Training Teaching, Prep for Classes, Seminars, Curriculum Prep	Misc. Conferences with BCM Display, Speaking, Travel, etc.	Total Hours	Average Hours per workday (actual)	Hours per day (con-tract)
Jan								
Feb								
March								
April								
May								
June								
July								
Aug								
Sept								
Oct								
Nov								
Dec								

Number of counseling sessions: _____
Average time per session: _____
Vacation days used: _____
Personal days used: _____
Other:

MILEAGE TALLY SHEET for Year _____ Name: _____

Purpose	Day	Place	Mi	Day	Place	Mi	Day	Mo	Qtr
Month:	1			16					
	2			17					
	3			18					
	4			19					
	5			20					
	6			21					
	7			22					
	8			23					
	9			24					
	10			25					
	11			26					
	12			27					
	13			28					
	14			29					
	15			30/31					
Month:	1			16					
	2			17					
	3			18					
	4			19					
	5			20					
	6			21					
	7			22					
	8			23					
	9			24					
	10			25					
	11			26					
	12			27					
	13			28					
	14			29					
	15			30/31					
Month:	1			16					
	2			17					
	3			18					
	4			19					
	5			20					
	6			21					
	7			22					
	8			23					
	9			24					
	10			25					
	11			26					
	12			27					
	13			28					
	14			29					
	15			30/31					

The table header spans: DAILY MILEAGE (covering Purpose, Day, Place, Mi, Day, Place, Mi) and TOTALS (covering Day, Mo, Qtr).

FIRST CONTACT TELEPHONE INFORMATION FORM

Name: _____   Date: _____

Source of referral: _____

Phone # _____   Address: _____

Work # _____   _____

Home Church _____

Description of Problem (s)

Attempted Solutions

Result of this Contact

FIRST CONTACT TELEPHONE INFORMATION FORM

Name: _____   Date: _____

Source of referral: _____

Phone # _____   Address: _____

Work # _____   _____

Home Church _____

Description of Problem (s)

Attempted Solutions

Result of this Contact

TO REFERRING PASTOR
Before giving this intake form (PDI) to your referred counselee:

- Please sign and date the PDI form on the line labeled "Referring Pastor's Signature" (top of page 1). Please sign and date the enclosed confidential envelope also.

- Requested donation for counseling is _____ per 50-minute session. Please discuss with your referred counselee how payment will be made. We suggest that the referring church consider helping counselees who are in financial need. Payments must be brought to sessions unless a monthly invoice is requested on this form. Invoices are sent to the referring church. Any other arrangements must be made *in advance* with the counselor.

- You or your counselee should return this completed referral form to our home office at the above address. Once the completed PDI and this referral form have been received in our home office, an appointment may be made.

- Thank you for allowing us to assist you! We look forward to serving you.

Please print legibly
Counselee Name: _____

Referring Pastor: Print _____ Signature _____

Church Name and Address: _____

_____

Church Phone (or Pastor's Phone): _____
Email: _____

☐ Counselee will pay in full at each session.

☐ Counselee will pay in part for each session in the amount of $_____. Balance of $_____ will be paid by referring church. Please have counselee bring payment to each session, unless other arrangements are made *in advance* with counselor.

☐ Church will pay in full for _____ sessions on a per-session basis.

☐ Church will pay in full for sessions on a monthly basis. Please send invoice to (if different from above church address):

☐ Other. Any other options must be approved by the counselor prior to first appointment. Please call our home office for assistance. Phone: _____

COUNSELEE INSTRUCTIONS

Welcome! In order to best serve you, we will need some preliminary information. The attached Personal Data Inventory form (PDI, our intake form) will give us background that will save us time in sessions and help your counselor to better understand your concerns. Please fill it out carefully. Read this sheet for instructions on returning your PDI and preparing for your first session. We look forward to working with you.

1. We offer counseling only by pastoral referral. If you do not have a referring pastor, you may contact one of the pastors at our home office for assistance: _____

    Ask your referring pastor to sign and date the top of the attached PDI form and the front of the confidential envelope if he has not already done so. He will also need to fill out the pastor's referral form he received with the PDI. He may send that separately, or you may include it with your completed PDI form.

2. Fill out this PDI form completely and sign the Terms of Counseling. This must be done before an appointment will be made.

3. The completed PDI should be sealed in an envelope and marked 'confidential.' The PDI envelope will not be opened by the secretary. Write your name on the outside of the envelope and have your pastor sign and date it. Then insert it into a larger envelope that can be addressed and stamped for mailing.

4. Mail or hand carry the PDI in the envelopes to:

5. Allow sufficient time for the PDI to be received by our office. Then you may call _____ or come in to make an appointment *preferably within two weeks*. You may be asked to provide your name, address, and other basic information to the secretary when the appointment is made.

6. Requested donation for counseling is $_____ per 50-minute session. If you are unable to cover the cost of the counseling, please contact your referring pastor for help. Please bring payment to each session. Checks may be made out to _____.

7. Bring your Bible, a pen, and a notebook to each session. We look forward to meeting you soon!

COUNSELING INFORMATION[1]

1. *Diagnostic Tools.* We use helpful counseling forms such as this intake form, homework journals, and other aids to gain an understanding of the central problems a person is experiencing.

2. *Intent Listening.* We encourage the counselee to speak his or her mind in an appropriate fashion and to discuss thoughts, anxieties, resentments, and fears so that the counselor will have a clear understanding of the central problems.

3. *Team Counseling.* There are times when a counseling situation may call for a team approach. If this is the case, we may have more than one counselor involved in a session. The counselors share insights and opinions with one another which pertain to the case. Team counseling can be especially helpful in marital counseling.

4. *Assignments.* Counselees make more rapid progress when they are required to study or to perform specific information-gathering or behavioral assignments which pertain to the problem. We tailor these assignments to the individual counselee and the circumstances.

5. *Accountability.* We are not interested in wasting the time of the counselors or the counselees. We are interested in believers learning how to experience the peace and joy that result from a walk of obedience to God's Word, and we hold the counselees accountable for doing the assignments on schedule.

How Long Does Counseling Take?

Each counseling session lasts for 50 minutes. Time required to complete biblical counseling will vary according to the individual, his or her motivation, and the particular problem. On the average, however, biblical counseling requires far less time than conventional secular counseling. Very simple problems are often solved in one session. Severe problems may require a longer period. Marital counseling may require as many as twelve to eighteen sessions or more. Substance abuse problems may require many more sessions, with intense accountability and follow-up.

How Much Does It Cost?

We ask for a _____ donation per 50-minute counseling session. Your referring church may agree to help you with counseling up to a designated number of sessions. Please discuss this possibility with the pastor who referred you.

About Confidentiality

We are careful to protect each counselee's confidentiality within biblical guidelines. There are times, however, when a counselor must consult with other counselors for advice. If information is revealed in counseling which indicates a genuine potential for harm to you or to others, the counselor may have to share that information with the appropriate authorities or family members. If the counselor has a supervisor, reports will be made to that supervisor, with the minimum necessary information revealed and with your identity being concealed if possible. See "Terms of Counseling" for more complete information concerning confidentiality.

---

1 This form was adapted. Source unknown.

TERMS OF COUNSELING

Reviewed with Counselee: _____
Date and Counselor Initials

Our goal in providing Christian counseling is to help you meet the challenges of life in a way that will please and honor the Lord Jesus Christ and allow you to fully enjoy His love for you and His plans for your life. We believe that the Bible provides thorough guidance and instruction for faith and life. Therefore, our counseling is based on scriptural principles rather than those of secular psychology or psychiatry. Neither the pastoral nor the lay counselors in this ministry are trained as psychotherapists or mental health professionals, nor should they be expected to follow the methods of such specialists. If you have specific legal, financial, medical, or other technical questions, you should seek advice from an independent professional. Our pastoral and lay counselors will help you to consider their counsel in light of relevant scriptural principles.

This counseling ministry is a non-profit, short term, biblically-counseling, peer-supported program of seminary-trained lay counselor(s) who are supervised by pastoral counselors, available to help members and friends of its home and host churches. We take a biblical approach to counseling. All problems will be addressed from principles and directives found in the Bible, unless the problem is organic. A counselee with an organic problem will be encouraged to seek medical assistance. This ministry is not a medical facility and is not equipped to treat organic problems. The counselor will make an effort to work alongside medical professionals on biological concerns. Information released to a medical professional would be provided only by prior written consent from the counselee unless that counselee's life or the lives of others are endangered.

Due to scheduled appointments, your counselor will not normally be available for telephone conversations during the week. If you have an emergency, please call to talk with the secretary. If she cannot help you, the counselor will return your call as soon as possible. Please seek appropriate protection if you are in danger and unable to reach your counselor immediately.

Donations for Counseling
Fees are required for seminars and workshops, and may be charged for various literary materials the counselor believes are important to the counseling process. In order to help meet our costs, a $_____ donation is requested at the completion of each counseling session. This form serves to provide the counselee with reasonable notification of donations requested. Please make checks out to _____. If you are unable to donate this amount, please discuss this in advance with your referring pastor. We also welcome gifts to the counseling ministry. All donations that are not for counseling sessions or materials are tax deductible. These donations should be given in cash or a separate check apart from the counseling session donation.

Supervision
To meet our objective of providing the highest level of care possible, all lay counselors are supervised by the executive director. Counselor notes may be reviewed periodically by the Executive Director or by the senior pastor of the home church to ensure sound biblical principles and counseling methods, and to comply with your church's discipline process. Lay counselors will refer any counselee in a suicidal condition to the referring pastor and the counselee's family or to the proper authorities. Lay counselors will report incidents of "reasonable suspected" child abuse, domestic violence, threats on life, or subpoenas to the appropriate authorities as required by law. The Executive Director or supervising pastor will review mediation agreements administered by counselors. Counselors are to report any incident worthy of church discipline to the Executive Director, who will cooperate with your church's discipline process on behalf of the counselor. The counselor may seek legal advice with regard to confidential information without counselee consent.

Confidentiality
Confidentiality is biblically guarded at all times. Certain laws require that counselors warn the appropriate individuals if the counselee intends to take harmful, dangerous, or criminal action. Counselors are also mandated to report any incidence of "reasonably suspected" child abuse (physical or sexual) and elderly abuse, or domestic violence to the appropriate authorities per the Supervision section above. Members of referring churches who reveal behavior worthy of church discipline, such as divorce without biblical basis, adultery, abuse of others, unethical or illegal practices, are subject to referral to the church disciplinary process by way of the executive director. If you are a member of a church, you have the prerogative of including your pastor in the counseling process, recognizing that this may limit the value of any privileged communication. Lay and pastoral counselors are not permitted to breach confidentiality to church discipline committees, or any other party except as provided in the Supervision section in this Terms of Counseling form, or by written permission from the counselee.
The counselee has a right to access his or her records and written information from those records in accordance with state and federal statutes.

Insurance
This ministry has no authorization for coverage with any insurance company or medical organization. Should a company offer to pay the requested donation for counseling, the payment will be accepted. All requested donations will be paid for by the counselee unless a church or other party chooses to pay. All counselees will be given a two-week notice of any change in requested donation.

Other counseling services are available in the community and the counselee has a right to freely choose among them, and to change practitioners after counseling has begun, within the limits of health insurance, medical assistance, or other health programs when there will be a change in the provider of counseling. We will provide information about other sources of counseling available and the counselee has a right to a coordinated transfer when there is a change. These rights can be exercised without retaliation by our ministry.

Appendix I

Terms of Counseling, page 2

Waiver of Liability
The undersigned, seeking biblical counseling as such as adhered to by our ministry, a non-profit religious organization, hereby acknowledges his or her understanding of the following conditions and further releases this ministry, its agents, counselors, and employees, from any liability or claim arising from the undersigned's participation in the above-mentioned biblical counseling program:

1. It is understood by the participant counselee that all biblical counseling will be provided by supervised counselors who counsel based upon their understanding of Scripture, not as licensed therapists;
2. That all counseling provided in the biblical counseling program is provided in accordance with the biblical principles adhered to by this ministry and are not necessarily provided in adherence to any local or national psychological or psychiatric association;
3. That no representation has been made, either expressly or implied, that the biblical counseling, as conducted by the above-mentioned lay counselors, is accepted as *customary* psychological and/or psychiatric therapy within the definitional terms utilized by those professions.
4. Certain statements may not be protected as privileged communications under law.

I, _____, affirm the accuracy of the personal information provided herein, and have read the
(Name)
information above and agree to the conditions set forth therein.

I agree and understand that all counseling that I receive from _____ will be based on the counselor's understanding of the Bible and its practical application. I am consenting to receive counseling from this ministry with full knowledge that biblical counselors believe and teach the authority of the Scriptures.

I hereby agree to the following conditions:
* I am committed to resolving my problems by coming into obedience to the Word of God.
* I will do the assigned weekly homework or the session will not be held.
* I will attend church each Sunday while I am in counseling.
* I understand that confidentiality cannot be absolutely guaranteed under the conditions indicated above.
* I will keep my financial responsibilities current.
* I will keep the appointment time, or will call to cancel or reschedule at least 48 hours in advance, with a legitimate reason. Three cancellations without prior notice will forfeit future sessions.
* I will pay a $20.00 fee if I cancel without a 24-hour notice.
* If I am unhappy in any way with the counseling, I will first discuss it with my counselor, then with my counselor and his or her supervisor, and then appeal it to the Board of Directors of this ministry. I agree to enter Christian mediation if I cannot solve my grievance, or, if necessary, a legally binding arbitration in accordance with the *Rules of Procedure* of the Institute of Christian Conciliation; judgment upon an arbitration award may be entered in any court having jurisdiction.
* I agree not to subpoena session notes for any reason.
* Sessions may be terminated at any time by the counselee or counselor.

Having clarified the principles and policies of our ministry, we welcome the opportunity to minister to you in the name of Christ and to be used by Him as He helps you to grow in spiritual maturity and prepares you for usefulness in His body. If you have any questions about these guidelines, please talk with the receptionist or one of our counselors. If these guidelines are acceptable to you, please sign below.

_____   _____
Counselee   Date

_____   _____
Counselee   Date

_____   _____
Counselee   Date

_____   _____
Counselor   Date

This Terms of Counseling form should be copied back-to-back.

COUNSELEE CONSENT FOR RELEASE OF INFORMATION[2]

I, _____, hereby authorize and consent to allow the herein designated individual(s) to release personal information gained through our counseling sessions to the individual(s) and/or organization(s) named below.

Individual(s) who may exchange information about me:

    1. _____

    2. _____

Specific information not to be released: (Check here if no restrictions ☐).

    1. _____

    2. _____

The purpose for this release is for biblical counseling at _____ **Church.**

I understand that I have no obligation to disclose this requested information and may revoke this consent at any time by informing any and all individuals or organizations listed above.

I waive, on behalf of myself and any persons who may have an interest in this matter, all provisions of the law relating to the disclosure of any confidential information and release _____ _____ and its counselors from all legal responsibility or liability that may arise from this authorization.

_____   _____

      Counselee   Date

_____   _____

      Legal Guardian   Date

_____   _____

      Witness   Date

---

2 Adapted from Howard Eyrich, *Christian Counseling Center Management: A Management Case Study Approach* (Growth Advantage Communications, 1996), 88.

COUNSELEE CONSENT FOR
OBSERVATION OF COUNSELING SESSIONS

A primary purpose of our ministry is to provide training in biblical discipleship for church leaders so that they may increase their skills in ministering to those under their care. We provide classes for instructional training, and we may provide opportunities for students to observe actual counseling sessions. By signing this form, you are agreeing to allow one or more advanced trainees** to observe one or more of your counseling sessions.

By checking and initialing the boxes below I hereby give my consent and permission to
_____ to

*_____ ☐ allow live observation of my sessions by one advanced trainee;
Initials

*_____ ☐ allow live observation of my sessions by more than one advanced trainee.
Initials

I agree to hold harmless the above named individuals and agencies of any liability in counseling observations.

_____	_____
Counselee	Date
_____	_____
Counselee's Legal Guardian	Date
_____	_____
Witness	Date
_____	_____
Counselor	Date

* Counselee should initial any or all of these options as appropriate.

** An advanced trainee is one who has completed our basic classes and has gone on to our advanced classes, or who has completed similar training in biblical counseling at an approved college or seminary and who wishes to obtain practical experience with counseling.

EVALUATION OF COUNSELING

Your Name (please print): _____

Your Counselor: _____

Please use the back of this form for further comments.

1. Please describe the changes that have occurred as a result of your counseling with us.

2. What principles or lessons did you find to be most helpful?

3. Suppose you know of someone who is struggling with a serious problem, but is hesitating to ask for counseling. What would you say to them?

4. Please give us suggestions for improving our ministry. How may we better serve our counselees?

May we have your permission to use your comments for promotional, educational, or encouragement purposes?
___ Yes ____No Your name will not be disclosed.

Please sign and date: _____

BUDGET (Year) _____
Annual Expense and Income Projection

Annual Expense Projection   Expense Category Totals

100 – Salary
    101   Counselor/Executive Director...
    102   Tax Liabilities ....
    170   Secretary ....

110 – Office
    111   Computer Supplies (toner cartridges, software updates) ....
    112   Office supplies (paper, copies, stationery) ....

120 – Communications
    120   Advertising (brochures, business cards) ....
    121   Postage and shipping ....
    122   Telephone (1 cell @$80/mo) ....
    124   Professional Consultation ....

130 – Professional Enrichment
    131   Library (books, videos, cassettes) ....
    132   Training/Education (registration) ....
    133   Travel (hotel, mileage, meals) ....

140 – Insurance and Fees
    141   Fees (NANC membership) ....
    142   Insurance (Church Mutual) ....
    143   Attorney Fees ....
    144   Government Fees ....

145 Internet Fees ....

150 – Training Center
    151   Videos (Independent Studies BSK 501) ....
    152   Classroom supplies ....
    153   Guest Teacher Honorarium (seminar, classes).....................
    157   Child Care (seminar) ....

160 – Travel
    161   Mileage for Counselor ....
    162   Accommodations ....
    163   Meals ....
    164   Guest Speaker airfare/mileage/accommodations ....

170 – Miscellaneous ....

180 – Designated Funds
    181   Books and Counseling Materials ....
    182   Counseling ....

Total Annual Expenses:

Annual Income Projection   Income Category Totals

Counseling ....

Donations: Home church   ....
                 Host church #1   ....
                 Host church #2   ....
                 Host church #3   ....
                 Helper churches   ....
                 Other Gifts and Misc. Donations.... ....

Seminar and Class Registrations ....

Books ....

Honorariums ....

Total Annual Income:

Budget overage or shortfall:

INVOICE REQUEST OR CREDIT FOR PAYMENT

Counselee: _____ Date of Session: _____

Referring Church: _____ Requested Donation: _____

☐ Payment of $_____ by _____ on (date) _____*
    ☐ Check number _____
    ☐ Cash

Next Appointment:

☐ Please send an invoice for $ _____ to:
    ☐ Referring church
    ☐   Other   (specify   name   and   address):

Payment received by _____ Date _____
* Provide a copy of this form as a receipt to payor.

INVOICE REQUEST OR CREDIT FOR PAYMENT

Counselee: _____ Date of Session: _____

Referring Church: _____ Requested Donation: _____

☐ Payment of $_____ by _____ on (date) _____*
    ☐ Check number _____
    ☐ Cash

Next Appointment:

☐ Please send an invoice for $ _____ to:
    ☐ Referring church
    ☐   Other   (specify   name   and   address):

Payment   received   by   _____   Date   _____
*   Provide   a   copy   of   this   form   as   a   receipt

REQUEST AND DISBURSEMENT VOUCHER (Blue)

This Box for Office Use Only
Check # _____
Date of Check _____

Date of Request _____

Amount of Check _____
(ATTACH RECEIPTS TO BACK. No checks will be written without receipts or other documentation.)

PAYEE/VENDOR (Person to write the check to):

_____

ITEMS REQUESTED _____

_____

_____

ACCOUNT TO DEBIT _____

Person Requesting Funds (Signature) _____

Check Preparer Signature _____

Authorized Signature _____

DEPOSIT VOUCHER (Pink)

This Box is For Office Use Only
Date _____ **Voucher #** _____

ACTIVITY ACCOUNT NAME _____

Reason money was collected: _____

_____

_____

_____

Checks $ _____

Cash $ _____

Coins $ _____

Total Deposit $ _____

PLEASE PREPARE MONEY FOR DEPOSIT AS FOLLOWS:

- *Add checks and clip or rubber band together with adding machine tape on top.*
- *Sort cash by ones, fives, tens, and twenties clipped together in numerical order.*
- *Put coins in a sealed envelope.*

READY FOR DEPOSIT IN CHECKING?   **YES** (Please circle)

Submitter Signature _____ Date _____

Authorized Signature _____

NON-CASH DONATION VOUCHER (Yellow)

This Box is For Office Use Only	
Date Received_____	Voucher # _____

AMOUNT: _____

DONOR: _____

Type of donation: _____

_____

_____

_____

Recipient Signature _____ Date _____

Authorized Signature _____

INCOME RECORD FOR COUNSELING SESSIONS

Counselor: Dates: to   , 20

Date	Counselee #	Session Amount	Amount Received by Cnslr.	Check if Office Receives Pmt.	Date	Counselee #	Session Amount	Amount Received by Cnslr.	Check if Office Receives Pmt.

YEAR-END FINANCIAL ACCOUNTABILITY FORM for _____

Auditor: Place a check mark before all items inspected and found correct or noted.

☐ I have reviewed the bank accounts from book to bank statement from the beginning of the year to the end of the year. Noted are any overdrafts or unusual items.
_____
_____

☐ I have reviewed outstanding checks for age and indicated all checks over 6 months outstanding.
_____
_____

☐ I have reviewed transfers between accounts, paying attention that transfers "out" are recorded as transfers "in" in opposite accounts and have found them to be
        ☐ correct   ☐ incorrect.

☐ I have reviewed large transactions and a 10% sample of the remaining invoices for expenditures or proper authorization by board/committee for moneys paid out. Listed are any exceptions:
_____
_____

☐ I have inspected tax deductible receipts to determine that they were properly accounted for.

☐ I have selected two months and checked math calculations on the monthly income and expense reports.

☐ I have reviewed the board/committee minutes regarding disposition of prior audit comments, approval of major expenditures and any compliance items called for in minutes.

☐ I have checked Federal Forms 941, W-2, and W-3 and have found all information to correlate.

☐ I have checked Wisconsin State Form WT-6 and have found all information to correlate.

☐ Form 990 has been filed for the past year.

*****************NOTE ANY FURTHER COMMENTS ON THE BACK.*******************

I have inspected the above marked areas of financial record keeping for _____ for the year _____ and have found them, to the best of my understanding, to be correct. I am a third party and am not on the board or staff of the corporation.

Signed _____ Date _____
This does not constitute a legal audit nor does the authorization signature necessarily represent that of a Certified Public Accountant.

REQUIREMENTS FOR COUNSELING OBSERVATION

1. Advanced students currently in our classes will be given priority in counseling supervision training, followed in priority by those who have completed our classes.

2. Student must be approved for counseling observation or supervision, as follows:
   a. Meets all qualifications for enrollment in our advanced classes.
   b. Letter of recommendation from current pastor.
   c. Letter of recommendation from one of our ministry board members if current pastor is not on the board of directors.
   d. Interview and approval by our ministry board of directors.
   e. Signs and adheres to statement of confidentiality and conduct.

3. Persons who do not meet the requirements of #2 above and are requesting counseling observation or supervision must meet the following requirements prior to the start of supervision:
   a. Has achieved the supervisory level of NANC certification process, or equivalent.
   b. Letter of recommendation from current NANC supervisor or current professor.
   c. Letter of recommendation from current pastor.
   d. Letter of recommendation from one of our ministry board member, if current pastor is not on our board of directors.
   e. Interview and approval by our ministry board of directors.
   f. Signs and adheres to statement of confidentiality and conduct.

COUNSELING OBSERVATION POLICY: CONDUCT AND CONFIDENTIALITY

The Bible teaches that Christians should carefully guard any personal and private information that others reveal to them. Protecting confidences is a sign of Christian love and respect (Matthew 7:12). It also discourages harmful gossip (Proverbs 16:28; 26:20), invites confession (Proverbs 11:13; 28:13; James 5:16), and encourages people to seek needed counseling (Proverbs 20:19; Romans 15:14). Since these goals are essential to the ministry of the gospel and the work of the church, all persons associated with our ministry are expected to refrain from gossip and to respect the confidences of others. In particular, our students and affiliates, pastors and counselors shall carefully protect all information that they receive through biblical counseling, subject to the following guidelines.

1. Identity of the counselee(s) is to be carefully protected unless the counselee(s) agrees in writing to allow the disclosure. Counselees must sign permission for observation before observed session(s) begin.
2. For the purposes of confidentiality, the observer is not to take written or otherwise recorded notes for personal use.
3. The observer is to remain silent and unobtrusive during the counseling session unless addressed directly by the session counselor.
4. The observer is not to communicate related to the session with the counselee or others outside the session, unless directed to do so by our ministry Board of Directors.

I, _____, agree to abide by the requirements and the counseling observation policy of (ministry name)_____ herein. I will exercise biblical integrity and discretion before, during, and following counseling sessions. In the event of dispute regarding counseling observation and/or supervision, I will submit to and abide by the ministry's disciplinary policies.

I understand that this permission is a privilege and not a right. Permission may be revoked or denied at any time and for any reason by our ministry's Board of Directors, our executive director or our counseling supervisor.

Requirements for Counseling Observation and Supervision, page 2

On behalf of myself and any persons who may have an interest in this matter, I release (ministry name) _____, its board of directors and its counselors from all legal responsibility or liability that may arise from this authorization.

_____   _____
            Applicant   Date

Please print clearly:
Name _____   Phone _____
Address _____   Cell _____
City_____ State _____ Zip _____   Email _____
Church membership _____
Church address _____
Pastor name _____ Phone _____
Current Seminary _____

Decision of the Board of Directors:

☐ After examining the required documents and completing interview(s), permission is granted by the Board of Directors to allow (name)_____ to observe live or taped counseling sessions under the conditions set herein for the period between (dates) _____ to _____.

Additional conditions set by the Board: (check and initial if none ☐ _____)

_____   _____
        Board Member   Date

_____   _____
        Board Member   Date

_____   _____
        Board Member   Date

☐ Permission has been denied by the board of Directors to allow observation of counseling sessions, for the following reason(s):

This Counseling Observation form should be copied back to back.

DISCIPLESHIP DEVELOPMENT STUDENT RECORD

Student Name:_____   Address:_____

Church: _____   _____

Phone and Email:

☐ Pursuing NANC Certification

Grade	Date completed	Course Title
____ ☐	_____	_____
____ ☐	_____	_____
____ ☐	_____	_____
____ ☐	_____	_____
____ ☐	_____	_____
____ ☐	_____	_____
____ ☐	_____	_____

Comments:

READING RECORD FORM

Name: _____

Class: _____

Date	Book Title	Number of Pages Read

CLASS ROSTER

Course Number and Title: _____

Class Dates: _____ **Project Due Date:** _____

Instructor: _____

Student Name									

This form is used to record class attendance and assignment completion.

Index

Index

Index